William Henry Margetson, George Alfred Henty

With Cochrane the Dauntless :

a Tale of the exploits of Lord Cochrane in South American waters

William Henry Margetson, George Alfred Henty

With Cochrane the Dauntless :
a Tale of the exploits of Lord Cochrane in South American waters

ISBN/EAN: 9783337024222

Printed in Europe, USA, Canada, Australia, Japan

Cover: Foto ©ninafisch / pixelio.de

More available books at **www.hansebooks.com**

With Cochrane the Dauntless

G. A. HENTY'S BOOKS

Illustrated by Eminent Artists

The Dragon and the Raven.
Wulf the Saxon.
Bonnie Prince Charlie.
By Conduct and Courage.
The Cat of Bubastes.
Maori and Settler.
Both Sides the Border.
In the Heart of the Rockies.
The Treasure of the Incas.
With Lee in Virginia.
By Pike and Dyke.
With Wolfe in Canada.
Under Wellington's Command.
True to the Old Flag.
The Tiger of Mysore.
One of the 28th.
In the Reign of Terror.
The Bravest of the Brave.
With Kitchener in the Soudan.
By England's Aid.
Beric the Briton.
Facing Death.
St. Bartholomew's Eve.
St. George for England.
When London Burned.
By Sheer Pluck.
Under Drake's Flag.
Redskin and Cowboy.

For Name and Fame.
Captain Bayley's Heir.
A March on London.
In Freedom's Cause.
Held Fast for England.
A Final Reckoning.
The Dash for Khartoum.
With Clive in India.
The Lion of the North.
At Agincourt.
The Lion of St. Mark.
With Moore at Corunna.
The Young Carthaginian.
At the Point of the Bayonet.
Through the Sikh War.
Through Russian Snows.
For the Temple.
Through the Fray.
With Cochrane the Dauntless.
Won by the Sword.
In Greek Waters.
On the Irrawaddy.
By Right of Conquest.
A Jacobite Exile.
At Aboukir and Acre.
To Herat and Cabul.
A Knight of the White Cross.
In the Irish Brigade.

LONDON: BLACKIE & SON, LTD., 50 OLD BAILEY, E.C.

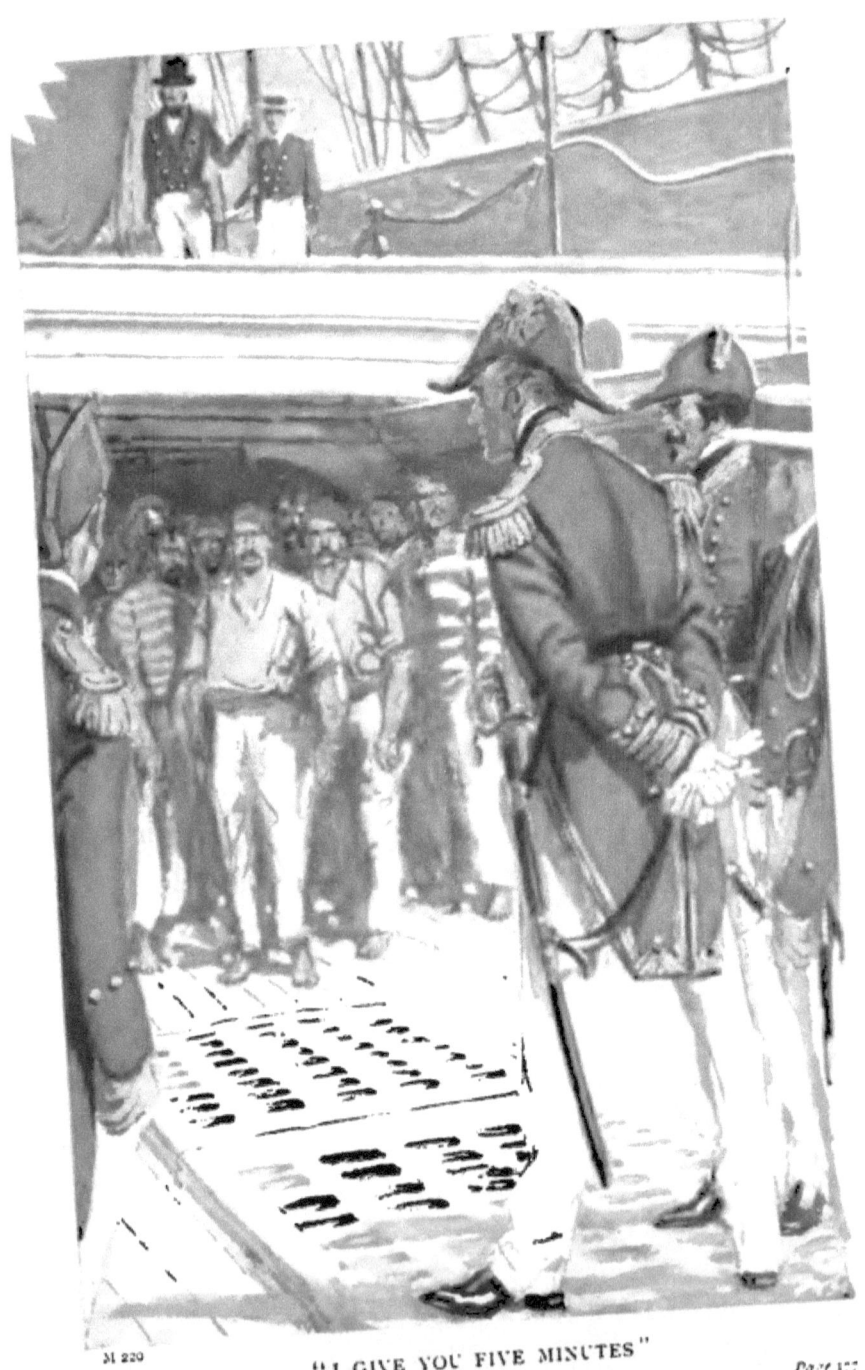

"I GIVE YOU FIVE MINUTES"

With Cochrane the Dauntless

A Tale of
the Exploits of Lord Cochrane in
South American Waters

BY

G. A. HENTY

Author of "Under Drake's Flag" "The Dash for Khartoum"
"In Greek Waters" "The Lion of St. Mark"
"Through Russian Snows" &c.

Illustrated

BLACKIE AND SON LIMITED
LONDON GLASGOW AND BOMBAY

*Printed in Great Britain by
Blackie & Son, Limited, Glasgow*

PREFACE

IN the annals of British sailors there is no name that should stand higher than that of Lord Cochrane. In some respects he resembled that daring leader and great military genius, the Earl of Peterborough. Both performed feats that most men would have regarded as impossible, both possessed extraordinary personal bravery and exceptional genius for war, and a love for adventure. Both accomplished marvels, and neither was appreciated at his full value by his countrymen, both having a touch of originality that amounted in the case of Peterborough to absolute eccentricity. In other respects they had little in common. Cochrane's life was passed in one long struggle on behalf of the oppressed. He ruined his career in our navy, and created for himself a host of bitter enemies by his crusade against the enormous abuses of our naval administration, and by the ardour with which he championed the cause of reform at home. Finding the English navy closed to him he threw himself into the cause of oppressed nationalities. His valour and genius saved Chili from being reconquered by the Spanish, rescued Peru from their grasp, and utterly broke their power in South America. Similarly he crushed the Portuguese power in Brazil and ensured its independence, and then took up the cause of Greece. In all four enterprises his efforts were hampered by the utter corruption of the governments of these countries, just as his efforts on behalf of British sailors and of the British people at large had brought upon him the hatred and persecution of a government as corrupt as those of Chili, Brazil, and Greece. He was rewarded only with the basest ingratitude, and returned home after having expended a large part of his fortune and permanently injured his health in the inestimable services he had rendered. In other respects besides those exploits connected with the sea, his genius was remarkable. After retiring from active service he devoted himself to inventions, and some of these paved the way to later scientific achievements, giving him a place alongside the Marquis of Worcester.

Of Lord Cochrane it can be said that he was the victim of his generous enthusiasm for the oppressed. During the greater portion of his life he rested under a heavy cloud, and it was only in extreme old age that he had the satisfaction of having his name rehabilitated, and of regaining the honours and rank of which he had been so unjustly deprived.

G. A. HENTY.

CONTENTS.

CHAP.		Page
I.	OFF TO SEA,	11
II.	IN THE MALAY ARCHIPELAGO,	30
III.	A CYCLONE,	50
IV.	A RESCUE,	69
V.	AGAIN ON THE ISLAND,	90
VI.	HOME,	109
VII.	COCHRANE'S CAREER,	128
VIII.	THE BASQUE ROADS,	146
IX.	IN CHILI,	158
X.	WRECKED,	176
XI.	A DANGEROUS COMPANION,	194
XII.	DEATH OF THE CAPTAIN,	214
XIII.	PRIZE-MONEY,	231
XIV.	A PRISONER,	249
XV.	FRIENDS IN NEED,	269
XVI.	AN INDIAN GUIDE,	287
XVII.	DOWN THE RIVER,	305
XVIII.	CAPTURED BY INDIANS,	323
XIX.	IN BRAZIL,	342
XX.	FRESH TRIUMPHS,	363

ILLUSTRATIONS

	Facing Page
"I GIVE YOU FIVE MINUTES"	*Frontispiece*
STEPHEN CRAWLS TO THE RESCUE OF HIS CHUM	88
COCHRANE SCATTERS THE FRENCH FLEET	152
STEPHEN BEATS OFF THE GREAT WAR-CANOE	224
PITA TRIES STEPHEN'S PLAN	320

WITH COCHRANE THE DAUNTLESS

CHAPTER I

OFF TO SEA

"I AM sure I do not know what to do with you, Steve," Lieutenant Embleton said one afternoon as he and his son were sitting upon a bench on the cliff at Ramsgate, looking over the sea. "Upon my word I don't see my way at all; this peace has stranded most of us, and at any rate, so far as I am concerned, there is not a ghost of a chance of my obtaining employment—not that I am fit for it if I could get it. I have been nearly ten years ashore. Every one of us who sailed under Cochrane has been a marked man ever since. However, that is an old story, and it is no use grumbling over what cannot be helped; besides, that wound in my hip has been troubling me a good deal of late, and I know I am not fit for sea. I don't think I should have minded so much if I had got post rank before being laid on the shelf. The difference of pension, too, would have been a help, for goodness knows it is hard work making ends meet on a lieutenant's half-pay. However, that is not the question now. The thing that I have got to consider is what is the best thing to do with you.

"Yes, I know you are ready to do anything, lad, and it is

not your fault that you are not in harness; but, in the first place, I found it hard to spare you, and in the next, I wanted you to stick to your books as long as you could. I grant there are many officers even in His Majesty's service who are as rough as if they had come in through the hawse-hole, but it tells against them. However, as you are past fifteen, I think now that you will do; and as you have been working steadily with me for the past four years, you have got a lot into your head that will give you an advantage over boys sent to sea two years younger.

"You are well up in navigation, and can take an observation as well as any old sailor, either by sun, moon, or stars. You can steer a boat in heavy weather, and knot and splice; you know the sails and ropes, and can go aloft as quickly as a monkey, and do anything that your strength permits. There have been plenty of opportunities for teaching you all this on short coasting voyages and on board ships driven in here by stress of weather. I suppose, Steve, however much we may talk of other professions, it comes to the sea at last. I know that you have always wanted it, but if I could have seen any opening for you on land I would rather that you had taken to it than that you should go afloat. You see what it has done for me, lad. It is a poor trade, though as long as it's war-time there is excitement enough to make up for the shortness of the pay. However, as I have told you many a time, there is no chance whatever of my getting you a midshipman's berth.

"I have not the slightest influence at the admiralty, and the navy has been so reduced since the war ended that they must have fifty applications for every vacancy; besides, now that there is no fighting to be done, I don't know that the merchant service isn't the best, for it is dull work indeed being years on a station when there is no chance of a brush with an enemy or the capture of a prize. In the merchant service you can have at least a change, and a smart young fellow who knows his business and has gentlemanly manners, has much better chances of coming to the front than he would have in the royal navy. So I think the time has come when I must bring myself to make a move in the matter."

"Thank you, father; I know very well that in studying with you I have learned a lot more than I should have done if I had gone to sea two years ago; but I do want to be working and earning something, instead of being an expense to you, and, as you know, I would prefer the sea to anything else."

"It is Hobson's choice, lad; it is the sea or nothing. And after all, I think the mercantile navy is as good a profession as a lad can take to, that is if he has no influence to back him on shore. I wrote a fortnight ago to a friend in London. He is the owner of four or five vessels, and it happened, a good many years ago now, that I recaptured one of them with a valuable cargo that had been taken by a French privateer. I was sent home in her, and when he came down to Plymouth, where I took her in, we became great friends. We were about the same age, and the loss at that time would have been a very serious one to him. I stayed with him once or twice when I was in town. I have not seen him for some years now—one cannot afford to run about on a lieutenant's half-pay—but I remembered him the other day when I was thinking things over in every light, and wrote to him. I told him how we were situated, and asked him if he would put you on board one of his ships, and this morning I had an answer from him saying that he would gladly do so. He said that he would take you as an apprentice without fees, and that at any time, should anything better turn up, or you see your way to getting into a firm with a larger fleet and better chance of advancement, he would cancel your indentures. No kinder offer could be made, and if you are willing I will write this evening to accept the offer, and tell him that I will go up with you in the hoy directly I hear from him that you are wanted."

"Thank you very much, father; I am awfully glad that it can be managed without expense, though I should be quite willing to go before the mast and work my way up."

"I know you would, Steve, but it is much better to start fair, for ship-owners prefer to take a young mate who has regularly served as an apprentice than a man who has only been trained before the mast; for although the latter may have picked up enough to scrape through his examination, he is rarely a good navigator, and works out his reckoning by rule of thumb, which is all very well as long as the weather is fine and he can get his observation at noon, but breaks down directly it comes to having to depend upon a glimpse of the moon through the clouds, or the chance of getting a star."

Lieutenant Embleton had been a dashing and gallant officer, but his career in the service had been ruined by the fact that he had served under Lord Cochrane, in the *Pallas*, in the *Impérieuse*, and in the *Speedy*. The latter was a little sloop mounting fourteen four-pounder guns, in which not only did Lord Cochrane capture many gun-boats and merchantmen, but on the 6th of May, 1801, he took the *Gamo*, a Spanish frigate, carrying six times as many men as the *Speedy* and seven times her weight of shot, an exploit that so aroused the jealousy of Earl St. Vincent that for a long time Lord Cochrane could not obtain employment. Three years later, when Lord Melville succeeded St. Vincent as first lord of the admiralty, Lord Cochrane was appointed to the *Pallas*, in which he again did excellent service; and distinguished himself still more when, in the *Impérieuse*, he attacked the whole French fleet in the Basque Roads, driving three or four of their battle-ships ashore, capturing three others, and compelling the rest to take to flight.

But the honour and popular applause gained by Lord

Cochrane was, in the opinion of the authorities, more than neutralized by his fearless exposure, from his place in Parliament, where he sat as one of the members for Westminster, of the scandalous abuses then prevailing in the navy. All attempts to silence him by the offers of valuable appointments being in vain, Lord Cochrane was subjected to a persecution altogether without precedent in parliamentary history. In the court-marshal which was held upon Lord Gambier for his failure to assist Cochrane in the action in the Basque Roads, the admiralty went so far as to forge charts, and so to show that the admiral could not come to Cochrane's assistance, and Gambier was not only acquitted, but received a vote of thanks from the House of Commons for the victory in which he had taken no part. For four years Lord Cochrane received no appointment, but at the close of 1813 his uncle, Sir Alexander Cochrane, was selected for the command of the fleet on the North American station, and nominated Cochrane his flag captain, an appointment resting entirely with him, and with which government could not interfere.

He did not, however, sail, for just as he was about to embark, a relation, who was engaged in stock exchange operations in conjunction with a foreign adventurer, carried out some dishonest transactions, those who were his dupes believing that he was acting under information obtained from Lord Cochrane. As soon as the latter heard a report of the affair he left his ship, came up to London, and demanded an investigation. Then followed one of the most disgraceful parodies of justice ever performed in this country. Lord Cochrane was arrested, tried, and by means of a partisan judge, false evidence, and measures more unscrupulous even than those of Judge Jeffreys, convicted and sentenced to imprisonment. A servile House of Commons obeyed the orders of ministers to expel him from their body. His name was struck off the order of the Bath, and his insignia torn down from St. George's Chapel with every mark of indignity.

Public indignation at the disgraceful means that had been taken to secure his conviction rose to such a height, that it was only by the persuasions of Lord Cochrane's friends that a riot was prevented. The citizens of Westminster at once re-elected him as their member, no one venturing to oppose him. After remaining in prison for some months he effected his escape and presented himself in the House of Commons. He was seized and carried back to prison, where he was thrown into a dungeon, and there kept until his health so suffered that his persecutors, fearing that fatal consequences would ensue, were obliged to place him in more wholesome quarters. Here he remained until the conclusion of his year's sentence. He then paid the fine of a thousand pounds, to which he had also been sentenced, and on the very day of his release from prison took his place in the House of Commons, and resumed his work as one of the leaders of the reform party.

Eighteen months later he was subjected to fresh persecution, and was tried for his escape from prison and fined a hundred pounds. A penny subscription was at once started, and eleven hundred pounds collected in this way, afforded a signal proof of the intensity of the feeling in his favour. This sum was used to pay the fine, and to reimburse him for the former fine to which he had been subjected. All Lord Cochrane's efforts to obtain a new trial, or an expression of an opinion from the House as to the illegality of the proceedings of his judge, Lord Ellenborough, were ineffective, the House, on each occasion when he brought the matter forward, obeying the orders of ministers and voting against his motions by an overwhelming majority. He had, however, the satisfaction of knowing that the nation at large was heartily with him, and recognized the gross injustice from which he had been a sufferer.

The hostility upon the part of the admiralty and government extended to those who had borne part in his glorious exploits at sea, and Lieutenant Embleton was put on half-pay after the action of the *Impérieuse* against the French fleet, and found himself without any prospect of future employment, and without even a chance of obtaining a nomination for his son to a midshipman's berth. The blow was at first a very keen one, but it was less bitterly felt after the conclusion of peace and the great reduction of the navy, as his fate was only that of thousands of other officers; and he had now come to feel that the effects of his wound, for which he received a small addition to his half-pay, rendered him unfit for further service, even could he have obtained an appointment. He had, since leaving the navy, lived in a little cottage at Ramsgate, where from his garden he could obtain a view of the sea and the passing ships. The education of his son afforded him employment for some hours a day. His favourite position was on a bench in the garden, from which he could watch through a telescope mounted on a tripod the passing ships, criticise the state of their rigging and sails, and form conjectures as to their destination.

It was a great pang to him to part with Stephen, but he felt that he could no longer keep him by his side; and he was sure that the careful training he had given him in all nautical matters would enable the lad to make his way in the mercantile navy. A fortnight after his conversation with Steve, the lieutenant received a letter from his friend in London, saying that one of his ships that had returned a fortnight before was now unloaded, and would at once begin to fit out for a fresh voyage, and it would be therefore as well for him to bring Stephen up, so that he might have the advantage of seeing the whole process of preparing a ship for sea. He gave a warm invitation to Lieutenant Embleton to stay with him for a week or two, and on the following day father and son went on board a

Ramsgate hoy, and thirty-six hours later arrived in the port of London. They were warmly received by Mr. Hewson.

"I think your boy is fortunate that the *Tiger* should be the first ship he will sail in," he said that evening. "I regard the captain as my best officer. He is a good seaman and a capital navigator, and he is of a most kindly disposition; therefore, I can put the boy under him with the certainty that he will be well treated and cared for. In the next place, the *Tiger* does not, like my other ships, make regular voyages to and from a foreign port, but carries on the business of a trader among the East Indian islands. It is not every one to whom such a business could be safely intrusted; but I have great confidence in Captain Pinder. He is a good man of business, thoroughly conscientious, and accustomed to the ways of the treacherous natives of those islands. The *Tiger* is more heavily armed than usual, and has more than once beaten off the attacks of their piratical craft, and there is no fear of Pinder's being caught napping.

"She will in the first place take a cargo to Calcutta, reserving a portion of her hold for my goods for trading among the islands. When she has landed her freight at Calcutta she will cruise in the Archipelago for some months, as long, in fact, as Pinder finds that he can carry on a really good business with the natives. Then she will return to Calcutta and fill up with freight for her return voyage. Thus, you see, your boy will gain a good deal of varied experience, and will see, perhaps, as much adventure and excitement as he would meet with in a score of ordinary voyages, and will have the advantage of being under a kind commander, who will instruct him in the rudiments of navigation."

"Nothing could be better," Mr. Embleton said warmly. "It is the voyage of all others that would be to the boy's taste, and I shall be satisfied indeed at his being in such good hands. As to navigation, it is practice only that he wants. I have taught him all that I know myself, and he can take a lunar, or work his reckoning out from a star observation, as accurately as I could do it myself."

"Is that so, Mr. Embleton? I am glad indeed to hear it. Then there is no doubt about the future of your boy, if he is steady and industrious. I am pleased to hear it for my own sake, if for nothing else; for although Pinder's mates are capital sailors, and in all other respects able officers, they are not men of Pinder's type. They can take, of course, a rough observation at noon, and work it out by rule of thumb and the aid of tables, but beyond that they can do nothing. They have not received the education to enable them to grapple with mathematical problems, even of the simplest kind; and although, in case of Pinder falling sick, they might manage under favourable circumstances to bring the ship home, they would fare very badly if they had a long spell of bad weather and could not get an observation at noon for days or even weeks together. It will be a satisfaction to me to know that in case of anything happening to the captain there is someone on board who could, in such a case, take a lunar or shoot a star. Well, tomorrow morning we will go down to the docks, and I will hand your boy over to Pinder. I should, of course, be very glad to have him here, but I think it is of great advantage to a boy to see everything done from the first step. She is going to have an entirely new fit-out both of standing and running rigging, so she has been stripped entirely, and has nothing but her three lower masts above the deck."

Accordingly, after breakfast next day Mr. Hewson sent for a hackney-coach and they drove down to the docks.

"That is the *Tiger*," Mr. Hewson said as he stopped at the side of a fine craft. "She is six hundred tons, three years old, and a fast sailer. She is not much to look at at present, but when she is in full dress she is a handsome vessel."

"She looks fast," Mr. Embleton said. "And for myself, I would rather command a craft of that size than one of greater tonnage."

The *Tiger* at present certainly did not show to advantage. Her deck was begrimed with dirt. A body of riggers were at work in parcelling and serving with spun yarn the eyes of the shrouds. An officer in a rough canvas suit was superintending the work.

"That is Mr. Staines, the first mate," Mr. Hewson said. "He would not be happy if he was not on board from the very first hour that the riggers were beginning their work. Good morning, Mr. Staines!" he went on, raising his voice. "Is Captain Pinder on board?"

"Yes, sir," the mate said, touching his cap, and then went aft to the poop-cabin, from which the captain came out as his visitor stepped on board. He also was in a working suit.

"Good morning, Mr. Hewson!" he said. "We are all in the rough, you see. One hardly expects visitors on her first day of fitting out."

"We all know that, captain. This is Lieutenant Embleton of the royal navy, and this is his son, of whom I was speaking to you two days ago."

"I am glad to meet you, sir," the captain said, shaking hands with Mr. Embleton "Every sailor knows you by reputation as being one of Lord Cochrane's officers. It will be a pleasure to me to do all I can for your son."

"You will find him very different to most of your apprentices, Pinder. He has had the advantage of his father's teaching, and, theoretically at any rate, he is already well up in his work. When I tell you that he can take a lunar, or an observation from a star, you may imagine that he will not require much teaching in navigation."

"I am glad indeed to hear it, Mr. Hewson—heartily glad;

there ought to be two men on board a ship who can do that, for there is never any saying what might happen if there is only one. It has made me anxious many a time, when we had a bad spell of weather, as to how the *Tiger* would get on if I happened to be washed overboard by a sea or killed by a falling spar. Well, Master Embleton, I can see that I shall have no difficulty in making a first-rate sailor of you. Have you come to stay?"

"Yes, sir. My father thought it would be good for me to be on board from the time the fitting-out began."

"Quite right, lad. You will then learn as much in a fortnight as you would in a year at sea. I always make a point of being here myself, and my first officer wouldn't allow anything to prevent his seeing that everything was right from first to last. But I don't think that you will be able to sleep on board for the next fortnight."

"Of course not," Mr. Embleton said. "I intend to take a lodging for him as close to the dock-gate as I can. Perhaps you may know of a tidy place."

"He can't do better than lodge with us," the captain said. "Mr. Staines and I always put up at the same place. We give them notice when we are going to begin to fit out, and they keep the rooms for us. We both slept there last night. The house is kept by a nice clean woman, the widow of a skipper who was lost with his craft about ten years ago. I have no doubt she can put the lad up too, and he can mess with us. I will go round with him myself; till we get the shrouds up, one is quite enough to look after the riggers."

"I thank you very much, captain. That will be in all respects more pleasant for the boy than lodging by himself."

The matter was speedily arranged. Mr. Embleton then took Stephen to a clothing shop and bought him two suits of rough canvas.

"You will find it dirty work, Steve. There is no keeping free of the tar. By the way, Captain Pinder, I have not ordered Steve's outfit yet, for I know that on some lines the apprentices dress like midshipmen, on others they don't; so I put it off until I saw you."

"I always like the apprentices on board my ship to be dressed as midshipmen," the captain replied. "There will only be three on board as far as I know. I make a point of messing with my officers, and if there are only two or three apprentices on board they take their meals with us, it does them good; and I don't at all approve of their mixing with the men forward. I should say, Mr. Embleton, get him one good suit for going ashore, another rougher suit for duty on board, half-a-dozen duck suits for the tropics, and two or three suits of dungaree for slipping on over the others when there is dirty work to be done. The cap is sufficient to indicate the officer. As for the rest of his outfit, your own experience will tell you what is needed. Railton in Leadenhall Street is a man I can recommend. He keeps the house badges for the caps, and turns out his work well. I generally get my togs there, and find him as cheap as anyone."

"Thank you! I will take Steve with me as far as that in the hackney-coach, and get him measured. Then he can be back here again by the time you knock off for dinner, and will then put on his slops and get to work."

Steve returned to the lodgings just as the captain and first mate came in to dinner. Then he carried one of his canvas suits down to the ship, put it on, and was soon at work having his first lesson in seizing ropes. For a fortnight the work continued, and Stephen greatly pleased the captain and first mate by his attention and willingness, working all the time as a rigger's boy, and paying the greatest attention to all the minutiæ of the work. Saturday afternoons and Sundays he spent at

Mr. Hewson's, where his father was still staying, his host refusing to listen to any talk of his leaving until the *Tiger* sailed. Another four days were spent in planing decks and painting inside and out. The work was scarcely finished when the cargo began to come on board. As soon as this was the case, the second and third mates and the other two apprentices joined. Like Mr. Staines, Towel and Pasley, the second and third mates, had both made their way up from the forecastle; both were active young men and good sailors, who had laboriously mastered the very small amount of bookwork that was needed, in addition to practical seamanship, to pass their examinations, but who, like the majority of their class of that time, knew nothing of navigation beyond taking a rough observation at mid-day and working it out by rule of thumb on the tables. Mr. Staines presented Stephen to them.

"This is our new apprentice," he said; "his father is a lieutenant in the royal navy, one of Lord Cochrane's men, and a great friend of the owner. Stephen Embleton is the lad's name, and some day he will make a fine officer. He has been at work here since the morning the riggers came on board, and is not afraid to put his hands into the tar-pot, as you can see from his appearance. He has learned a lot from his father, so we won't have the trouble with him we generally do have with Johnny-raws."

"That is right, youngster," the second mate said heartily; "if you will learn anywhere, you will learn here, for a better captain never commanded a ship. No passengers, I hope, Staines?"

"No; I believe that the skipper has had two or three applications, but although the owner has no objection to his taking them, he considers the trouble is more than they are worth. Of course, he would make something out of their passage, but there would, almost certainly, be some cantankerous beggars among them, and of course the table costs a good deal more when there are passengers, especially as he will have the apprentices to mess with him. I am sure I am glad indeed that we sha'n't be bothered with them."

The other two apprentices were about Stephen's age. Both had made one trip in the *Tiger*, and were at first a little inclined to patronize the new-comer. The day before the *Tiger* hauled out into the river, the owner and Mr. Embleton came down to look over her. Great was the change that three weeks had made in her appearance. Her deck was beautifully white, the lofty spars well scraped and freshly varnished, and the network of new rigging set her off to the greatest advantage. The new suit of sails were all bent, and lay loose in their gaskets ready for dropping. Four guns were ranged along either side.

"She is a handsome craft indeed," Mr. Embleton said as he stood on the wharf alongside, taking in every detail of her outfit with the eye of a seaman. "What are the guns—twelve-pounders?"

"Yes, but there is a long eighteen down in the hold, which will be mounted as a pivot as soon as she gets among the islands. The others are well enough when you come to close quarters, but the long gun generally keeps the pirates from getting there; they don't like being peppered before they come within fighting distance. I believe the captain would rather part with all the other guns than sail without Long Tom."

"That I would," Captain Pinder, who had just joined, remarked. "Five times has the pivot-gun made them sheer off without venturing to come to close quarters; and indeed I have never had to loose the broadside guns but three times, in each of which they came suddenly round the corner into a bay where we were lying at anchor."

As they had had notice of the owner's intention to come down, the officers were all in their new uniforms, and after Captain Pinder had shown his guests round the ship, they sat down together to dinner in the cabin.

"You have plenty of freeboard, I see," Mr. Embleton said, as, after returning on deck, he looked over the side.

"Yes, I never will load down my ships," Mr. Hewson said, "and will never take cargo within twenty per cent of their full carrying power. I have as little as possible stowed either quite forward or quite aft, so that they have not only plenty of freeboard, but are buoyant in a heavy sea. I am sure it pays. I don't insure my ships, and I have not lost one in the last sixteen years. The insurance money saved makes up for the loss of freight, and I have the satisfaction of knowing that I have done all in my power to ensure the safety of my officers and men."

"And very good policy, Hewson," Mr. Embleton said warmly. "I see scores of ships passing inside the Goodwins so loaded down that I would not be on board in a heavy gale for all the money in the bank, and the state of their sails often shows that they are badly cared for in all other respects. The system of insurance is no doubt a good one, but it has been so scandalously abused that it may safely be said that it has largely increased the annual number of wrecks and loss of life. Were it not for insurance, owners would, in their own interest, be driven to see that their ships were made in every respect seaworthy, well provided with gear of all kinds, well manned, and above all, not overloaded. Insurances are responsible for a large proportion of our marine disasters."

As, if the wind continued favourable, the *Tiger* would drop down the river as soon as she got out of dock, which would be at a very early hour the next morning, it was necessary that Stephen should be on board that evening. He, however, went back with his father to Mr. Hewson's, spent the afternoon at Exeter 'Change seeing the wild beasts, and returned by eight o'clock to the ship.

The *Tiger* made a quick voyage to Calcutta. She rounded the Cape without encountering bad weather, and was only twice obliged to shorten sail during the whole passage. Stephen enjoyed his life exceedingly. He was in the first officer's watch, and became a great favourite with Mr. Staines. He astonished his fellow-apprentices, as soon as they were fairly on their way, by producing his quadrant and taking observations at the same time as did the captain and mates; still more so when he took lunar and star observations, working them all out by figures instead of from the tables in the nautical almanac. He found at first some little difficulty in obtaining accuracy when the vessel was rolling, but he was not long in overcoming this, and the captain found that he was able to place the ship's position on the chart quite as correctly as he did himself.

"I would give a lot, Steve," the first mate said, when they had been out a fortnight, "if I could work things out as you do. I have gone over and over again to fellows who advertise that they teach navigation, but it is of no use, I can't make head or tail of all the letters and zigzigs and things. I have tried and I have tried till my head ached, but the more I study it the more fogged I get about it. There does not seem to me to be any sense in the thing, and when I see you sit down and figure away with all those letters and things, it beats me altogether."

"It is not difficult when you have begun from the beginning," Stephen said. "Of course, as my father wanted to teach me navigation, he taught me just the things that led up to the problems that you are talking about, so that it really was not hard, but if I had to do any other sort of mathematical questions I should be just as much puzzled as you are. Then you see, my father explained every step as it came, and as one led to another, I learnt them without meeting with any one special difficulty; but I can quite see that it would be very hard for anyone to learn to work it out without having been coached from the start."

"I shall never try again. I think I could find a port by reckoning and the sun, but as for the moon and stars I give them up altogether. There are hundreds of skippers, nay thousands of them, who don't know more than I do."

This was indeed the case, and the skilful navigators had less advantage over experienced men who worked by rule of thumb than is now the case, as the instruments were comparatively rough and the chronometers far less accurate than at present, and even those most skilful in their use were well satisfied if at the end of a long voyage they found that they were within twenty miles of their reckoning.

"It is different work now, lad, to what it used to be two years ago. Now one walks up and down the deck, and though there may be twenty sail in sight, one pays no more attention to them than one would to as many sea-birds. Then every sail was watched, and one was up in the tops with one's glass twenty times a day, for there was no saying whether it was a friend or an enemy. One's watch at night was a watch then, for there was never any saying whether a French privateer might not come looming out of the darkness at any moment; and if a vessel of about our size was made out a mile off, it was all hands on deck, and cast the lashings off the guns, and stand by till she was out of sight again. Now one jogs along, and all that you have got to look out for, is to see that you don't run foul of another craft, or let one run foul of you. Yes, we had a rough time of it in those days, and I ain't sorry that they are over."

"But you look out sharp for pirates when you are among the islands, don't you, Mr. Staines?"

"Ay, lad; but when one sees a Malay pirate, there is no mistaking her for anything else. At night it is generally a stark calm, and whether one is lying idle, with the sails hanging flat against the mast, or whether one is at anchor, one knows that they can't come upon us under sail, and on a still night one can hear the beat of their oars miles away. There is never any fear of being surprised as long as there is a hand wide awake and watchful on deck. Calms are the greatest curse out there; the ship lies sometimes for days, ay and for weeks, with the water as smooth as grease, and everything that has been thrown overboard floating alongside, and the sun coming down until your brain is on the boil."

"You have storms sometimes, don't you?"

"Sometimes, not very often; but when it does blow, it blows fit to take your head off, and you have nothing to do but to cruise under bare poles, and hope that nothing will get in your way. There is one thing, they are not gales like we have here, but cyclones, and instead of getting blown along for hundreds of miles, you go round and round, so that if there is no land within fifty miles of you when the storm strikes, the chances are that you are safe. If you can but lie to, you can manage at last to edge out of it on the side that is furthest from land. A cyclone is no joke, I can tell you; but if you get warning enough to get your canvas stowed and to send down your light spars, and have got a ship like the *Tiger* under you in good trim,—not too light, not too heavy,—you ought to be able to live through it. There is no better sailor nor one more familiar with the islands than the skipper. He is not fond of carrying on, and perhaps at times we think him a little too prudent, but he generally turns out right; anyhow, it is a fault on the right side.

"I have sailed under him fifteen years now. I was third mate when I first joined his ship; not this, you know, but the old *Gertrude*. I have never had a cross word with him, nor have the other two mates. He expects every man to do his duty, as is right enough; but if that is done well, everything goes on smooth. I don't think that there are ten of the crew who have not been with the skipper for years. When we get back to port and the crew are paid off, it is always, 'When will you want us again, captain?' and no matter whether it is in a fortnight or in a couple of months, pretty nearly every man will turn up."

"That speaks for itself, both as to the owner and the skipper, and the mates too, Mr. Staines."

"Well, we have not much to do with it. Unless a man does his duty, and does it pleasantly and without cursing and swearing, he won't make two voyages under the skipper; indeed he won't make one. Three years ago Towel was laid up with a hurt he got on the voyage before, and we had to get a new second mate at the last moment, for Pasley had not got his certificate then, and couldn't take Towel's place. The man was highly recommended, and was a good sailor, but he was a bully, and a foul-mouthed one, and the skipper put him on shore at the Cape, and paid his passage home out of his own pocket—though I know the owner returned it to him afterwards, and said that he had done quite right. I tell you, lad, you are lucky in making your first voyage on board the *Tiger*, for, putting aside everything else, I don't know a single ship, except Hewson's, where the apprentices mess with the master and mates, and are treated as they are here.

"I daresay you wonder why some of us have not been apprentices, but it is only the last two or three years that Hewson's ships have carried them. Before that there was always a fourth mate to each of his ships, so that there were two officers in each watch; but the ships have such a good name, and the owner had so many applications from friends with sons who wanted to go to sea, that three years ago he made the change. But he is mighty particular who he takes, and all his indentures contain a clause that unless the reports by the captains they sail under are favourable, the owner has the right of returning the premium he received and of cancelling the indentures. I can tell you, lad, that if every owner took as much pains for the comfort of his officers and crews as Mr. Howson does, Jack would have a deal better life than is now the case."

CHAPTER II.

IN THE MALAY ARCHIPELAGO.

THE stay at Calcutta was a short one, and as soon as the cargo for that port was unladen, the *Tiger* again sailed. The apprentices had a run ashore, but each had gone with one of the mates, as in so large a city the boys, if alone, might well have got into trouble. Stephen went with the first mate, and was glad at the arrangement, as Mr. Staines had frequently been there before and knew the town well, and Stephen therefore saw a great deal more of it than he would have done had he been alone. He was delighted with the native bazaar, and would have laid out much of his spare cash there, had not Mr. Staines prevented him.

"Time enough when you get back, Stephen. But if you have got any money to spend you had better go with me to a stall where, the last two voyages I have been here, I laid in a stock of articles useful for trading with the Malays—looking.

glasses, beads, brass buttons, bright handkerchiefs, and things of that sort. I don't say but that one might get them cheaper in London; but in the first place, one always finds plenty of things there to spend one's money on; and in the second place, the people here know exactly the sort of goods needed in the islands, and one can get them all at one stall instead of having to hunt about in a dozen shops for them. We are each allowed to trade on our own account up to a certain amount; and, as a rule, I find that when I get back here I can sell the curiosities I buy down in the islands, for about four times as much as the goods cost me, so if you do the same you will have more money to buy things with here than if you bought them now. But for most of the things you pick up you will find you can get a much better price in London than you can here."

"What sort of things do you buy there, Mr. Staines?"

"The skins of birds, carved wood-work, Malay arms, models of canoes, and things of that kind. The bird skins are the best, especially if you know anything about them. I have got as much as two or three pounds for a rare skin that I exchanged for a twopenny looking-glass and half a dozen brass buttons, but of course that was an exceptional case; for, as a rule, they will average two or three shillings apiece. You had better buy a big pot of arsenical soap, which acts as a preservative to keep away insects, also two or three air-tight tin boxes; they will hold the things you buy here, and you can fill them with trade goods."

Steve took the advice, and expended four out of the five pounds his father had given him on sailing. The mate laid out twenty pounds in similar purchases, and then they returned to the ship, which was anchored a mile down the river, followed by three coolies carrying their purchases. The other apprentices similarly laid out their spare cash.

"You have done well, lads," the captain said, as they were

at dinner on the evening before sailing. "You must not expect to make a very great deal by your trading, although, no doubt, you will get a handsome return for your money. To do really well you must have some knowledge of what birds are rare and what are common, and I should advise you when we get home to spend any time that you have to spare in visiting the Museum and examining the birds there. No doubt you will be able to find out from one of the attendants which are rare ones, and might be able to consult some books on the subject. You may have the luck to come across skins that are altogether new; and, at any rate, a little knowledge would enable you to exchange your goods to a very much greater advantage than you could otherwise do. A knowledge of that kind is always useful to a sailor, who in his wanderings may well get from the natives rare and valuable specimens in natural history, and there are always plenty of collectors ready to pay good prices for them. I have often regretted that I did not pay attention to such matters when I was young; for besides paying well, it gives a great interest to visits to little-known places, and I have heard of two or three captains who have made a good deal of money by it."

For two months after getting among the islands no serious adventures were met with. Trading went on steadily. Several times large native craft were seen, but these sheered off when they saw that the *Tiger* was well armed and prepared for defence. As most of the places touched at had been visited by the captain on previous voyages, the natives hailed his return with expressions of apparent pleasure; but however friendly their bearing, there was never any abatement of the vigilance by the captain and his officers. Only a certain number were allowed to come on board to trade. The seamen always carried cutlasses by their side and a brace of pistols in their belts, and even when they went ashore for wood or water two boats were always sent, half the men with loaded muskets keeping guard while the others worked, and the guns of the ship were loaded and trained in readiness to open fire in case of any hostile demonstration on the part of the natives. Occasionally, when a chief had paid a visit to the ship and invited the captain to a feast on shore, a strong guard armed to the teeth accompanied him, and a boat lay by the ship's side in readiness to land another party if necessary.

"They are the most treacherous race on earth," the captain said one day when the third officer remarked that they seemed very friendly. "You can never trust them for a moment; they will shake hands with you with one hand and stab you with the other. Numbers of ships' companies have been massacred owing to the captains putting faith in appearances, and allowing too many of the copper-coloured scoundrels to get on board at once. As long as you make a rule that not more than twenty or thirty can come on the deck, and that all boats must keep at a distance, you are safe, but you must never let yourself be caught napping. I have had one or two very narrow escapes, for it is twenty-five years now since I first came among these islands.

"I had just passed as a third mate when I made my first voyage here. The captain was an easy-going man, and was quite taken in by the appearance of friendliness on the part of the natives. The first mate, too, was a good sailor, but new to the islands, and too fond of his grog; but luckily the second mate had been here before. His ship had once been attacked and nearly half the men killed before they could beat the Malays overboard, and he was always in a fidget.

"I was only about twenty at the time, and, like a young fool, thought that it was pure cowardice on his part; however, at his earnest request I carried a brace of double-barrelled pistols in my pocket, and, unknown to the captain and the first mate, he persuaded a dozen of the crew to do the same, and got the captain to let him keep the cannon loaded with grape, though the latter made no secret that he regarded this precaution as altogether uncalled for. The natives came on board as usual, at first only two or three canoe loads, but gradually the number of Malays on deck became larger and larger, and quite a crowd of boats were clustered round. I could see that Pearson, the second mate, was in a fidget; he glanced at me significantly two or three times, and I began to think myself that he might be right. We were both of us engaged in bartering with the natives, and I noticed that Pearson put the goods under his charge close to one side of the deck, so that standing behind them he leant against the bulwark and could not be taken in rear. I ordered a couple of the men to move my lot also. Both of those I spoke to were, I knew, among those Pearson had persuaded to carry pistols in their pockets.

"'I don't like the look of things, Mr. Pinder,' one of them, an old hand, whispered to me.

"'No more do I, Jack,' I said. 'Just slip below and bring up four of those boarding-axes. Put one of them down among Mr. Pearson's goods and make a sign to him that it is for his use, put the other three down in front of me, and then do you and Bob Hawkins take your places between me and Mr. Pearson, as if you were going to lend us a hand with the trade; then if there is a shindy the four of us will be able to make a hard fight of it anyhow.'

"He did as I told him, and the second officer nodded to me approvingly. Things went on quietly for another five minutes, then I heard a heavy blow given, followed by a fall; and, as if this was the signal, the quiet crowd of natives became in a moment a mob of yelling fiends; screams filled the air, pistol-shots rang out, and you may guess we fell to work in earnest. I fancy we did not throw away a shot between us, and cleared a space in front of us, then snatching up the axes we made at them tooth and nail. We first fought our way aft. The first mate was fighting like a demon; he had caught up a handspike, and, being a very powerful man, kept off his assailants fairly till we cut our way through and joined him. The moment he was free from the group that was attacking him, he rushed forward, sweeping the natives over with his handspike like ninepins. Two of us kept on each side of him. There was just breadth enough on the deck to give free play to our axes, and though the Malays came at us furiously, they could not stand the blows of our heavy weapons. The cook and the steward came rushing up behind us.

"'Turn the cannon on the canoes!' Pearson shouted. 'Depress them as much as you can, and give it them hot.'

"I had no time to look round, but half a minute later I heard one of the cannon go off, followed by yells and screams from the water.

"'Train two of them along the deck,' I shouted, 'but don't fire until you have orders.'

"The Malays were swarming up from the canoes and joining the crowd in front of us, and I saw a rush of some of our fellows up on to the top of the forecastle. We could make no way now, and it was as much as we could do to hold our own. I fought on until I thought the guns were ready; then, looking round, saw the two men standing behind them with lighted matches.

"'The cannon are trained to sweep the deck, Conklin!' but it was not until I touched him and shouted in his ear again that the mate heard me.

"'Now!' Pearson yelled, 'throw yourselves on to them, cut down one or two of the rascals, and when I shout 'Run!' get back behind the guns.'

"The thought of what was coming gave us fresh strength.

We went at them with a will, and drove them back a couple of yards. Then Pearson shouted 'Run!' and back we went aft as hard as we could tear, Pearson and I almost dragging Conklin with us. As we passed between the guns, with the Malays close at our heels, both men fired; the guns were crammed almost to the mouth with bullets, and the execution was awful. In a moment we dashed at them again, while the men forward, who had armed themselves with the capstan-bars, ran down the ladder and fell upon them. In another minute it was all over. The Malays who remained alive sprang over the bulwark, and we discharged the remaining five cannons into the canoes, smashing up numbers of them, and the rest paddled for the shore for their lives. We had time now to look around. It was an awful sight. Over fifty Malays lay dead, together with eleven of our men, besides the captain. If it had not been for Pearson not a soul would have lived to tell the tale. After it was over, we found that, as the crowds on deck had increased, most of our old hands, who were the men that had taken the pistols, had gradually gathered near the forecastle. Some of the others had joined them, and when the outbreak came, they had for a time been able to make a stout resistance, until one of their number, who was on the forecastle when the fight began, shouted to them that we were training the cannon forward, and they then made a rush up and joined him.

"Every man who had been among the natives had been cut down at the first alarm. Out of the twenty-eight hands on board when the fight began only sixteen remained. Many of these had desperate wounds from the Malay creases, and two of them died a day or two afterwards. Conklin had been very badly cut about. None of the wounds ought to have been dangerous, but he had heated his blood by drink, and that in in a hot climate is fatal, so we buried him ten days after the fight. Thus, you see, we lost two officers and thirteen men, and all for want of taking precautions. Of course we sailed at once for Calcutta, and luckily had fine weather on the way; we should have fared badly with but half a crew had we fallen in with a hurricane. Pearson was a good navigator, and, after taking six more hands on board at Calcutta, he brought her home safely. The owners made us both handsome presents, and the next voyage he sailed as first mate and I as second. So it turned out a lucky stroke for both of us. Three years later he went as captain, and a year afterwards I sailed as his first mate."

"When was it you had your other adventure, captain?"

"That was in the year before. I did not sail with Pearson that year, for he was promoted suddenly to a ship ready to sail. It was a piece of luck for him. One of the owners went down to the docks late one afternoon and found the captain blind drunk. So he was sent straight on shore, and Pearson got his billet. I was very sorry that I could not go with him, as after that business we became great friends, and in his report of the affair he gave me more credit than I deserved for my idea of getting those hatchets up, which, he said, alone enabled us to make a successful defence. I had the more cause to regret his transfer, since the captain was an obstinate man, as we found out during the voyage, and just as much inclined to treat the natives with contempt as my former skipper had been. However, the man appointed to take Pearson's place as first mate was a sharp fellow, and lucky he was so. We were lying one night in a harbour where the natives had appeared particularly friendly the day before. Purvis, the mate, suggested to the captain that it would be as well to have the watches kept as if at sea, but the old man pooh-poohed the idea.

"'I don't like it,' the mate said to me; 'those fellows were too friendly. They did not bargain over the goods, but took them at our own terms, which is not their way. I believe they did it just to lull us into a sense of security. As soon as the skipper turns in for the night I will get the guns quietly loaded, and you and I will keep watch, while I will order the crew to turn in all standing, so as to be ready to tumble out at once. It is mighty hard to keep awake on these soft nights when the anchor is down, and with neither you nor I on deck the betting is two to one that the hands on anchor watch will drop off to sleep. The skipper will be snoring by ten o'clock, and you had better turn in now. I will see to getting the guns loaded, and to having plenty of ammunition handy. I will call you at four bells. If we are going to be attacked it is likely to be just as day is breaking.'

"'You had better call me at two bells,' I said, 'and then you can get three hours' sleep and be up at eight bells. It won't begin to get light until after that, and you may be sure that if I hear any sound I will wake you at once.'

"So we arranged it, and at one o'clock he came down quietly. I had only taken off my shoes and carried these in my hand, so as to avoid making any noise that might wake the skipper, as I went out on deck.

"'Everything is quiet,' the mate said, 'and has been ever since you turned in. Even that is not natural, for, as you know, the natives when they have been doing a trade generally keep on feasting and making a row half the night. Keep your ears well open, for there is no trusting the watch. Every time I have gone forward I have found them sound asleep. Naturally they think that, as there is only an anchor watch, there can be no fear of disturbance; so you must trust to your own ears and not to theirs.'

"'All right!' I said; 'I will keep awake—never fear.'

"I think if I had not been confident that the first mate was not the man to take alarm easily, I should have had difficulty in keeping my eyes open, for the night was sultry and not a breath of air was moving. I went forward to the two men on watch and told them that they must keep a sharp look-out, for that it was likely enough we might be attacked before morning. Then I lit my pipe and paced up and down the deck, stopping occasionally to listen intently. It was nearly eight bells when I thought I heard a grating sound on shore. I walked forward and found, as I expected, that the two men on watch were half-asleep. 'Wake up, you fools!' I said; "there is something moving.' Again I heard the low grating sound.

"'Did you hear that?' I asked.

"The men were wide awake now.

"'Yes, sir, I heard a noise; but I don't know what it was.'

"'They are launching their canoes,' I said. 'I will call the first officer.'

"I went aft. Purvis woke directly I touched him.

"'I fancy they are launching their canoes,' I said. 'I have twice heard a grating sound.'

"He was up in a moment. We stood listening intently for some minutes. There was certainly a movement on shore, but it was difficult to say of what kind. It was just a low confused murmur.

"'You are right,' the mate said presently; 'look at the water.'

"For a moment I scarcely understood him; then I saw what he meant. It had been as smooth as oil before; it was no longer so, but it was broken with tiny ripples as if disturbed by the faintest possible breeze.

"'These ripples must be made by launching the canoes,' he went on. 'A strong body of men might carry them almost noiselessly down that sandy beach and put them in the water without making a splash, but the stir made in wading and in lowering them down, however quietly, would break up this glassy surface, and the ripples once started would run out here. Anyhow we will get the men out. Tell them to come noiselessly. We will serve out the arms and ammunition to them, but we won't load the guns till we have something more to go upon. It may be some time before they attack. I think it is likely enough that they will wait until they hear the boats—which I have no doubt they have sent for—coming up, before they make a move.'

"'Shall I wake the skipper?'

"'Certainly not. As likely as not he would blow us all up and send the men back to their bunks again. He has made up his mind that there is no danger, and the obstinate beggar would risk our having all our throats cut rather than own there was any ground for alarm.'

"I went into the forecastle and roused the men, warning them to muster as quietly as possible. Half an hour passed without the slightest sound being heard. Then the men fidgeted and whispered together, and were evidently of opinion that they had been turned out on a false alarm.

"'Hush, men!' Purvis said sharply, 'I can hear something.'

"You could have heard a pin drop in a moment, and I believe every man held his breath. There was a sort of quiver in the air rather than a sound, and Watkins the boatswain, who had been years and years in vessels trading among the islands, said: 'You are right, Mr. Purvis, that is sweeps; and what is more, it is not one boat, but I should say half a dozen.'

"'That is what I think,' the mate said. 'How far off should you say they were?'

"'It is difficult to tell. I should say three or four miles. That is the best of these proas. A canoe, if the men take pains with their paddling, will come within a hundred yards of you before you hear them, but as the proas row oars, you can make them out a long way off on a still night like this.'

"'Well, we will wait a few minutes longer before we wake the skipper,' Purvis said to me. 'He will swear that he does not hear any noise at all, and that it is all our fancy. In ten minutes there will be no mistaking it. Watkins, you had better get up that boarding-netting'—for among these islands all the ships carry them, and very useful they are in repelling an attack.

"'I have got it handy,' the boatswain said, and soon brought it on deck. 'Shall we lash it up, sir?'

"'No; we had better wait till the captain comes out. It won't take above a couple of minutes, especially if you run it all along by the bulwarks.'

"In a few minutes the sound of the oars was unmistakable, and Purvis went in to call the captain.

"'What is it?' the skipper said as the mate knocked.

"'There are five or six proas coming towards us, sir, and we have reason to believe that the canoes on shore are all launched and ready to attack us.'

"'I believe it is all nonsense,' the skipper said angrily as he came from his door. 'You are always fidgeting about pirates, Mr. Purvis.'

"He came out on deck, listened a moment, and then said: 'Stuff and nonsense! What, have you got the men out? Send them to their bunks at once!'

"'With the greatest respect to you, sir, I shall do nothing of the sort, and if I did the men would not obey me. They can all hear the proas, and we are not going to submit to have our throats cut tamely. Mr. Pinder thoroughly agrees with me, and so does the boatswain, that these proas can be coming for no good purpose at this time of night, and it were madness not to be ready for them. What do you say, Mr. Pinder?'

"'I entirely agree with you, sir,' I replied.

"'This is rank mutiny!' the skipper said furiously.

"'I would rather be tried for mutiny than have my throat cut here. Now, sir, will you give orders, or shall I?'

"'I will give no orders,' the captain said. 'In the morning I will have you put in irons.'

"Purvis, giving a short laugh, turned on his heel. 'My lads,' he said, 'you have heard the sound of the oars, and know as well as I do that we shall shortly be attacked, and shall have to fight hard for our lives. The captain is of opinion that we are all mistaken, and wants us to turn in again. What do you say? Will you have your throats cut or not?'

"There was an angry growl from the sailors.

"'Very well, then, set to work and load the guns—ball at first, but keep your grape handy, we shall want it before we have done. Do it quietly; it is as well these fellows on shore should not know what we are up to. As soon as you have loaded, rig up the boarding-nettings.'

"In a moment all was bustle. There was no need to run the guns in, for that was already done, the captain insisting upon our always having the ports closed, in order, as he said, that the natives might see that our intentions were perfectly friendly. Consequently, the men were enabled to load the guns without noise, moving about the deck on their naked feet like shadows. Then the boarding-nettings were triced up, arms distributed amongst the men, each having a boarding-pike, a cutlass, and a brace of pistols. By the time that this was done, we judged by the sound of the sweeps that the pirates were not more than a mile away. Lanterns were got up on deck and placed in readiness to be lighted and run up to the yard-arm, so as to throw some light down on the water.

"'Now, we will call the old man again. Obstinate as he

is he can't help hearing the oars now, and I know that he is plucky enough, and will fight the ship well as soon as he is once convinced that there is danger.'

"We went together to the skipper's.

"Captain,' Purvis said in a loud voice, 'Pinder and I have come to tell you that the proas are within a mile of us, and to ask you to take the command and fight the ship.'

"We heard the skipper tumble out of his bunk again with an angry exclamation. He opened the door without a word and went straight up on to the poop. He listened a moment, and then ran down again.

"'I beg your pardon, Mr. Purvis,' he said hastily, 'but I have been wrong, and there is no doubt we are going to be attacked. I am heartily sorry for what I have said, and I thank you for your watchfulness."

"'Say no more about it, captain. We are ready to begin as soon as you give the orders.'

"'I will throw on some things and be out again in a minute;' and in less than that time he turned out again.

"'You have the guns loaded?' he asked.

"'Ay, ay, sir, and the boarding-nettings up.'

"'Can you make them out yet?'

"'No, sir. By the sound, they are keeping close in to the shore. I have got the kedge anchor in a boat. Shall I lower it and row a couple of ship's-lengths and drop it there, then we can warp her round, so as to bring all our guns to bear? I deferred doing that to the last, so that the fellows on shore should not know we were on the alert.'

"'Yes; do so at once, Mr. Purvis.'

"The boatswain and two hands were at once called to the boat, which was then lowered and rowed off in the direction the mate pointed out. The anchor was let drop, and the boat returned to the ship, paying out the hawser over the stern. The captain had taken his place on the forecastle, and was looking anxiously ahead.

"'I see them,' he exclaimed at last; 'they are coming out from behind that low point half a mile away. Haul on the hawser and bring her broadside to bear on them. Get the guns across to the starboard side, Mr. Pinder.'

"The ship was pierced for eight guns a side, and by the time the ship was swung round, they were all in position. The proas, now no more than a quarter of a mile away, were heading straight for us.

"'Take a steady aim, lads,' the captain said, 'and fire as soon as you are sure of your shot.'

"In quick succession the guns spoke out. At the reports wild yells broke from the proas, and from the shore, now astern of us.

"'Load as quick as you can with grape,' the captain shouted.

"There had been five proas when the first gun was fired, but before we had reloaded one had disappeared, and there was shouting and confusion in one of the others. It was evident that she also was in difficulties.

"'Don't fire until I give the word.'

"The three proas were within fifty yards of us when he gave the order, and the eight guns poured their contents into the crowded decks. The effect was terrible. Two of the proas ceased rowing altogether, and some of the oars of the other dropped into the water and hampered the efforts of those who still continued to row.

"'The port watch will repel boarders. The starboard watch will load again,' the captain ordered.

"There was way enough on the proas to bring them all alongside, but either the men at the steering oars were all killed or they had lost their heads, for, instead of bringing them up alongside, they simply came up bows on. As they struck the side the Malays tried to climb up, but, attacking as they did only at three points, our men had little difficulty in keeping them off, thrusting through the nettings with their boarding-pikes, and giving the Malays no time to attempt to chop down the nettings with their creases.

"'Are you all loaded?' the captain shouted.

"'Ay, ay, sir,' came from the guns.

"'Train them so as to take the proas between wind and water,' the captain said; 'then run the port guns back to their places; we shall be attacked on that side directly.'

"The sea indeed was sparkling with phosphoric fire, as a crowd of canoes from the shore paddled out towards us. The steward now lit and ran up half a dozen lanterns. We got the guns over in time, but before we could load them the Malays were swarming up the side.

"'Take three men, Pinder, and load the guns,' cried the captain; 'we will keep these fellows off.'

"The same order was given to the boatswain with regard to the guns on the starboard side. It was exciting work, for spears were flying in showers, stink-pots were hurled over the nettings, and the yelling and shouting were deafening. Our men were sticking to their pikes, for they had been ordered to keep their pistols in reserve in case the pirates obtained a footing on deck. There were two little guns on the poop, and when I had loaded the guns on the port side the captain sent me up to load these. I crammed them with bullets up to the muzzle, and then ran them to the poop railing, and placed one of the hands there with a lighted match. We had a tough ten minutes of it, and if the canoes had come up at the same time as the proas it would have gone hard with us; but the last broadside that had been poured in had sunk two of the big craft, and the other had drifted away, so that, in fact, we had only the shore canoes to cope with. We had hard work to keep them back, but none of the natives managed to cross the netting along the waist of the ship, though a few shoved themselves through holes that they hacked with their creases.

"Some managed to swarm up by the cable on to the bows, but three men who were stationed there disposed of them before enough could gain a footing to be dangerous. The captain had been keeping the guns in reserve in case the proa that had dropped behind at first should come on, but he now saw that she was low in the water, and that many of the Malays were jumping overboard. He therefore shouted out:

"'Give them both broadsides. Aim into the thick of them.'

"That broadside settled it; seven or eight of their big canoes were smashed up; several of the others turned and paddled to the shore; and a moment later, the men who were attacking us leapt into the boats alongside and followed their example.

"'Load as quickly as you can,' the captain cried, 'and give them a parting salute.' We ran the two little quarter-deck guns over and peppered them with bullets, and the other guns joined in as soon as they were reloaded.'

"That finished the matter. Our loss was not heavy, considering what a hard fight it had been. We had but two killed, and seven or eight wounded by their spears; while they must have suffered frightfully. In the morning the captain called the crew aft, and made a speech thanking them for their conduct, and saying that they owed their safety and that of the ship to the first mate and myself, and that the night's work would be a lesson that he should never forget. He privately said the same thing to us, and there was no doubt that it was the first mate who saved the ship.

"This and the other affair were a lesson to me as well as to the captain. No matter how friendly the natives might appear, from that day I have never anchored among the islands without having half my guns double-shotted, and the other half loaded with grape; and there is always an officer and half a watch on deck, so that, whatever happens to us, it will not be because I have been caught napping. On both those occasions the captains well-nigh lost ship and crew by their carelessness."

For several weeks they cruised among the islands bartering goods with the natives of sea-coast villages. At most of these the captain had touched on previous voyages, and as soon as the ship was recognized the canoes came off freely. Stephen gradually got rid of the goods he had purchased at Calcutta. Knowing nothing of the respective value of the bird skins, he was guided simply by their rarity. Of skins of which numbers were brought on board, he bought none, however brilliant the plumage; but whenever he saw one that was new to him he at once made an offer for it. But as this was seldom, his box filled but slowly, until one day he went ashore with the captain, the first mate, and twelve sailors armed to the teeth, to pay a visit to the chief. On the few occasions on which he had landed he always carried with him a hand-bag filled full of trade goods. On the present occasion, after the feasting had gone on for some time, he stole out from the chief's hut. The men were sitting down in front drinking palm wine, but keeping a vigilant eye upon the movements of the natives. Presently one of the Malays came up to him and touched his bag, as if to ask what were its contents. He brought out two or three small looking-glasses, some large brass necklaces, and a few of the cheap bangles and rings set with coloured glass, used by the Hindoo peasant women. The native pointed to a hut near, and beckoned to Steve to follow him.

"Jim, you may as well come with me," Stephen said to one of the sailors. "I think this fellow wants to trade with me; but they are treacherous beggars, and I don't care about going with him by myself."

The sailor got up and followed him across to the hut. The

Malay was evidently a chief of some importance, and Stephen thought that he might be possessed of articles of a better class than those usually offered. In one corner of the hut stood a seaman's chest with several small cases round it. It needed but a glance to show that the latter were two chronometers and three quadrants.

'The scoundrels have been plundering a ship, Jim."

"Ay, ay, your honour, there is not much doubt about that. I should like to knock the black villain on the head."

The chief caught the tone of anger, and made a variety of signs to the effect that there had been a great storm, and that a ship had been driven ashore and wrecked.

"Ay, ay, that is all very well," the sailor growled; "but that won't do for us. Those chronometers would never have floated, and them polished cases have never been in the water."

"Never mind, Jim; it won't do to look suspicious." He pointed to the chronometers, and asked by signs how much was wanted for them. He took out four looking-glasses, two brass chains, and three or four bead necklaces. The chief looked doubtful; but when Stephen added a crimson silk handkerchief he closed with the bargain at once. He would indeed have given them for the looking-glasses alone if Stephen had held out for them, for he regarded the chronometers with a certain sense of dread; they were to him mysteries, having made, when first brought ashore, a ticking noise, and were generally considered to be in some way alive. They were, therefore, left out in the air for some days, and it was then found that they were, as supposed, dead. None of the other natives would have given them house-room; but the chief, who was less superstitious than the majority of the tribe, had brought them into his hut, although he had not had sufficient courage to break them up for the sake of the brass.

Having disposed of these the chief opened the lid of the chest. He took out some clothes and held them up, but Stephen shook his head decidedly. Then he brought out a gold watch and a heavy bag; he untied the latter, and handed it to Stephen for inspection. The lad had difficulty in repressing an exclamation, for it was full of guineas, but put it down and placed the watch beside it, assumed an air of indifference, and then made up another pile of about equal value to the first, but threw in a couple of dozen brass buttons. The chief nodded, and Stephen slipped the bag and watch into his coat pocket. While this transaction had been going on, Jim had carried the boxes containing the chronometers and quadrants to his comrades.

"Anything more, sir?" he asked, as he appeared at the door of the hut.

"Nothing more to carry, Jim, as far as I am concerned; but there is a good pea-jacket and some togs in that chest. I have no doubt that it belonged to the captain of the ship; they have cut off all the buttons. I will buy them for you."

The coat and trousers, and half a dozen shirts were, to Jim's great delight, purchased for him. Stephen then examined the whole contents of the chest, thinking that some papers might be found that would give a clue to the name of the ship that it had belonged to, but nothing of the sort was discovered. However, he bought the whole of the clothes, and, calling in the sailors one by one, divided them among them, and then went back and joined the captain.

"I have been doing some trading, captain," he whispered to him. "It is white plunder; and I have no doubt that a ship has been surprised and her crew massacred somewhere near here. I have bought the chronometers and quadrants, and they have certainly not been in the water; also the contents of a sea-chest, which I divided among the men. There were no papers of any kind, but from the appearance of the chronometers, I should say that they cannot have been here long."

The captain nodded.

"We will talk it over when we get on board, Steve. We will be off at once, for these fellows are beginning to get drunk with this beastly liquor of theirs, and it is best that we should get out of the place before there is any excuse for a quarrel."

A few minutes later they took their seats in the boat and rowed off to the ship.

CHAPTER III.

A CYCLONE.

AS soon as they arrived on board, Captain Pinder examined the chronometers and pronounced them to be excellent ones.

"I would not wind them up until it is Greenwich time as they now stand, and would then compare them with our own."

"Of course, sir," Stephen said, "I have bought these not for myself but for the ship."

"Not at all, Steve; you have traded as you have a right to do, and the ship has nothing to do with it. At the same time I don't know whether you will be able to keep or sell them. I must give notice on our return home that such things have been found here under circumstances that leave no doubt that the crew of the ship to which they belonged have been massacred, and the ship herself burned. No doubt owners of vessels that have been missing will call at the office to inspect the chronometers. I do not say that anyone would have a legal right to them; they have been absolutely lost and gone out of their possession, and you have bought them in the way of fair trade."

"If they wish to have them back again, sir, of course I will give them up."

"Well, at any rate, if you did so, lad, you would get a reward proportionate to their value. However, they may never be claimed. Owners whose ships are missing, and who have received the insurance money, are not likely to trouble themselves further in the matter."

"This is not all I have, sir," Stephen went on. "I also got this gold watch and this bag of money. I suppose the chest belonged to the captain, and that he carried this gold with him for the purchase of stores."

"You are a lucky fellow, Steve. Come down into my cabin and we will count the money. Two hundred guineas," he went on, when they had finished; "well, that is about the best bit of trade that I have seen done; you had better hand this over to me to keep."

"Oh, I don't mean it to be kept, sir," Stephen said; "it would not be fair at all. I would not think of it. It is like prize-money, and ought to be divided in the same way. I don't mind keeping the gold watch just now, but if we find out the name of the ship when we get back to England, I should wish to send it to the widow of the captain, and the money too, if it belonged to him."

"There is no chance whatever of that, lad. No captain would be fool enough to bring out a lot of gold like that on his own account. It was certainly ship's money that he would hold for making advances to the crew; as for the purchase of stores, he would pay for them by bills on the owner. But still, you are no doubt right about the watch, and the poor fellow's widow would, doubtless, be glad to have it; as to the gold, I will take charge of it for the present. We will talk the matter over again later on; there is no occasion to come to any decision about it. At present it is entirely yours. I don't think that you have any right to give up a sum of money like this without, at any rate, very careful consideration. It is a sum that, divided up into shares, would give but a very small amount to each on board, while it might be of the most material service to you some day or other. But please oblige me by saying nothing whatever about it at present. Whatever decision is arrived at in matters of this sort, somebody is sure to feel aggrieved, and it is astonishing what little things upset a crew, especially on a voyage of this kind, where there is no such controlling influence over the men's minds as that exercised by touching at ports where there are authorities to whom, in case of necessity, the captain can appeal."

"Very well, sir, I will, of course, do as you wish. Shall I say anything about the watch?"

"Yes; there is no objection to your doing that, especially as that must be mentioned in any inquiries we may make as to any ship being missing, and there is no need for any secrecy about it. I shall also mention the money to the officers; they will appreciate the offer that you have made, and agree with me, I am sure, that it will be better that nothing should be said to the crew."

That evening the first mate said to Stephen: "The captain has been telling us about that bag of money you got hold of, Steve, and we all think that your offer to treat it as if it were prize-money is a very kind one, but we agree with him that it would be a mistake. In the first place, the money wouldn't go far. In any matter of that sort the ship, that is to say the owners, take a large share to begin with, the officers take some shares, and the men's shares would not come to a pound a head. A pound a head would only suffice for them to have a drunken spree on shore, but they are just as well without that, and, as the captain says, it is astonishing what little things upset sailors' minds. They might take it into their head that as you got two hundred pounds in that hut there might be a lot more, and they would be wanting to land and to turn the village upside down, and there would be bloodshed and all sorts of trouble. The old saying, 'Least said, soonest mended', comes in here strongly. We have, so far, got on very well with the natives this voyage, and I hope that we shall continue to do so to the end. I quite allow that we should all of us be glad to give a sharp lesson to that village ashore. They have been plundering, and I have no doubt murdering, the crew of some ship. Still, we have no evidence of that, and we can't attack the village on mere supposition. They have been friendly enough with us, partly because we have been here before, and the captain gets on well with them, but more because they are perfectly well aware that we are always on guard, and that there is no chance whatever of their catching us asleep. In nine cases out of ten it is the carelessness and over-confidence of sailors that tempt the natives to take advantage of it; they would never have shown you these things if they had had any idea of attacking us."

Next morning the operation of filling up the water-tanks was completed, and at noon the orders were given to weigh anchor. Steve saw how rightly the captain had foreseen what was likely to happen, for no sooner was the order given than two of the men came aft as a deputation from the crew.

"What is it, lads?" he asked.

"Well, captain, the boat's crew that went ashore yesterday came off with a lot of togs that must, in course, have been taken from some seaman's chest. Now, it seems to us as that chest could not have been there by fair means, and that, like enough, they had been murdering and looting some vessel here; and, for aught we know, the place may be full of plunder of some sort or another, and that, may be, there are twenty or thirty other seamen's chests there, and other goods. It seems to us, sir, that these chaps ought to be punished, and that we should try to get as much of the plunder they have got hidden as we can; therefore, the crew beg that you will sanction our going ashore and tackling them."

"No, lads, I can't sanction that," the captain said. "It is true that Mr. Embleton was offered by one of their chiefs some chronometers and the contents of a sea-chest. He bought the chronometers, and he also bought the contents of the chest and divided them among the men who went ashore. The chief made signs to him that these things had been saved from a ship that had been wrecked, and it is possible that it may be so. It may not have been wrecked on this island, and those things may have been the share of one of the canoes from here that assisted in looting her; at any rate, we have no proof that the vessel was boarded and captured. If it had been done here, I think we should have seen more signs of it among the natives who have come out to the ship or on shore. There would have been more trade goods about—handkerchiefs, and beads, and so on, and they would not have been anxious to trade with us. At any rate, there are no grounds for attacking a village that has, during the last three or four days, traded peacefully with us, as they have done on several different occasions when I have put in here. Even if there were no other reason, I should refuse to allow them to be attacked, because the news of the affair would spread from island to island, and next time we were in these seas we should do no trade, and should certainly be attacked if we gave them a chance. Of course I shall report the circumstances connected with the discovery of this chest at Calcutta, and endeavour to find out what ship has been lately missing; beyond that we can do nothing in the matter. We are traders; if we are attacked we do our best to beat off the assailants, but it would be altogether beyond our business to attack sea-side villages because we find that they are in the possession of ships' goods, for were we to do so we should soon put an end to all trade in these islands. Go back and tell your comrades this, and then muster at once and heave the cable short."

The orders were obeyed, but it was evident that there was a lack of the usual briskness and willingness. However, before the ship had been many hours on her way, matters settled down and the work went on as usual.

"You see, lad," the first officer said to Stephen as the sails were sheeted home, and the *Tiger* glided away from her anchorage, "the captain was quite right, and if it had been known on the ship that you had got that money, there would have been a good deal more trouble than there was. It would have been no good to tell them that, no doubt, it was the ship's money. Sailors are like children; they would have argued that if you could obtain two hundred pounds from one hut, they would each be likely to get as much in a general loot of the village. You see, giving them those togs you bought was enough to stir them up, and things would not have passed off so pleasantly had they known about the money.

"I do not say that there would have been a mutiny, or anything of that sort, because the great majority of them have sailed for years under the skipper; still, there would have been great discontent and grumbling, and if there happened to be among the new hands one or two sea-lawyers, they might have worked upon the men, and caused a great deal of trouble."

"I see that, sir," Steve said.

"Well, there is no harm done, lad, and you will see that in a day or two the matter will have been forgotten. But it is a lesson that you may profit by; it is always best to avoid anything that, even remotely, is likely to set sailors talking together. All crews are not as trustworthy as the *Tiger's*, and you would be astonished what mischief two or three cunning plausible rascals can do among a crew, if they have got ever so small a grievance to work upon."

A week later the ship was passing along the coast of a small island when Joyce, the eldest apprentice, who was examining the shore through a glass, said to the second officer:

"There is a wreck of some sort, sir, in among those black rocks."

"So there is," the mate said, shading his eyes with his hand. "I see it plainly enough now that you call my attention to it."

He went aft and reported it to the captain, who came out and examined it carefully with his glass.

"It is a wreck certainly, and not the work of the natives this time," he said. "She has been blown on shore and left almost high and dry; her spars are all gone, the bulwarks are swept away, and though I cannot see the line of her broadside, I fancy that she has broken in two. Anyhow, as we have hardly steerage way, we shall lose no time by sending to find out what ship she is. Mr. Towel, you might as well lower the gig. Take six men; let them all take muskets and pistols with them. As Mr. Joyce was the first to make her out he may as well go with you. If you see no signs of natives, you can land and ascertain whether she has been plundered. It may be that she has not been discovered yet by the natives. If you see any of them about, content yourself with getting the ship's name and port from her stern."

The boat was lowered.

"You may go too, Steve," he added as Stephen was looking down into the boat. "It is Mr. Archer's turn; but as he had got a touch of fever this morning, he is better sitting under the shade of that sail than in an open boat."

"Thank you very much, sir," Stephen said, and, running below, shoved his pistols into his pocket.

"You have got water in the boat?" the captain asked the mate just as Steve returned on deck.

"The keg is about half-full, sir," he said as one of the sailors lifted and shook it.

"Hand them another down from the long-boat," the captain said, turning to one of the men; "it is better always to make sure. Mr. Towel," he went on, leaning over the side, "one is never sure of the weather for an hour, and I don't altogether like the colour of the sky now. But if there are no signs of change aloft, and you see the natives have not been near the place, give a look round beyond the rocks for anything that might show whether some of the crew got ashore—fires made, or anything of that sort. Should you see signs, we will fire a gun or two when you return, and lay off for a few hours to give them a chance of coming down to the beach."

"Ay, ay, sir," the mate said, "I will take a look round for them; but from the way she has been thrown up I should doubt whether there is the slightest chance of anyone having got ashore.'

The captain nodded, then the mate gave the word, and the boat pushed off from the ship. Four men rowed, two sat in the bow, Mr. Towel and the two apprentices sat aft. They were some three miles from shore. There was a ripple on the water, but the wind was very light. There was, however, a ground-swell that had caused the *Tiger* to roll, but which was scarcely perceptible in the boat. Steve remarked on this.

"No," the mate said, "these long swells do not affect a boat in the least. I have often gone ashore on the west coast of Africa, when one was scarcely conscious in the boat of there being any swell on at all, and yet the vessels at anchor outside were rolling almost gunwale under. Still, I would rather that we had not got it, it is a sign that there is wind somewhere, and I agree with the skipper that it is an unnatural-looking sky. Still, it may be hours yet before there is any change."

Half an hour's rowing took them to shore. "She could not have picked out a worse place, lads," the mate said when they approached the wreck. "You see there are black heads sticking out of the water all round, and it must have been a tremendous sea to have carried that ship right through them and chucked her up there where there are not two feet of water."

"The *Lady Vernon*, London," Joyce exclaimed at this moment, "I can make out her name plainly."

"Then your eyes are better than mine, Joyce, for I can't say I can read it yet. Row easy, men, and you in the bow keep a sharp look-out on the water. If we were to come bow-on to a hidden rock we should have to wait ashore until another boat came out to fetch us."

Rowing very gently the boat kept on her course until within half a length of the ship, then she ran quietly up on a flat rock some seven or eight inches under water. They could see now that the captain's conjecture was correct. The ship had broken her back, having, as she was carried in on the crest of a great wave, dropped on a sharp ledge of rocks about amidships. The sea had rushed in through the hole in her side, and had torn away all her planking and most of her timbers forward, while the after part of the ship had held together. The hold, however, was gutted of its contents.

"The natives have not been here since," Steve said as he pointed ahead where, apparently far out of reach of the water, lay a quantity of wreckage, splinters of planks, bits of timber, bales of goods, and a great litter of loose cargo.

"It is of no use climbing up above," the mate said in answer to an offer on Joyce's part to endeavour to reach the deck "The waves, you see, have rushed in through the stern windows, and have made a clean sweep of everything. Half the deck has burst up and gone. We will have a look at the things on shore. Step out, lads, and pull the boat a bit higher up."

This was done, and they waded through the water knee-deep to shore. The wreckage lay a hundred yards further up, on ground quite twenty feet higher than that on which they were standing. The bales were all marked with the ship's name. There were no signs of casks or boxes, these had doubtless been smashed into splinters. Among the wreckage five skeletons were found. They searched further inland, but could discover no sign whatever of life between the shore and a dense forest that began four or five hundred yards away.

"It is certain that no one has escaped," the mate said. "In the first place, no living creature could have ever gained his feet if cast up by such a sea as that must have been. The first wave that struck her after she was thrown up there must have swept the decks clean and finished them all at one blow. In the next place, if by a miracle any of them did get safely ashore, you may be sure that they would have buried their comrades the next morning. You see, it is sand up there where the wreckage lies, and it would not have taken long to scrape a hole deep enough and large enough to bury them. Ah! the captain is getting impatient," he exclaimed, as the sound of a gun came across the water. "No wonder," he went on as he looked at the sky.

They had been about an hour on shore, and had been so fully occupied in examining the wreckage, and in looking for some signs that might tell them if any of the crew had gained the shore, that they had paid no attention whatever to the weather. A great change had taken place since they had left the ship. The wind had entirely died away, and a darkness had crept over the sky; it was not a cloud, but a sort of dull vapour.

"Quick, lads, to the boat," the mate said, "there is not a moment to be lost. There is a storm brewing, and the sooner we are on board the better."

They ran through the water, got into the boat, and pushed her off.

"Be careful, men; paddle quietly until we are well beyond the rocks. Keep a sharp look-out forward." Another gun was fired from the ship as he spoke. "Steady, men, steady!" he said; "you can row as hard as you like when we get outside, but it is of no use knocking a hole in her to start with."

As soon as they were beyond the rocks they bent to the oars. At the mate's orders, the two apprentices and the sailors in the bow took their seats by the rowers and double-banked the oars.

"The skipper is getting every rag of sail off her," the mate said, as he looked ahead. "There is another gun! It is getting darker and darker, I don't suppose they can make us out. Give way, lads."

The gloom deepened rapidly. The ship continued to fire guns every minute or two, and it was well she did so, for the mate had now lost sight of her.

"Which way do you think it will come, sir?" Stephen, who was at the stroke-oar, asked.

The mate shook his head. "There is no knowing," he said. "If it is inshore, the *Tiger* will lay her bones by that wreck behind us. We can't be above a mile away from her by the sound of that last gun. But it will be a close thing, I can hear the wind coming."

Even those rowing were conscious of a low moaning sound.

"It comes from behind I think," the mate said in answer to a look from Stephen. Suddenly a puff of wind from behind rippled the water round them and then died away again. "Row, lads," the mate exclaimed, "I can see the ship now, she is not half a mile away; five minutes will do it."

The men strained at the oars and the boat sprang forward at every stroke. They could hear the moaning sound growing louder and louder.

"The captain has got her head off shore," the mate said; "he has been towing her round. They have just hoisted the boat up. He has got the little storm-jib on her. Now, lads, another four or five hundred yards and we shall be alongside."

It was a race with the storm, but the odds were too great. They were but a hundred yards from the ship when the roar rose into a wild scream, and a line of white water sprang towards them with fearful velocity.

"In oars, men!" the mate shouted. "Throw yourselves flat in the bottom of the boat,—quick!"

The order was executed almost as soon as given. The mate, too, slipped off his seat on to the floor-board, while still retaining hold of the tiller. The next moment the storm struck them. It was well that the boat was still flying through the water with the way full on her; had she been lying motionless she would probably have sunk like a stone under the force of the blow. As it was she leapt forward like a horse under a spur. They passed but half a length or so from the ship. The latter had not yet gathered way, but lay pressed down until her bow was well-nigh level with the water. As the mate looked up he saw the captain holding on by the shrouds. Each waved a hand and then the boat flew on, and in a minute the ship was out of sight. The mate shouted in the ear of the sailor who rowed the stroke-oar and who was lying next to him:

"Crawl forward and try and fix the floor-board there, so as to show a few inches above the bow to act as a head-sail. If she broaches to, it is all up with us. As you go along tell each man to shift himself a bit more aft. Her stern must be well down or I can never keep her straight. If you can't fix the floor-board, get up the mast; tie up the foresail in a roll, and then hoist it, that will give hold enough to the wind."

The man nodded and made his way forward; he endeavoured to carry out the first part of his orders, but the moment he raised the floor-board above the level of the gunwale it was wrenched from his hands and blown ahead. With the aid of two other men he managed to step the mast. The mate waved his hand to him to say that that would do for the present. The man, however, prepared the sail ready for hoisting, rolling it up tightly and winding a cord round and round it; then he hooked the head on to the traveller on the mast, and lay down at its foot, holding the halliard in readiness to hoist it. The water was still perfectly smooth, and the boat flew straight before the wind without any tendency to broach to. Stephen, after the stroke-oar had gone forward, crept aft until he was beside the mate, and there lay for a time, feeling half-stupefied by the tremendous roar of the cyclone.

Captain Pinder was, as every good officer should be, most particular about his boats, and always had them built specially from his own design. They were broader than usual, and had a flat floor and a deep keel, thus they were extremely buoyant, their lines resembling those of the surf-boats on the west coasts of India and Africa, while their deep keels enabled them to sail close to the wind. The men chafed sometimes when, on their way to shore, they found themselves passed by the narrow boats of other ships; but the captain was perfectly indifferent to this, and used to say to other skippers who laughed at him for what they called his "walnut shells":

"A boat is not made for racing; she is made to carry her crew in a heavy sea. My boats will live where yours would be swamped in five minutes, and with their great beam they will carry all sail, while you would not dare show a shred of canvas. It makes no difference to me whether I get to shore five minutes earlier or later; properly handled, the smallest of my boats ought to weather any ordinary gale, while the long-boat would be as safe to cross the Atlantic in as the *Tiger* herself, though I don't say that she would be as comfortable."

The crew, every one of whom had many a time grumbled at the contrast between their beamy craft and the smart gigs of most other ships, now felt the advantage. The boat sped lightly along, raising her head higher and higher out of the water whenever a fresh blast of wind added to her speed, and, save for the sound of the rushing water against the sides, might have been at rest, for any motion that could be perceived. In half an hour the sea began to get up; as soon as it did so the mate made a signal to the man at the halliards, and the sail was drawn up. Tightly as it was rolled, the difference was at once perceptible, and the boat flew along faster than before. The men were now sitting up in the bottom of the boat; they knew that the battle with the storm had as yet scarcely begun, and that when the sea once got up they would have a terrible time of it. In an ordinary ship's-boat the prospect would have been absolutely hopeless; but the Norwegian pilot-boats—whose model the captain had pretty closely followed—are able successfully to ride out the heaviest gale in the North Sea, and the mate and the two apprentices, the latter of whom had often heard from Captain Pinder, with whom the matter was a pet hobby, of the wonderful power of these craft in a gale, entertained a strong hope that she would live through whatever might come. As the sea rose, a small portion of the foresail was loosed, then more was freed, until the whole of the little sail was drawing, and the speed with which it dragged the boat along saved her from being swamped by the following waves. But in another hour the water no longer ran in waves, it was broken up in a confused and tumultuous sea; the greater part of the sail was again bound up, for there was no longer the same risk of being swamped, and it was necessary to moderate the boat's speed in such a tumult of water.

"What makes it like this?" Stephen shouted.

"The circular motion of the wind," the mate replied in a

similar tone of voice. "I dare say we have made two or three circles already."

"There is a compass in the locker behind you, sir."

The mate nodded.

"That may be useful when the storm is over, but would not help us now, and might get broken."

That Stephen could quite understand, for the motions of the boat were so sudden and unexpected that the crew often grasped at the thwarts and gunwale, fearing they would be thrown right out of her. At one moment a wave seemed to rise underneath her, and almost chuck her into the air, then she would sink between two masses of water, that looked as if they would tumble over and fill her, then she would dash head-forward at a wave that rose suddenly in front of her. For a time it seemed to all on board as if her destruction was imminent, but as the buoyant little craft struggled bravely on,—shipping no more water than one man with the bailer could free her of as fast as it came aboard, in the shape of spray,—they began to breathe again more freely.

It was now nine hours since the gale had burst upon them, and there were no signs of an abatement, when, as they were on the top of a wave, the mate shouted:

"There are breakers ahead."

Every head was lifted, and when the boat rose again on a wave they could see a line of white foam ahead of them as far on either side as the eye could see through the mist.

"Keep a look-out for a break in the line, Wilcox," the mate shouted.

The man forward waved his hand, and, holding to the mast, stood up. A minute later he turned and shouted something to the man next to him, and the message was passed from mouth to mouth to the mate.

"It is not a reef, sir; it is a low sandy coast."

"Take your places on the thwarts," the mate shouted, "and get your oars out."

The men did so. Then, in a momentary lull in the blast, the officer said:

"Get ready to pull for your lives when I give the word. Our only chance is to go in on the top of a wave. The instant we touch the ground and she loses her way, jump out and stick your heels in the sand."

They approached the edge of the surf rapidly.

"Stick your oars in deep and check her way," the mate shouted.

He stood up in the boat when they were within fifty yards of the point where the waves curled over and fell with a roar like thunder on the beach. Two or three waves passed under her, then he saw one of greater height approaching.

"Row, lads! row for your lives!"

The wind helping them, they flew forward. The wave rose higher and higher behind them—it looked almost as steep as a wall—and an involuntary cry broke from several of the men as the boat's stern rose up it.

"Row! row!" the mate shouted.

But six strokes were pulled and then the wave fell over with a crash, and in a moment they were shooting along with the speed of an arrow in the midst of a mass of seething foam.

"Get ready to jump!" the mate shouted.

His voice was lost, but the action which accompanied it was understood. They were flying up a steep slope, when suddenly the motion became slower, then there was a bump.

"Hold to her, lads, if you can; every man spring overboard."

For a moment they seemed drawn backwards by the rush of the water, then the boat became fixed, and a moment later the water left them.

"Now, all together before the next wave reaches her."

With a united effort they lifted and ran the boat her own length further up. The next wave barely reached the boat's stern. Before another came she was well up on the sand. Then the mate pointed upwards. The roar of the surf and the howl of the wind would have drowned any words, but his gesture was sufficient. Most of the men had, like their officer, lost their hats, but those who had not done so took them off. Several of them, including Stephen and Joyce, threw themselves on their knees, the others stood with bent heads, and all uttered a fervent thanksgiving for their preservation from what had seemed almost certain death. The mate was the first to move. He went to the side of the boat, and began to take double handfuls of sand, and to throw them into her. The others looked at him in surprise, but he made signs that the wind might lift the boat up, whirl her round, and dash her to pieces; then all set to at the work, which they continued until the boat was half-full of sand. Then the two barrels of water were carried up, together with a bag of biscuits and a bottle of rum from the locker, where a supply was always kept in case of an emergency like the present. They went on beyond the brow of the sand-hill, and ensconced themselves in a hollow at its foot, where they were completely sheltered from the wind. The mate got out his jack-knife, and managed to get the cork out of the bottle, and pouring water from one of the breakers into a tin pannikin that formed part of the boat's equipment, gave a ration of grog to each, and served out a biscuit all round.

As soon as these were eaten and the grog drank, they threw themselves on the sand and were soon fast asleep, utterly worn out with the prolonged strain they had gone through.

When they woke, day was just breaking. The mate was the first to leap to his feet.

"Tumble up, lads," he said, "we must have had twelve hours' sleep. The storm is over."

All were soon at the top of the sand-hill. A heavy sea was still breaking on the sands, but there was scarce a breath of wind, and the sea, though rough and agitated, was no longer covered with white heads, and looked bright in the rosy light. The boat lay where they had left it, securely anchored by the weight of the sand it contained. Their next glance was inland. For a quarter of a mile away the sand covered everything, then a few bushes rose from it; beyond were some stunted trees, and a hundred yards further a thick forest bordered the sandy belt as far as they could see on either hand. It was evidently a large island, for two or three miles away the country rose hill beyond hill, culminating in a jagged mountain dome twenty miles distant.

"Do you know where we are, sir?" Stephen asked, as the mate stood silently looking at the peak.

"No, I wish I did. I have either never seen that hill before, or, if I have, it has been from some other side that gave it quite a different outline. You see, we were nine hours in the gale, and during that time I fancy we must have run nearly a hundred miles; but I do not suppose we are half that distance from the point where we started, for we are sure to have gone round and round several times in the first hour or two. The island we were at, was some fifty or sixty miles from the coast of Sumatra, and possibly it is there that we have been cast ashore; but, on the other hand, we may have gone quite in another direction. Anyhow, there is no denying that we are in an awkward fix. It matters little enough which of the islands we have hit upon, the natives are all pirates and scoundrels, and the possession they prize most is a human head. The first thing to do, lads, is to draw the charges from our muskets and pistols and to reload them, then we will have a consultation."

This was done, and then they went down to the boat.

"I half expected it," the mate went on, after examining her; "the shock has started the butts of three planks on one side, and two on the other. We will get the sand out first and turn her over, bottom upwards."

This was done.

"I think we might make a shift to cobble it up," the mate said. "Some of the wood here is as hard as iron, and we might cut some pegs and fasten the planks into their place again. I don't suppose we shall be able to make them water-tight, but we might caulk them up with pitch or gum from some of the trees. But that is not the first thing to think of; it is no use having a boat if we have not food or water to put into her. These biscuits would last us two or three days, and the water, if we are careful, as long again, but that is not enough to start with on a long cruise. The place we have to make for is Timor. Do you think that you could find your way there, Steve, and how far is it?"

"I was looking at the chart the last day I was on board, sir, and I noticed that Timor lay to the south of where we were then, and I should say it was something like six or seven hundred miles away."

"Well, it is of no use starting on such an expedition as that with such a stock of provisions as ours, so I propose that, in the first place, we see what is to be found in the forest. It will be hard if we do not find a supply of fruit. If we can collect a store enough we might venture upon making a start. You see, we must keep well off the land, for if we were made out from any of the coast villages, we should have one of their craft after us in no time; but, in any case, I should say we had better stay here for a week. If the *Tiger* got safely through that gale, you may be sure the captain will be cruising about looking for us. He has sufficient faith in his boats to feel pretty positive that if we have not been cast ashore we are still afloat."

CHAPTER IV.

A RESCUE.

THEY were soon in the forest. It required care and caution to make their way through the tangled growth of climbing canes and vines. Some of these were armed with terrible thorns, and as they had no hatchets to chop their way through them they were often obliged to make detours to escape these obstacles. Orchids of brilliant colours and fantastic shapes grew thickly on the trees, ants in countless numbers swarmed up and down the trunks, and many an angry exclamation was wrung from the seamen as a bite as sharp as the sting of a wasp told that some of these insects had crawled up the legs of their trousers or made their way down their neck.

"Unless we are going to live on ants," the mate said ruefully as he gave a savage slap at his leg, "it seems to me we are likely to starve, for I have seen nothing whatever to eat since we entered the wood. Even if some of the trees did bear fruit I don't see how we are going to get at it, for one would be eaten alive by these little brutes before we reached the top."

"I vote we turn back, Mr. Towel," one of the men said. "I would rather put to sea and take my chance than keep on being stung by these ants, when there doesn't seem the least hope of our finding anything."

"There doesn't seem much chance here, Nixon. I think we had best get out of the wood and follow the edge along. We may come to some place where it is more open, and may even strike on a stream. If we could do that we might patch up the boat and pull up stream a bit. Anyhow, I don't think it is any use pushing on here. My jacket is torn in a dozen places already by the thorns."

"One of them has nearly taken my eye out," another grumbled; and indeed all were bleeding from the gashes they had received from the thorns. They made their way back carefully, and there was a general exclamation of satisfaction when the light could be seen ahead through the trees. As soon as they were out on the sands shirts were hastily pulled off and a hunt for ants carried out.

"It is lucky the bites don't swell up," Joyce said, "or I should be a mass of bumps. It is as bad as if one had been attacked by a swarm of bees. Yet there is only a little red spot to show for each bite."

As soon as they had freed themselves from the ants they started along the edge of the forest. After walking for two miles they gave a shout of joy, for a river some fifty yards wide issued from the forest. The sand-hills had hidden it from sight until they were close upon it.

"Thank God, we sha'n't die of thirst," the mate said. "It will be a hard job to get our boat here, but it has got to be done. Even if we could launch it through the surf there would be no getting in through the rollers on the bar, at least I should not like to try it. So we have got to drag her here somehow. It will be a tough job, but as there seems no chance of getting food in any other way we must undertake it. Hurrah!" he exclaimed suddenly, "there are some cocoa-nut trees on the other side of the river. That settles it. Let us be off back again at once."

They returned in much better spirits than they had before felt. On the way they went a short distance into the forest, and cut off a number of thorns some two inches long and seemingly as hard as iron. They breakfasted on a biscuit, with a full allowance of water, and then set to work at the boat. The thorns answered their purpose as nails admirably, and the planks soon were securely fastened into their places against the stem; but without nails to clench the planks together, it was evident to them all that the boat would not float five minutes. They stood looking at it discontentedly.

"What is to be done with it?" said Mr. Towel. "Can anyone make a suggestion?"

"I should think, sir," Stephen said, "that if we could get some strong fibre, or some of those thin climbers that barred our way—they were not thicker than string, but there was no breaking them, and I should think that they would do—that with them we could sew the planks together and caulk them afterwards with the threads from a bit of the leg of one of our drill trousers."

"A capital idea, Stephen. At any rate, it would be worth trying."

"I will go and fetch some of those climbers, sir, and some long thorns to make the holes with."

"We may as well all go, Stephen; we have nothing to do here, and at any rate it is cooler in the forest than it is on the sands. We shall want a good stock of thorns, for we are sure to break lots of them in making the holes."

"I have a thing in my knife that will do for that, sir," Joyce said; and he produced from his pocket a knife with many blades, one of them being a long pricker. "It was given to me the day before we sailed, and I have always wondered what use that thing could ever be. Here is a use for it at last."

"Capital, Joyce! That is just the thing. There is flint and steel, and a tinder-box in the locker, and our best plan will be to make a fire and heat that pricker of yours red-hot. It would make the work a great deal easier, and there will be less risk of breaking it or of splitting the wood. So now we will collect dry wood and creepers and leave the thorns alone."

This was done; but when they returned to the edge of the forest all agreed that they should lie down there in the shade until the sun had lost its power, for their position being almost on the equator the heat out on the sand was unbearable.

"It will be as well for one to keep a watch, lads," the mate said. "We have seen no signs of natives, but there may be some about. The sun is nearly overhead, so it will be another four or five hours before we can set to work. I will take the first watch. In an hour I will wake Mr. Joyce; Mr. Embleton will follow him; then you, Nixon; that will take us on till it's time to move."

These arrangements were carried out, and as the sun sank towards the horizon the party went down to the beach. Some rotten wood was crumbled up and a fire quickly made, then the work of boring the holes began, and was kept up all night. As it was necessary to put them very closely together, and the piercer had to be heated two or three times for each hole, two worked by turns while the rest slept, and by sunrise the holes were all finished. Then the work of sewing the planks together began, the boat being turned on its side to allow the string, as they called it, to be passed backwards and forwards. In two hours their work was completed. Stephen cut off four or five inches of duck from the bottom of each leg of his trousers, and unravelling the thread he and the mate pressed it into the seams as fast as the sewing was completed.

"I think that that will do," the mate said, looking with a satisfied air at the work. "Now, what it wants is a little tallow to rub in; but there is no candle handy."

"When I was on watch, sir, I saw lots of bees flying in and out of the trees. If we could light on a hive the wax would do first-rate."

"So it would, Steve. However, until we can find one I fancy we shall get on well enough. Five minutes' bailing occasionally will keep her dry enough, I am sure, at any rate for river work. Now we have got the big job before us; let us have a try how we can move her."

The nine men put their strength to the boat, but they found that the deep keel buried itself in the sand, and that they could not drag her along. Then they tried carrying her, the mate, the two boys, and two men on one side, and the other four men on the other. She was a heavy weight, but they could just manage it, and carried her for some twenty yards before they put her down.

"This will never do," the mate said. "We can't use our strength to advantage, else the weight would not be too great for us. Let us go up to the wood, lads, and chop four poles, turn her over, and lay her down on them. In that way I don't think we shall have much difficulty about it."

It took them longer than they expected, for the wood was so tough that their cutlasses produced but little impression upon it. After an hour's hard work, however, they cut four poles, each about twelve feet long. With these they returned to the boat, laid the poles down on the sand at equal distances apart, and turned the boat over upon them; then a man took each end of a pole, the two boys taking one end together, and at a word lifted the boat with comparative ease. It was very hard work under the blazing sun, and they had to stop every hundred yards or so to rest their arms. Still they were successful, and after three hours' toil they reached the river. The oars had been lost when they landed, and they determined to take the bottom boards out and cut them into paddles The first thing, however, was to bathe.

"Don't go far out," the mate said, "there may be sharks or alligators in the river for aught we know."

Greatly refreshed by their dip, they took the boards out of the boat, carried them up into the shade of the trees, and with their jack-knives fashioned them into rude paddles, with thin creepers strips of wood tying down the handles to add to their strength. This took them all the afternoon. When the sun had lost its power they put the boat into the water, and made an experimental trip in her, and were glad to see that the seams were almost water-tight, and that it would need but an occasional use of the bailer to keep her clear. They at once paddled across the river to the opposite side, and then pulling the boat up made a rush for the cocoa-nut trees that they had seen the day before.

"How are we to get up?" Joyce inquired, looking with dismay at the smooth trunks.

"I learnt that on the west coast of Africa," the mate replied. "I was there two years and got to know, I think, all there was to know with regard to steering a boat in a surf; climbing a cocoa-nut tree is easy work in comparison. Fetch the head-rope of the boat."

This was done, and he asked who volunteered for the first climb.

"I will try it, Mr. Towel," Joyce said, "if you will show me how."

"Stand by the side of the tree, Joyce. Now I will put this rope round you and round the tree, leaving a certain amount of slack in the loop. Now you get a grip of the tree with your knees. Then with your hands you shift the loop up as high as you can, and lean against it. Get a sort of purchase, and so shift your knees a bit higher. No doubt you will feel it awkward at first, but after a little practice you will find no difficulty whatever in going up at a fair rate of speed."

In spite of his experience aloft Joyce found it hard work to climb the tree As soon as he was at the top he broke off the nuts and dropped them; when he had picked two nuts for each of the party he descended.

"They are not a bit like cocoa-nuts," Stephen remarked as the first came to the ground. "They look more like queer-shaped gourds."

"They do, lad," the mate agreed. "But you see they are not ripe yet, while those we get in England are over-ripe; instead of the inside nut being enveloped in fibre the whole thing is soft, and, you see '—here he suited the action to the word—"you can cut a hole down right through, and then all that you have got to do is to drink the milk."

The men followed the officer's example, and were soon taking long draughts of the sweet, cool liquor, which differs widely indeed from that of the ripe cocoa-nut.

"How is it that the milk is so cool, sir?" Steve asked.

"That is more than I can tell you, for no matter how hot the weather, the milk of fresh cocoa-nuts is always cool; why it should be so I have no idea."

After they had drunk the milk they broke open the nuts and scraped the soft cream-like paste which lined the inside, and which, when the nut ripened, would have become hard and solid.

"You will find them of different degrees of ripeness," the mate said. "Some of them will furnish us with drink, some with food, and as there are trees along here as far as we can see, we need not worry ourselves as to victuals. Well, we have done our work for the day and will make this our camp, and talk over what is the best thing to do next."

After much deliberation it was decided that they should paddle up the river the next day, leaving two of their number at the edge of the forest to keep a look-out for the ship.

"It is as well to see what there is on the river," the mate said. "Of course if we come to a village we shall let ourselves drop down quietly again. And we must keep a sharp look-out as we go; it would never do to let them get a sight of us, for none of the natives of these islands are to be trusted, and I am sure that none of us wish to have our heads used as a decoration in their huts. What I hope to come upon is the site of an abandoned village. These people often shift their quarters. They have no belongings to speak of to move, and a couple of days' labour is enough for them to put up fresh huts. But in the places they have occupied we are sure to find bananas; and if we can but get a boat-load of them we shall be victualled for a voyage, and after waiting long enough to give the ship a chance of finding us, the sooner we are off the better. Many of these islands are inhabited by tribes that spare no one who falls into their hands, and it would be better to take our chance on the sea than to remain here. There are a good many little Dutch settlements scattered about. What we have got to do is to light upon one of these. There is no mistaking them for native villages, and once we can get a point of departure we shall have no difficulty in laying our course either for Timor or Java. Stephen, I shall leave you as the junior officer here to-morrow. Wilcox will stay with you. If you see the ship you will light a big fire and throw green leaves on it to make as big a smoke as possible. They would know at once that it was a signal, for the natives would do nothing to attract notice, especially if their intentions were hostile."

"All right, sir! We will keep a sharp look-out. You won't be away many hours, I suppose?"

"Certainly not. We don't want to do any exploring. All we want to do is to look for food, and the most likely food for us to find is a troop of monkeys among the trees overhanging the river. As a rule, I should not like to shoot the beasts. They are too much like human beings. But if we can get a supply of meat it will be welcome, no matter what it may be. Of course we should not shoot many, for a couple of days would be the outside that meat would keep good here."

"But might not firing a gun bring the natives down on you, sir?" Stephen said.

"Oh, we have seen no signs of natives!" the mate said impatiently, "and there mayn't be any within miles and miles of us, probably not nearer than those hills; for I believe it is there that they principally do what cultivation there is—in the first place, because it is cooler, and in the next place because there are, we know, tremendous swamps in the low land of Sumatra, though whether this is Sumatra or not I cannot say."

The next morning the boat started as soon as a supply of cocoa-nuts, sufficient for the day, had been thrown down, two or three of the sailors adopting the means the mate had taught Joyce, and going up the trees very much more quickly than he had done.

"What do you think of this 'ere business, Master Stephen?" Wilcox said as they watched the boat making its way slowly against the current.

"I don't know, Wilcox, what to think of it."

"I calls it a risky affair," the sailor said after a pause. "Mr. Towel is a good officer, I don't say as he isn't, but I would rather see an older head on his shoulders just at present. It is all very well for him to say as there may be no natives within twenty miles; but how is he to know that? There may be a village just round the turn of the river. All these chaps are pirates when they get a chance, every mother's son of them, and there may be half a dozen war-canoes lying a mile up this river. It would be natural that they should be somewhere near its mouth, ready to start out if a sail is sighted, or news is brought to them that there is a ship anchored off a coast village within a few hours' row. As to firing a gun, in my opinion it is just madness. As he says himself, meat won't keep two days, and it is just flying in the face of Providence to risk attracting the attention of the natives, for the sake of a day's rations of fresh meat.

"It was all very well to bring the boat up here so as to lie out of sight of any canoes that happened to be passing along the shore; but I would much rather have left her where she was, though I allows it would have been risky. I would have just chucked the sail over her and covered that with an inch or so of sand, so that it would not have been noticed by a boat a short way out. But if there is a village up here, why, a boat might come down any moment to do some fishing, and there we should be caught at once; as for getting away with them makeshift paddles, it would not be worth even thinking of. I hope our chaps will come back without having seen a monkey or a village, or as much as a banana, then the mate won't be hankering to go up again; and I should make free to advise him to get the boat up amongst the trees here till we have decided that the ship won't come, and agree to make a start."

"I am with you to some extent, Wilcox, and I do think that it is a risky thing going up the river. If we were to fill up with cocoa-nuts they would last us for a week anyhow, and then when we saw another grove of them we could land and load up again."

"You can't take an observation, I suppose, Mr. Stephen, and find out in a rough way whereabouts we are?"

Steve shook his head. "No, Wilcox. If I had had my quadrant I might have got near enough to have made a rough guess, for I have got that watch I bought in my pocket, and I have timed it every day with the chronometers, and find that it does not gain more than half a minute a day, so that at the present moment it is not much more than a minute out by them, and if I had had the quadrant I could have made a pretty close calculation. We were about a degree and a half south at noon before that cyclone struck us, but I don't see that that would help us now."

"It is a pity, sir," the sailor said, "for it would help us wonderful if we could find out our position within fifty miles or so."

"I wish we could, Wilcox;" and Stephen sat for some time thinking. At last he said, "I might, anyhow, find out in a rough sort of way whether we have been blown north or south. We will see if we can find a perfectly straight stick, ten or twelve feet long. If I fix that upright in sand the shadow would help us. It was the 25th of March yesterday, and the sun at noon would therefore be exactly overhead of the line at twelve o'clock. Therefore, if we have been blown north, we should get a very short shadow to the south at twelve o'clock; whereas if we have been blown south, there would be a shadow north. It might not be more than an inch long; but even that would tell us something."

They selected a long straight stick, drove it deeply into the sand, walked round it several times so as to assure themselves that it was perfectly upright, and then returned again to the shelter of the trees. An hour later the sound of a gun came to their ears.

"He has found some of them monkeys," Wilcox growled.

Three more shots were heard. "How far are they off, do you think?" Stephen asked.

"I dunno, sir. If it was on the open sea and calm like this, I should say they might be two or three miles, but in this 'ere forest there ain't no saying at all. I don't reckon they would be above two miles anyhow, that is if the stream is as strong up there as it is here. They were making very slow way against it when they started. I reckon they have been gone about an hour, and they would not have got more than two miles away against this stream. Well, I hope that they will be content now and turn back again."

Half an hour passed, then they heard a gun again; it was quickly followed by another and another.

"More monkeys," Wilcox exclaimed in a tone of disgust.

"I hope it is monkeys," Stephen said. "Listen. There are four more shots close together."

The sailor leapt to his feet. "I believe you are right, sir, that cussed firing has brought the natives down upon them. They would not want to keep on firing at the monkeys. We shall hear in a minute if they fire again. They have all emptied their pieces. If they load quick and fire again it will be a bad sign. There they are!" he broke off as two shots were heard. "I am afraid that settles it, sir, and settles us too, for if they are attacked there ain't a ghost of a chance of their getting away, and there won't be much more chance of our doing so."

Four more shots were heard, and then all was quiet. "Now, sir, we will be getting pretty deep in among these trees, keeping close to the bank, so that we can look through the bushes without being seen. If the boat comes along all right, there ain't no harm done; if it don't come along after a bit, we shall know what has happened."

Picking up his gun, Wilcox was about to turn off into the wood when Stephen said:

"We had better take three or four cocoa-nuts each, Wilcox. There is no saying whether we shall come back to this place, and it is as well to have something to eat."

Each tied some nuts together, threw them over their shoulders, and started along the river bank. The stream was bordered by a thick undergrowth, which afforded an effectual screen for any one behind it. After going for about a quarter of a mile they stopped to listen. There was a faint throbbing sound in the air.

"Paddles!" Steve exclaimed.

"Ay, and native paddles, sir. Our men don't paddle like that, and I fancy," he went on after listening again, "there is more than one canoe. That settles it, sir. There isn't a chance of our ever seeing our mates again."

"Oh, don't say that, Wilcox! Even if some have been killed, the others may have been taken prisoners. I can't believe they have all been murdered."

"Well, I hope not, sir, but it looks very black. If they had pounced upon them sudden, and there had been no fighting, they might have kept them prisoners a day or two till they made a grand feast and killed them; but that firing we heard settles it to my mind. I should say there ain't no manner of doubt that our fellows will have killed some of the niggers, and I expect that the two canoes closed in on them, and then it would be all over in a minute."

When the canoes were within a quarter of a mile the rowers broke into a sort of chant, with occasional wild shouts and yells.

"There they come," Wilcox said as two long canoes, paddling abreast, rounded a turn in the river a short distance away. "There must be something like fifty men in each canoe."

In a short time the canoes came along at a high rate of speed. The sailor gave a sudden exclamation of fury.

"What is it?" Steve asked.

"Don't you see, sir, in the stern of each of the canoes, piled up by the steering oar, there are some heads."

"I can't look at them," Steven said, drawing back from his peep-hole through the leaves.

"They are whites," the sailor muttered. "There ain't no doubt about it. I would give all my pay for the voyage to have the *Tiger's* crew here, that we might give them murdering villains a volley."

But Stephen did not hear him; he had thrown himself down, and the tears were running down his cheeks. The loss of the second mate, who had always been cheery and kind, and of his fellow apprentice, Joyce, completely unnerved him. Up to now he had hoped, but what before had been doubt as to their fate had now been converted into certainty.

"Don't give way, Master Steve," the sailor said, stooping over him and laying his hand on his shoulder. "It is a bad job, there ain't no denying it. What happened to them half an hour ago may happen to us before long; we have got to be up and doing, sir."

"You are right, Wilcox," Steve said, as he rose to his feet. "In the first place, could you count the heads?"

"No; there was a pile of them in each boat; there may have been three, there may have been four in each."

"Well, one thing is certain, Wilcox; we must find out if any of them are still alive, and if so we must try and get them out of the Malays' hands."

"I am ready to try, sir. When a chap sees such a thing as that he don't seem to care much for his life; and at least if we are caught we can polish off a few of the villains before we go under, so I am game to do anything you may order."

"It is not for me to order, Wilcox; I am only a young apprentice, and you are an experienced sailor; and now that we are alone and in danger together, it is for you to lead."

"Well, if that is the way you look at it, sir, I am willing to do all I can; and if we find there is any of our mates alive we will get them out if it is possible, never fear."

"Do you think those canoes are going to put to sea?" Steve asked.

"Not they; they have just gone down to the mouth of the river to see whether that boat came from a ship lying off the shore or whether it was alone. There, do you hear those yells?

They have got out of the canoes, and found the place where we camped last night. We walked about there a good bit, and it ain't likely they will be able to find out whether there was seven or nine of us. Besides, I don't think they will look much, for they would take it for certain we should all go up the river together; and so we should have done if it had not been that you and I were left behind to look out for a sail."

In half an hour the two canoes came back again. They both kept well over to the opposite side of the river to avoid the full force of the current, and the sailor and Stephen attempted to count the heads in their sterns. They could not make out the number, but were inclined to agree that the two dark masses were about the same size.

"I think there can only be three in each boat," Steven said. "In that case one man may have been made prisoner; at any rate, Wilcox, we will go on and see."

As soon as the canoes had gone round the bend of the river, they proceeded on their way. The ground presently became exceedingly swampy, and they could see by the pieces of dead wood and litter caught among the bushes, that in times of flood the river must overflow its banks and extend a long distance into the forest. From time to time they had to wade waist-deep across channels by which the water from the marsh was draining slowly into the river. Before crossing these, at Wilcox's suggestion they each cut down a bush and beat the water with it.

"I expect there are no end of alligators in this swamp," the sailor said; "and I know that the natives, before they cross streams where the brutes are likely to be hiding, beat the water with sticks or bushes to frighten them away."

It was hard work walking, for they often sunk knee-deep in the wet soil, but after toiling for nearly an hour they heard a confused noise ahead, and could ere long make out the beating of drums and the wild shouts of Malays, mingled with a deep roaring sound made by horns. They now went on more cautiously, and presently could make out through the trees a large native village standing upon rising ground by the side of the river. Creeping cautiously to the edge of the bush they could see that a large number of men, women, and children were assembled in an open space between the houses and the water. The women were bringing bundles of wood, and a column of smoke rising in the centre of the crowd showed that the preparation for a feast had begun.

"If we had but one of our ten-pounders loaded with grape with us," Wilcox said, "I would pour a volley into those black devils if it cost me my life afterwards."

"What do you think they are going to do, Wilcox?"

"I reckon there ain't much doubt about it," the sailor replied; "they are going to make a feast of our mess-mates."

Stephen uttered an exclamation of horror and disgust. "Do you mean to say that they are cannibals, Wilcox?"

"In course I can't say for certain, Master Steve. Some of these tribes are cannibals and some ain't, and I reckon by what I see going on that those villains are. Are you a good climber, sir?"

"Do you mean climbing a tree. I have never had much practice at that, Wilcox, but I dare say I could manage it."

"Well, sir, you are lighter and more active than I am, and I was thinking that if you could get up to the top of this tree you would have a view down over the village. The leaves are pretty thick, and as the niggers are busy there is not much chance of their looking about for a man up a tree. You see the village ain't above a hundred and fifty yards away, and the ground ain't more than twenty feet above the river. I should say that this tree was seventy or eighty feet high, so that from the top you can get a view pretty well over the place; if there is one of our chaps there he may be lying tied up somewhere. Of course he might be in a hut, but it is much more likely that they would have just chucked him down until they wanted him. I think if you got on my shoulder you would be able to get hold of that lowest branch where it bends down, and climb along it to the trunk; after that the branches come pretty thick together."

"I think I could manage that easily enough."

"Well, then, here goes," the sailor said, and took up his post beneath where the bough was lowest. "If you can't reach it from my shoulder, sir, you step on my head. I can hold you easy enough. You keep the trunk as far as possible between you and the village."

"The leaves are thick up high," Steve said, looking up at the tree; "directly it gets above the level of these smaller trees it spreads its branches out well."

"Now, jump upon my back, sir, and then climb upon my shoulders. You had best take hold of my hands to steady yourself."

It was necessary, as the sailor had suggested, for Steve to stand upon his supporter's head before he could get hold of a branch sufficiently strong to bear his weight. As soon as he did so he drew himself up, and was soon climbing the main trunk. The higher he got the more convinced was he that he would not be observed by the natives, for the trees behind him formed a background, and therefore he could not be seen against the sky. He kept, however, as the sailor had told him, on the other side of the trunk, and when he had gained the smaller branches at the top of the tree he looked out through an opening in the foliage. The village seemed to lie almost at his feet, and he could see every object on the ground. It was not long before he perceived a figure lying full length in front of one of the huts, close to the spot where the people were gathered. It was certainly an European, and from the whiteness of the trousers he felt sure that it was either the mate or Joyce. He counted the number of huts, and found that the one beside which the figure was lying was the eighth in the line facing the river. There were two lines of huts with a sort of street between them. Behind the second row the rise on which the village was situated fell rapidly away and the jungle grew almost up to the back of the huts. Those in the second line stood somewhat further apart than those in the first, and he observed that the sixth house in the back line was opposite the eighth in the front. Having gathered this information he descended the tree.

"What news, sir?" the sailor asked, as Stephen dropped from the bough to his side.

"There is one of our comrades lying by the huts, Wilcox. I can tell by his white ducks that it is either Mr. Towel or Joyce; whether he is alive or dead, of course I can't say. I did not see him move, but no doubt he would be tied hand and foot. I saw nothing of the others, and there would be no reason why he should be treated differently from them if he were dead."

"You may be sure of that. Well, that is better than I had hoped. If we can save one it will be something."

"I have been examining the ground," Stephen went on, "and we could work round close up to the second row of huts. We must count six of them, then go along by the side of the sixth and cross the street to the hut opposite. The prisoner is lying in front of that, I mean on the river side of it. Of course, there is no doing anything until the sun has set, except that we might work round to that hut. It will be easier to get through this horrid swamp before it gets dark than afterwards, and there will be less fear of our stumbling and breaking a branch. What time do you think it is now?"

A RESCUE.

"I don't think it is more than eight bells yet," Wilcox said. "It is a lot of hours to wait, and I would give a good bit to be out of the swamp before it gets dark. Howsomever, if we keep along by the river coming back we can't lose our way, that is one comfort. Well, let us work round at once, and then we shall see how the land lies. It is like enough that as soon as they have got a big fire made up, and the cooking begun, they will most of them turn in for a sleep till the heat of the day is over, and begin their feast after sundown. They generally do sleep half the day, and then keep it up half the night."

Accordingly they started through the wood, and in a quarter of an hour found themselves at the foot of the rising ground on which the village stood. They had counted the huts, and now crawled up through the thick bushes and stood within a few yards of the sixth hut. The swamp had been very deep on the way, and they had had the greatest difficulty in getting through it. Stephen had once sunk below his waist in the mud, and would have been unable to extricate himself, had not the sailor held on by a young tree with one hand while he stretched out the other to him.

"I am all right now as far as colour goes, Wilcox. Now, do you stay here and I will crawl along by the side of the hut and have a look up and down the street. I did not see a soul between the row of huts when I was in the tree."

When Stephen peeped out by the side of the hut he saw that there were several people about, apparently returning from the spot where they had congregated. He rejoined his companion, and they waited an hour. By this time perfect silence had fallen on the village. The heat was intense, and even in the forest all sound had ceased, as if birds and insects were alike indulging in a mid-day sleep.

"I will go and have a look again now," Stephen said. "It

I find no one about I will cross the street and try to cut the ropes, and bring him here at once. If there is a guard over him I will come back again to you. We ought to be able to silence the guard without his giving the alarm, especially as he is likely to be half-asleep.

"You had better leave your pistols here, Master Steve, and take your cutlass. A pistol-shot now would bring the whole village down on us, and we should have no chance of getting through the swamp with a hundred of those fellows after us. You had better draw your sword, and leave the scabbard and belt here. In the first place, it is handier to have the sword ready; and it is not so likely to knock against anything when you have got it in your hand as it would be trailing behind you as you crawl along. I shall be on the look-out, sir, and shall be by your side in a brace of shakes if you hail."

Stephen parted the bushes, and then stepped lightly to the corner of the hut. Not a soul was to be seen moving about, and he dashed across to the house opposite, crawled along by its side, and then looked round. The great fire had burned low, and Stephen shuddered as his eye fell upon the mass of embers and thought of what was lying below them. There was no one about—the whole of the natives had retired to their huts. In another moment he was beside the prisoner. It was Joyce. Bands of cord-like creepers were wrapped round his legs; his wrists were tied together, and from them a rope went to a peg four feet beyond him, extending his arms at full length beyond his head. A similar fastening from his ankles kept his legs at full stretch in the other direction. Fastened thus, the Malays evidently considered that there was no necessity for a guard over him.

"Joyce, old fellow," Stephen whispered in his ear, "are you conscious?"

The lad opened his closed eyes with a start.

STEPHEN CRAWLS TO THE RESCUE OF HIS CHUM

Page 88

"Don't speak," Stephen went on.

"Is it really you, Steve, or am I dreaming?"

"You are awake enough, Tom. I am here with Wilcox and will soon get these things off you." Drawing his jack-knife he cut the bonds. "Do you think that you can walk, Tom?"

"Yes, the things were not very tight, only being pegged out like this I could not move an inch."

Stephen was lying down by his side while he cut the fastenings. He now looked round again.

"There is no one in sight, Tom, but you had better wriggle yourself along until you get to the corner of the hut."

As soon as they were round the corner they stood up. As they did so, the sailor put his head out through the bushes and waved them a silent cheer. Stephen went first, and as soon as he saw that the street was empty he beckoned to his companion, and they ran across to the other side; a moment later they joined the sailor. The latter gave a grip to Joyce's hand, and then held out to him a cocoa-nut he had just cut open in readiness. This he seized eagerly and took a long drink.

"I was choking with thirst," Joyce gasped, as he finished the contents of the nut.

"Take care how you go through the bushes," the sailor whispered, as he turned and led the way; "everything is so quiet that a rustle might be heard."

They went along with the greatest caution. Their bare feet fell noiselessly on the spongy soil, but sometimes as they sank into the mud the suck of the air as they drew them out made a sound that startled them. At last they reached the tree where they had left all the cocoa-nuts with the exception of the one that the sailor had brought on. When they stopped, Joyce threw himself down and burst into tears.

"Leave me alone," he said, as Stephen began to speak to him, "I shall be better directly, but it has been awful. I will tell you about it afterwards. I tried to make up my mind to stand it bravely, and it is the getting out of it when there did not seem to be a chance in the world that has upset me."

In five minutes he rose again to his feet. "I am ready to go on now," he said.

"Yes, I think it is time to be moving, sir. As soon as those beggars wake up and find you have gone, they will set out in chase, and the longer start we get the better."

CHAPTER V.

AGAIN ON THE ISLAND.

OVER such ground it was impossible to hurry, but in three-quarters of an hour they reached the edge of the wood.

"I have been thinking that we had better take to the water for a bit," Stephen said. "They are sure to think that you have made for the coast, and they will not be long in finding our footmarks. Though I don't know much about the Malays, I expect they can follow a track like all other savages. The only thing to settle is whether we shall swim across the river and go along in that direction, or keep on this side. We have not seen anything of alligators, and I don't think the sharks ever cross the bars and come into fresh water."

"All right, sir! If you think it is best to cross, I am ready," Wilcox said. "A dip will do us good, for the heat in that wood is enough to roast an ox; besides, it will wash the mud off us. But we must look about for a log to put the gun and our pistols and the ammunition on, we must not risk wetting that."

There were many pieces of drift-wood by the edge of the

water, and choosing one of them they fastened the weapons and cartridges on the top, and then, entering the water and pushing it before them, swam over to the opposite side. Then taking the arms again they let the log drift down the river, and keeping in the water ankle-deep they followed the stream down to the sea, and continued their course along the sand washed by the surf.

"How long a start do you think we shall get, Wilcox?" Stephen asked.

"I should say that two hours is as much as we can hope for."

"Well, we shall be a good long way off by that time. I feel a new man after that swim."

"So do I," Joyce said, speaking more briskly than he had hitherto done.

"Well, we had better set off at a trot," the sailor said. "I expect those beggars can run a good deal faster than we can. The great thing is for us to get so far away before it gets dark that they won't be able to see our figures. If it is eight bells before they fairly set off after us, they will only have a little better than two hours and a half. They are sure to be thrown out for a bit at the mouth of the river. They will see our footsteps at the water side, but won't know whether we have crossed or have kept along on that side. Very likely some of them will go one way and some the other, still they are sure to have a talk and a delay. They ought not to travel twice as fast as we have, at any rate, and they would have to do that to catch us before it is dark."

They set off at a brisk trot. The sand was fairly hard below the spot where the surf rushed up over it, and the walking was easy in comparison to that in the swamp or on loose sand. Still it was hot work. The sun blazed down upon them, there was not a breath of wind, and they were drenched with perspiration. They kept on steadily, however, slackening only occasionally into a walk for two or three minutes, and then going on again at a sharp pace.

"They won't catch us before it gets dark," the sailor said confidently. "I reckon we must be making near seven knots an hour, and even a Malay could not go at fourteen; besides, they will have to keep a sharp look-out for footmarks in the sand above water-mark, as we might at any time come up from the water and take to the forest. Anyhow, we must keep it up as long as we can go. We ain't running for amusement, it is for a big prize, for our lives depend on our keeping ahead."

Anxiously they watched the sun as it sank down towards the horizon, and there was an exclamation of satisfaction as it disappeared below the water.

"Another half-hour and we shall be able to take it easy," Stephen said. "I should not think they would keep up the search after dark, and then we could safely take to the forest. The wind is springing up already, and this light drifting sand will cover all signs of our footsteps before morning."

"We had better keep in the water as long as we can, Master Steve. They can't trace our footsteps here, but they might under the trees. These sort of chaps are like dogs. I expect they can pretty well follow you by smell, and the hope of getting heads will keep them at it as long as there is the slightest chance of their overtaking us."

"Well, we may as well be on the safe side anyhow, Wilcox, and will keep on here as long as we can drag our feet along. We have got no boots to pinch our corns, and every time the surf rushes up it cools our feet, so we ought to be able to keep on till eight bells in the middle watch, by that time I should think we shall have gone something like forty miles from that river."

"All that," the sailor agreed. "It was about four bells

when we swam across, and in the four hours we have certainly gone twenty-four knots, and I should say a bit further than that. If we only make three knots for the next six hours, we shall have logged over forty by eight bells, and I should say that even the Malays will hardly come as far as that, especially as the men who take this side won't be sure that we have not gone the other, and have been caught by their mates."

They kept steadily on, but their speed gradually abated, and for the last two hours before the hands of Stephen's watch pointed to twelve o'clock, they stumbled rather than walked.

"I think that will do," he said at last, "it is nearly eight bells now. Let us tread in each other's footsteps as well as we can, so that there shall only be one line of marks."

The change from the firm sand to the yielding drift—in which their feet sank three or four inches—finished them, and although they had not more than a hundred yards to walk to the trees, it seemed to them that they would never get there. At last they reached the edge of the forest, staggered a few paces in, and then without a word dropped down and almost instantaneously fell asleep.

The sun was high when they woke. Stephen was the first to get on to his feet. He went to the edge of the trees and looked across. To his satisfaction he saw that the drifting sand had obliterated all trace of their passage.

"Then I vote," Wilcox said, when he was told the news, "that we go a bit further into the wood and camp there for the day. I am just aching from head to foot."

"I think we must go on a bit further, Wilcox. You see there are no cocoa-nuts here, and we must keep on until we come to a grove of them. The trees are never far apart, and we may not have a mile to go. We certainly can't stay here all day without something to eat and drink. You see we threw our nuts away when we started."

"I suppose you are right, sir," the sailor said, slowly getting up on to his feet; "but it is hard, after such a run as we made yesterday, to have to get up anchor again."

"Well, we can take it easily, Wilcox, and we will stop at the first cocoa-nut tree we come to. Now, Tom, as we go along you shall tell us about yesterday, we have not heard a word yet."

"Well," began Joyce, "we paddled up the river, as you know. It was as much as we could do sometimes to make head against the current. I suppose we had been gone about an hour when we saw a troop of monkeys on the boughs of a tree overhanging the water. They did not seem a bit afraid of us, but chattered and screamed. We shot three of them. I did not fire, for I could not bring myself to kill one of them. It was like shooting at a child. We picked them out of the water and put them in the boat, and then paddled on again. We had just got to a turn in the river when two big canoes came round the corner. It was of no use our trying to get away, for they could go six feet to our one. Mr. Towel stood up in the stern and held both his arms up to show that we were friendly, but directly afterwards a shower of spears came whizzing down at us. One hit Jackson, who was in the bow, somewhere in the body. He fired at them, and then fell down in the bottom of the boat. Then the rest of us fired, and for a moment they sheered off, but the men had just time to reload their guns when the Malays came at us. The men fired again, and a moment later the canoes ran alongside. We took to our pistols, but the Malays came leaping on board like demons.

"I don't know anything more about that part of the business, for I got a crack on the head with a club, and did not know anything more till I was hauled on shore and chucked down. Then I saw them bring from the canoes the heads of all the others. It was frightful. Then they dragged the bodies out from the bottom of the canoes. They had all been stripped, and I believe I should have fainted if a big Malay had not given me a tremendous kick, and made me walk up to the village. As soon as I got there they tied me up and staked me out. There was a tremendous noise and shouting and yelling, but what was done I don't know, as I could see nothing but the sky and the wall of the hut. It was an awful time; first because I knew that sooner or later they would kill me, and in the next place, because I was driven pretty nearly mad by the flies and things that settled on my face. Of course I could not brush them away, and all that I could do was to shake my head, and they did not seem to mind that. It seems ridiculous that, after seeing one's friends killed and knowing that one is going to be killed oneself, one should worry over flies, but I can tell you I went nearly out of my mind with irritation at the tickling of their feet. It seemed to me that I was there for ages, though I knew by the height of the sun that it was only about noon. The thirst, too, was fearful, and I made up my mind that the sooner they came and killed me the better. I found myself talking all sorts of nonsense, and I do think that I should have gone out of my mind before the day was over. When first I heard your voice I thought it must be a dream, like some of the other ideas that came into my mind. I had thought of you both when I was first fastened up, and wondered whether the Malays would find you. I had even thought at first that if you only knew where I was you might try to get me away after dark if I was not killed before that, and you can guess my feelings when I became convinced that it was really you. How did you know what had happened?"

"You must have been insensible for a good bit, Tom. We heard the firing, and thought that there was too much of it for shooting monkeys, and that you must have been attacked, so we made our way along among the bushes by the bank. Presently the two canoes came down, and we made out some heads in the stern of each boat. They went to the mouth of the river, to see, no doubt, if there was a ship there. They came back again in half an hour. We tried to count the heads, and both of us thought that there were about the same number in each boat. Of course we could not be sure, but we determined to come on to the village and find out for certain. I climbed up a high tree a short distance from it—the one where we came upon the cocoa-nuts—and made you out lying beside a hut. I knew by the white ducks that it was either you or poor Towel. Then we worked round, waited until the village had gone off to sleep, and then came for you. You see the Malays had no idea that there were any more whites about, and therefore took no trouble about you. No doubt they thought that the boat had escaped from a wreck, and that all who had got away in her had gone up the river together. Ah! there is a cocoa-nut. I am glad our walk is over, for I am beginning to feel hot and thirsty."

"So am I, and stiff and sore all over."

The cocoa-nut tree was the first of a grove. Stephen, who was by far the most active of the party, soon climbed one of the trees, and threw a score of nuts down. They went a little distance further back into the forest. Each consumed the contents of four nuts, then two of them lay down to sleep again, while the other kept watch. The march was not resumed until after sunset. They had another meal of cocoa-nuts before they started, and each took three nuts for use on the journey. They again walked at the edge of the water, as they had done the day before. It was by far the pleasantest way, and they kept on until daylight appeared, and then again went into the wood.

"I should think now," Stephen said, as after a good sleep

they ate a cocoa-nut breakfast, "that we need not bother any more about the Malays of that village. It is quite possible that we passed another last night, though of course the sand-hills would have prevented our seeing it. The question is now, what are we to do next?"

"That is what I was thinking all the time that we were walking last night," Joyce said. "We can't keep on tramping and living on cocoa-nuts for ever."

"That is quite certain, Tom, but there is no reason why we should do so. There must be some villages on this coast, and when we start this evening I vote we keep along here instead of going down to the water. Where there is a village there must be fishing canoes, and all we have got to do is to take one, and put to sea. I don't mean to say that we can get in and push straight away, for we must have some provisions; but when we have found a village we can hide up near it, and get as many cocoa-nuts as we can carry. Besides, there are sure to be bananas and other fruit-trees close by, and after laying our cocoa-nuts down by the edge of the water, we can go up and cut as many bananas as we like, and then we shall have enough food to last us ten days or so. There is one comfort, wherever we may land there cannot be a worse lot of Malays than there are about here."

"That is a capital plan, Master Stephen," Wilcox said. "I have not been thinking of a village, except as to how to get past it; but, as you say, there is no reason why we should not make off in a canoe."

The next night they kept along just inside the trees, and had walked but two hours when they found that these ended abruptly, and that they stood on the edge of a clearing.

"Here is your village, Stephen."

"Yes; one hardly hoped to find one so soon. Well, the first thing is to go down and search in the sand-hills for canoes."

Four or five were found lying together in a hollow some twenty yards beyond high-water mark. They examined them carefully.

"Any of them will do," Wilcox said, "but I think this is the best one. It is a little larger than the others, and the wood feels newer and sounder. I expect she is meant for four paddlers, and she will carry us and a fair cargo well."

"That is settled, then," Stephen said. "I propose that we go back some little distance from the village, get our cocoa-nuts at once, and bring them back and hide them in the bushes not far from where the clearing begins. It will save time to-morrow."

"Why should we not go to-night?" Joyce asked. "It is only about nine o'clock now, and if we get the cocoa-nuts near here, we can make two or three journeys down to the boat with them, and be off before midnight."

"So we might, Tom. What do you say, Wilcox?"

"The sooner the better, says I," the sailor replied. "As Mr. Joyce says, we can be off by eight bells easy, and we shall be out of sight of this village long before daybreak."

"Well, Wilcox, will you and Mr. Joyce get the cocoa-nuts, and while you are doing it I will creep round this clearing and get bananas. I can see lots of their broad leaves over there. As I get them I will bring them to this corner, and by the time you have got a store of nuts, I shall have a pile of bananas. I think you had better go four or five hundred yards away before you cut the nuts, for they come down with such a thump that any native who is awake here might very well hear them."

"We will go a bit away, sir," Wilcox said, "but if we take pains to let them drop each time just as there is a puff of wind, there is no fear of their hearing them."

They separated, and Stephen, entering the clearing, soon

came upon a banana tree with long bunches of the fruit. Two of these were as much as he could carry, and his portion of the work was soon done, and indeed he had carried them down to the water's edge before his companions had brought three loads of cocoa-nuts to the point where he had left them. He helped to take these down, then the canoe was lifted and carried to the edge of the water, being taken in far enough to float each time the surf ran up. Then the fruit was placed in it.

"I wish we had poor Mr. Towel with us to take her through the surf," Wilcox said.

"I wish we had; but fortunately it is not very heavy."

"No, sir; it is sure not to be," the sailor said. "I have noticed that they always put their villages at points where the surf is lighter than usual. I suppose the water is shallower, or deeper, or something. I don't know what it is, but there is certainly a difference. Besides, there has been no wind to speak of since we landed, and the waves are nothing to what they were then. Now, gentlemen, as I am more accustomed to this sort of thing than you are, I will take the place in the stern, where I can steer her a bit. The moment she floats as the surf comes in, and I see the chance is a good one, I will give the word; then we will all paddle as hard as we can, and go out as the surf draws back, so as to meet the next wave before it breaks. Everything depends on that."

They took their places in the canoe, and grasped the paddles that they had found in her. Two or three waves passed under them, and then they saw one higher than the others approaching them.

"We will go out on the back of this one," Wilcox said. "Paddle the moment the surf lifts the canoe, and don't let her be washed up a foot."

The wave fell over with a crash, and a torrent of foam rushed up towards them.

"Now," Wilcox exclaimed, as the white line reached the bow, "paddle for your lives!"

For a moment, in spite of their desperate efforts, they were carried upwards, then the canoe seemed to hang in the air, and they were riding forward with the speed of an arrow on the receding water.

"All you know," Wilcox shouted, and as the rush of water ceased they drove her ahead to meet the next wave. It rose higher and higher. The canoe reached it, and, as it passed under them, stood almost upright. Two or three more desperate strokes, and they heard a crash behind them.

"Row, row!" Wilcox shouted, as they felt the boat drawn backwards. It was but for a few seconds, then they moved ahead again, passed over the next wave, and were safe. They now settled to steady paddling, and before they had gone many hundred yards from shore they no longer felt the long smooth rollers, over which the canoe glided insensibly.

By daylight the land they had left was far behind them, the low-lying coast had sunk from their view, and the hills behind were almost shrouded from sight by the mist that rose from the swamps.

"It was well we rescued Mr. Joyce before it was dark," the sailor said to Stephen. "One night in those swamps is enough to lay any white man up with fever. That was why I was so anxious to get him away at once. I did not think that they would kill him straight off. If they had wanted him for the feast they would have cut off his head when they caught him. I expect they would have kept him for some other occasion; but I wanted to get him out of it before the mists began to rise from the swamps. Now, sir, as we are well away, shall I put her head north or south?"

"I don't think it matters much, Wilcox. There is some high land just ahead now, we may as well make in that direction as any other; but if we get to a small island on the way, I should think that it would be safest to land there, and wait for a few days anyhow, as we agreed before, to see if there are any signs of a sail. At any rate, we won't go near, by daylight, any island likely to be inhabited."

After paddling for some hours they saw a low island that seemed to be about a quarter of a mile in diameter, and headed towards it. Before they reached it, however, Wilcox said:

"Do you know, Mr. Joyce, I have been thinking for some time that I knew that hill we were pointing to, and, now we have opened it out a bit more, I feel sure of it."

The lads ceased paddling, and looked intently at the hill, now some twelve miles away. It had a flat top that seemed to be split asunder by a crack running through it.

"I know it now," Stephen exclaimed excitedly, "it is the island where that wreck was."

"That is it, sure enough, sir. I have been thinking it was so for some time, but it is only now that I have caught the light through that gap at the top. It was more open from the point where the *Tiger* lay when we started for shore, but if we row on for a mile or two and then make straight for it, I think we shall just about strike the point where the wreck is lying. No, I think we had better wait a while, Mr. Joyce," he said, as the latter dipped his paddle in the water and turned the boat's head towards the island.

"I think we had better wait till the sun gets pretty low. We know there ain't any villages near the wreck, for she must have been there a good month afore we found her, and it was certain then that no native had been near her. Still there may be some higher up on the slopes, and they might make us out, so it is better that we should not get within six or eight miles of land before it begins to be dark. We could not go to a better place. First of all, there are no natives; secondly, we may pick up all sorts of useful things about the shore. We did not see anything but bales and wreckage where we landed, but it was all rock there. Now some of the casks and things may have floated along, and have been cast up upon the sand. Then, it is about the likeliest point for sighting the *Tiger*. The skipper would naturally say to himself, There is no saying where the boat has gone to, but if it is anywhere near the island where we lost them, they would be likely to make for the wreck in hopes of finding some provisions cast up there; and so he would sail round to have a look."

"I think he would," the boys both agreed, letting the boat drift quietly. They made a hearty meal of bananas and cocoa-nut milk, and then all lay down in the canoe and dozed for some hours. The two lads were roused by Wilcox saying:

"I think, gentlemen, we can paddle on quietly now; the sun will be setting in less than an hour."

Resuming their seats, they paddled gently on until the sun disappeared, then quickened their pace, and in another hour reached the shore. They had no difficulty in landing, for the side on which the wreck was lying was sheltered by the island itself from the rollers, and it was a sandy beach.

"I don't think that we are far from the spot," Wilcox said, "for we made straight for that crack on the hill, and kept it open all the while. I reckon we can't be more than half a mile from where the wreck was lying.

"I don't suppose we shall see anything of that, the cyclone must have finished it. However, we will walk along the shore till we get to the spot. We cannot mistake that. We will keep a bit back from the sea. We may light upon something as we go, but it will be sure to be well inland; you know we saw how far the sea washed things up beside the wreck."

The night was too dark, however, for them to distinguish objects ten yards away, and they soon came down to the water's edge again, following it until the character of the shore changed and rocks took the place of the sand.

"That is all right," the sailor said; "now I think we had better go back to the boat again till we get daylight. It would never do to walk across these rocks in the dark with naked feet. It was bad enough when it was light, but we should cut our feet to pieces if we tried it now. There is no hurry about it, as we are within half a mile of the wreck. We know that everything is pretty well smashed up that went ashore there, so that we are far more likely to find something on the sands, and we shall see the *Tiger* just as well from where the canoe is as from the wreck. The first thing to look for is water. I don't say that the cocoa-nuts would not supply us for another week; but if we are going to stay here long—and for my part I don't see anything better to do—we must either find another cocoa-nut grove or water."

"I don't think we are likely to find another cocoa-nut grove," Stephen said.

"Why not, sir? They have them mostly on all these islands."

"That is true," Stephen agreed; "but I should say it is just because there are none here that there are no villages anywhere about."

"I did not think of that, sir; yes, I expect you are right; and in that case it is still more necessary to hunt for water. If we can find it within four or five miles either side of the wreck we are all right, because the *Tiger* could not come here without our seeing her; but I should not like to be much further away. However, most of these islands have water, especially when they are hilly; and as we have been lucky so far, it will be hard if we don't find a stream of some sort along ten miles of shore."

The next morning they set out on a tour of exploration. They were not long before they came upon many relics of the wreck: planks, spars, and remains of the cargo. They lay nearly two hundred yards from the shore, and bore no signs of the rough usage that had marked the wreckage among the rocks.

"Hurrah! there are some tubs," Joyce shouted, as they reached the top of a low sand-hill. They broke into a run, and were soon standing beside six casks, lying a short distance apart.

"Salt junk," Wilcox said, as they looked at the cask they first came to, "and no bad thing either; cocoa-nuts are good for drink, but that soft, pulpy stuff inside don't go very far; and after a chap has been eating it for a week he wants to get his teeth into something more substantial. This ain't no good," he went on, giving a kick at the next cask, "unless the natives come up and we open trade with them. These are goods they shipped at Calcutta. This is better," he went on, as he looked at the next; "this 'ere is biscuits; and with biscuits and salt junk, and a banana now and then, no man need grumble."

The next two were, like the second, filled with trade articles; the last was a cask of flour.

"Well, we can stop here a couple of months if we like, gentlemen, if we can but hit upon water; for that, of course, we must look beyond the line of sand; a river can cut through it, but a little stream would find its way underneath the sand to the sea."

As they approached the rocky ground, which rose like a ridge, and could be traced far inland, the sailor said: "This is the most likely spot. Any water that came down from the hills would run along at the foot of these rocks to the sea."

"I think that you are right, Wilcox; the foliage looks

brighter along by the rocks than it does anywhere else, and I should not be surprised if we found a stream there."

As they approached the rocks within a hundred yards, the hope became a certainty, for there was some growth of verdure. They quickened their steps and ran forward, but, to their disappointment, there was no stream, however small.

"We have got to dig for it," Wilcox said; "there is water not far down, I will swear."

The soil was chiefly composed of sand, and they set to work with their hands to scrape a hole in it. They had got but a foot down when the soil became moist, and a foot lower water began to ooze out of the sides into the hole.

"Thank God for that!" the sailor said reverently, "that makes it safe. This evening, when it gets cool, we will bring the paddles here, and will soon dig a hole for our well. We can't do better than roll a tub here and sink it in the hole, and bring the canoe to the edge of that rock down by the sea, then we have only got to chop some boughs and make a sort of hut, and we shall be as comfortable as if we were back home."

"It is curious finding a rock here," Joyce said presently, as they made their way over to it. "For all the distance that we have gone along by the sea, it has been nothing but sand: it is rum black-looking stuff, too."

"I expect it is lava," Stephen said. "There are lots of volcanoes among these islands, and I believe that high hill is one, and that if we were to climb up we should find there was a crater there. You see we are just in a line with that gap, and this rock goes exactly in that direction. I expect that in some eruption ever so long ago, the crater split there, and the lava poured down here into the sea."

"Very likely that is it, Stephen; it must have been a long time ago anyhow, you see there are big trees growing on it."

In ten minutes they arrived at the spot where the wreck

had been; her keel remained there, but with this exception she had entirely disappeared. They took another look among the wreckage, cut off some lengths of rope and coiled them up, and also a sail, which the sailor pronounced to be a topgallant sail. This they rolled up, fastened it by short pieces of rope, and then, the sailor taking the middle and the lads the ends on their shoulders, they carried it to what they already called their "well".

"We will set to work at once to rig up a tent under the shade of these trees," the sailor said, "it will keep the night mists off better than branches; and we will bring another sail over to cover the ground and keep the mist from rising inside."

"What are we going to cook our junk in?" Joyce asked suddenly.

The sailor looked at his companion in dismay. "Dash my timbers," he said, "I never thought of that; that is a go. Perhaps we can manage it in the native way: they boil things by putting water into a big shell, and dropping hot stones into it until it boils. We have not got any shells, but we might find a hollow in the rock that will hold water."

"That is all very well, Wilcox; but how are we going to heat our stones?"

"You have done me there, Master Stephen," the sailor said, in a tone of utter disgust; "we have not got flint or tinder."

"We might manage the tinder easily enough," Stephen said, "by using rotten wood; but tinder is of no use without steel. We shall have to eat our biscuits without meat, Wilcox, unless we can light a fire by rubbing two sticks together."

"That ain't to be done, sir; I have seen white men try it over and over again, and I have tried it myself, but it ain't no manner of good. The Almighty has given us a lot of knowledge that he has not given to these black fellows, but he has balanced it up by giving them the knack of lighting a fire which he has not given to us. I never heard of a white man who could make fire in that way."

"Well, I will have a try, anyhow," Joyce said; "there can't be anything special about a Malay that he can make fire more than a white man."

"You may try as much as you like, Master Joyce," the sailor said, shaking his head solemnly, "but mark my words, you won't be able to do it. It is a pity, too, for with all this wood that has been drying as if on purpose for us, we could have had one without being afraid of the smoke."

"Well, we must not grumble; we have got a lot to be thankful for; and we can do without meat well enough."

"Yes, Mr. Joyce," Wilcox said reluctantly; "only, you know, I wish we had not come across that cask of salt junk, then one would never have thought about it; but seeing it there, and not being able to cook it, is enough to make a saint grumble, I should say."

"Not if he were really a saint, Wilcox. However, don't make up your mind that you are not going to get your teeth into that junk till I give up the hope of making a fire."

"Well, sir, we will roll the three barrels over here, and then set about rigging up the tent. There is nothing like being busy."

By nightfall they had got the tent up. They had had some argument over the best site. All would have preferred to have erected it on the low ground, near their well, but finally a point was decided upon, some little distance higher—a level spot being found on the rock where some trees offered every convenience for pitching it, and the surface of the rock was fairly flat. A few armfuls of coarse grass sufficed to fill up the inequalities, and render it even enough for sleeping on. Here they had the advantage of getting the sea-breeze, and of having a wide view across the water, while trees growing behind them completely hid the tent from being seen from the higher ground. Before erecting it they had deepened the well, and found that the water was clear and good, and that it flowed in so abundantly there was no fear whatever of the supply falling short.

The next morning Wilcox and Joyce started for an early walk, with a view to seeing whether there were any things thrown up on the sand beyond the rock. Stephen was to stay behind at the tent and keep watch for a sail.

"I will leave the gun behind with you, Master Stephen," Wilcox said; "Mr. Joyce has got his pistols, and I have my cutlass. If you want us back, or if you make out a sail, you fire it off; we will come back as quick as we can. Don't you fidget if we are some time away; casks may have floated a good bit along before they got thrown up, and it is just as well to see the thing through now, and then we sha'n't have to do it again. We will keep a good look-out for a sail too, for it is like enough that we may be a long way beyond the sound of the gun. You see we can make out from here that a mile further on the trees come down to near the sea again, just as they did on the other island. We will take some cocoa-nuts with us, in case we should not light upon any there. We sha'n't be uneasy about you, because we know for certain that there ain't any natives near; and, in the same way, you need not trouble yourself about us."

"All right, Wilcox! I will see whether I can't get some junk cooked for you, ready for a meal at sunset."

The sailor smiled grimly. "All right, sir; if I find some meat cooked for me, I will guarantee that I will eat it, even if it is as tough as an alligator."

CHAPTER VI.

HOME.

AS soon as his companions had left him, Stephen went off and brought up as much dried wood as he could carry, among it a piece of plank that was almost rotten. This he crumbled up. Then he set the cask of salt junk on end, and with a heavy piece of rock hammered away until he forced the head in. Then he took out a good-sized piece of meat and put it into the well. The water here was constantly changing, a current flowing through it towards the sea. Then he brought up two or three more loads of wreckage and sat down under the awning, for it could scarcely be termed a tent, as both ends were open to allow a free passage for the air. Here he sat for some hours, occasionally getting up and looking over the sea to the right and left. It was not until it was nearly noon and the sun was overhead that he could try the experiment upon which he relied to obtain fire. When it was nearly vertical he went down to the well, opened his watch-case, and dipped the glass carefully into the water. He thought of trying to take it out of the case, but the risk of breaking it would have been too great. Carrying it very carefully, he went up to the tent again and sat down beside his little heap of crumbled wood and held the watch-glass full of water over it.

As he expected he found that it made an admirable burning-glass, its only drawback being that it was only available when the sun was overhead. Almost instantaneously as the focus fell upon the wood the latter began to smoke, and in less than a minute a flame sprang up. Some small splinters that he had got ready were placed on it, and in a very short time a fire was blazing. As soon as the wood was well alight he had poured off the water and very carefully wiped the glass and the rim that held it. He went a short distance away as soon as the fire was burning well, and was pleased to find that no smoke was given off, the sun having dried the wreckage until not the slightest particle of moisture remained in it. He now kept a sharp look-out along the shore, but it was not until nearly five o'clock that he saw his companions issue from the trees a mile and a half away and move along the sand. He went down to the well, took out the meat, and brought it up and laid it on the rock to dry. He felt sure that by this time the water would have removed the greater portion of the salt, and that he would now be able to roast it satisfactorily.

He had already got two forked twigs as a support for his spit, and, taking the ramrod from the gun, thrust it through the meat. He had ceased putting on fresh wood the moment he saw the others come from the forest. The fire soon sank down to a mass of glowing embers, over which he put the meat, the ends of the ramrod being supported by the forked twigs. He turned it round and round occasionally to prevent it from burning, and although he had himself been indifferent as to whether they could obtain means for cooking the junk, he felt a ravenous appetite as the odour of the meat rose. Just as he came to the conclusion that the meat must be cooked through, Wilcox and Joyce arrived. They stopped in amazement as their eyes fell on the fire.

"Come on, Wilcox," Stephen said with a laugh. "Don't stand staring there. Dinner is ready, and I am only waiting for you to begin."

"I am downright famished," the sailor said as he came up. "I would not have believed it if I had not seen it. How on earth did you manage it?"

"Not by rubbing pieces of wood together, Wilcox, but by filling my watch-glass with water and using it as a burning-glass; it lit the wood in less than a minute; only it would not do, you know, unless the sun was right overhead, and I had to wait until twelve o'clock before I tried the experiment."

The meat was cut up into three huge portions, and using biscuits as plates they speedily set to work upon it.

"You have pretty well got rid of the salt," Wilcox said after his first mouthful. "It is well-nigh as good as roast meat. How did you do that, sir?"

"It was in the well for seven or eight hours," Stephen replied. "The water was running through it, so that it was as good as putting it into a river. Salt meat is best boiled, but as I had no pot to boil it in, I thought I would try and roast it; and, as you say, the water has got rid of the salt altogether."

"It is the best bit of meat that I have eaten since I left England," Wilcox said. "Well, I don't mind now if we stop here for another month. We have meat and biscuits, and I reckon, Mr. Stephen, that you will be able to think of some plan for making flap-jacks out of the flour, and we have found a cocoa-nut grove. So we shall be able to live like kings."

The next morning Stephen was again left in charge of the fire, and the other two started to fetch a fresh load of cocoa-nuts, saying that they should be back by twelve o'clock, and should expect to find that he had got something new for them. After putting a piece of meat into the well Stephen made a fresh experiment. Fishing out a great lump of fat from the cask, he first washed it carefully to get rid of the salt, then put it into half a cocoa-nut shell, placed this on some hot embers and fried the fat until most of it melted, and then squeezed the remainder between two flat stones. Then he poured the fat into another cocoa-nut half full of milk, put three or four pounds of flour on a flat rock, made a hollow in the middle as he had seen the servant do at home while making pastry, poured the liquor gradually into this, mixing it up with the flour until he had made the whole into dough. Then he cleared away a portion of the embers, and dividing the dough into flat cakes placed these on the hot ground. Half an hour later he cleared another space from embers, and turned the cakes over, and in twenty minutes they were baked through. They were pronounced excellent by his companions as they ate them with their meat.

"We must not be too lavish," Stephen said, "as we do not know how long we may have to wait here. I propose for breakfast that we have biscuits only, then for dinner we will have some meat and biscuits again, and for supper cold meat and cakes. How much meat do you think there is, Wilcox?"

"There is supposed to be a hundred and a half in that cask, Mr. Embleton."

"Well, that will last us just about a month," Stephen said, "at a pound and a half each a day. I propose that we have that allowance for a fortnight, and if there are no signs of the ship by that time we can then reduce ourselves to three-quarters of a pound a day. At that rate it will last for six weeks altogether. The flour and the biscuits would last twice as long, but we must keep a good stock of them on hand, so as to have a store if we take to the canoe again."

This proposal was agreed to. They had, however, been there about a week when early one morning Joyce discovered a sail far away on the horizon. In great excitement they hurried down to the canoe, which had been brought along and hauled up on the rocks.

"Put her into the water to see if the sun has opened her seams."

Finding that it had done so, they filled her and then hauled her just beyond the edge of the water. Then they went up to their tent again.

"There ain't much wind," the sailor said, "and it will die away altogether in an hour or two. It is no good our doing anything until we see which way she is heading. If it is the *Tiger*, I reckon she is making for this spot, and we can wait till the afternoon anyhow before we take to the canoe. If it is only a chance ship, and we find she is bearing a course that brings her anywhere near us, we must take to the canoe at once. I should say she is a good five-and-twenty miles away, but anyhow we can get out to her before the evening breeze springs up."

By nine o'clock they made out that the ship was certainly heading in their direction. Then the wind left her, and presently they saw her swing broadside on to them.

"She is very like the *Tiger*," Joyce said. "She is just about the same size and barque-rigged, but we cannot see her hull."

"She is the *Tiger* sure enough," Wilcox said. "Her heading this way made it pretty well certain, but I think I could swear to her now."

"Well, I vote we start for her at once. What do you say, Stephen?"

"I think so, Tom. Certainly it will be a long row in the heat, but that does not matter. We had better put a stock of biscuits and cocoa-nuts on board. One never knows about the weather here, and before night there might be another cyclone, then she might have to run for it. We should have to make for the nearest land, and might not be able to get back here for two or three days."

As they had eaten their first meal there was no reason for any delay. The canoe was emptied out, a store sufficient for two or three days put on board, and they were soon on their way. They took the bearings of the ship by various points of the island before they started, lest it should come over thick.

"It ain't no use hurrying," Wilcox said as they dipped their paddles in the water. "We have got a good five hours' pull before us, and whether it is five or seven it don't make much difference."

They had each cut a square of canvas with which to cover their heads and shoulders, and at short intervals they dipped these in the sea and so kept off at least a portion of the extreme heat. The boat was much less heavily laden than it had been on their previous journey, and went lightly through the water. In spite of their agreement to take it easy their impatience to reach the ship, on whose upper sails their eyes were fixed as they paddled, prevented their doing so, and for the first two hours they rowed at almost racing pace. Then the heat of the sun began to tell upon them, their efforts slackened, and their pace decreased materially. However, they could now make out the line of the hull above the horizon, and knew that she could not be at most more than some eight miles away, and in little more than two hours they were within half a mile of her. It was their old ship the *Tiger*. By this time they could see that they were objects of eager curiosity on board, and presently they heard loud cheers come across the water.

"They have made us out," Joyce said. "Of course, at first they took us for a native canoe, for they would be looking for the gig. They don't know yet what bad news we have to tell them."

In a few minutes they were alongside, but as soon as they were within hail the captain had shouted out:

"Are all well?"

"No, sir," Joyce, who was in the bow, shouted back, "I am sorry to say that Mr. Towel and the rest have all been killed by the Malays."

The news effectually damped the feeling of delight that had been excited on board when it was known that the canoe contained three of the boat's party, for whose safety the greatest anxiety had been felt, the captain alone having entertained any hopes that the gig could have lived through the storm. However, as they climbed up the ladder to the deck they were shaken warmly by the hand by officers and crew, and then the captain requested Joyce and Stephen to come down to his cabin, while Wilcox went forward to tell the story to the crew. The first and third mates also came into the cabin. Joyce then, as the senior, told the story of all that had happened from the time the cyclone had burst upon them.

"You see, sir," he said when he came to the conclusion, "I owe my life entirely to Stephen and Wilcox."

"I see that plainly enough, Mr. Joyce," the captain said gravely. "They behaved admirably both in that and in the whole subsequent proceedings. You were lucky indeed in hitting on the spot where we were separated. We were four hundred miles away when we got out of the cyclone. The wind has been very light, and we have gone close to every island we have passed on our way here. It was, of course, most doubtful whether you would be able to find the place where the wreck was, for you too might have been carried hundreds of miles in an entirely different direction, and without your instruments you would have had but a small chance of discovering your position or finding your way here. Still, it seemed the only chance. Of course I could not tell whether when you landed you found the wreck had been stripped by the natives; but if you had not done so it seemed to me you would certainly make your way there if you could, for you would know there were no natives near, and you might, for all I could tell, have found various stores cast up that would enable you to live for a long time.

"It has been, as you say, a sad business indeed. Six lives have been lost, and, as it appears to me from your story, unnecessarily; it was a grievous mistake going up that river. I can understand Mr. Towel's anxiety to obtain a stock of provisions of some sort to victual the boat for a long cruise, but he should have endeavoured to ascertain first, by following the bank on foot, whether there were any native villages there before venturing up in the boat; and to fire guns until he had ascertained that there were no enemy near, is another instance of that fatal carelessness that costs so many lives. However, the poor fellow of course acted for the best, and he has paid dearly for his error. That expedient of yours for lighting a fire, Steve, was a very ingenious one, and does you a great deal of credit. I don't think that it would have occurred to me. Altogether, young gentlemen, you seem to have behaved extremely prudently and well. I am sorry to tell you that your comrade Archer was washed overboard in the cyclone, and two of the men were killed by being struck by a spar that got adrift."

The news of Archer's death greatly destroyed the pleasure of the lads at finding themselves safely on board the *Tiger* again, and they took up their work with very sorrowful hearts.

For another two months the *Tiger* continued her cruise among the islands without any adventure occurring. By the end of that time they had disposed of their goods and had taken in a large number of the native productions in exchange, and the ship's course was laid north again for Calcutta, where they filled up with Indian produce and then sailed for home.

Five months later they arrived in the Thames, the only bad weather they had encountered being a storm as they entered the Channel. They anchored at Gravesend, and the captain told Stephen to land and take a post-chaise up to London, and report to Mr. Hewson that the *Tiger* would come up on the tide next morning. It was eight o'clock in the evening when Stephen arrived at his employer's. Mr. Hewson received him with great kindness.

"I am always very glad when I hear that one of my ships is safe in port," he said; "for however great my confidence, there are times when human skill and strength are of no avail. I did not expect that the *Tiger* would be back for another month or so, and am heartily glad to hear that she has returned. All has gone well, I hope?"

"I am sorry to say, sir, that we have lost altogether nine lives, including those of Mr. Towel, the second officer, and Archer, my fellow apprentice."

"That is bad indeed," Mr. Hewson said in a tone of great concern. "How did it happen?"

Stephen related briefly the events that had brought about the misfortunes. "I am sorry indeed," Mr. Hewson said when he had concluded; "but it is a consolation to me that none of the lives were lost from any deficiency in the ship's gear or appointments. The boat must have been an excellent one indeed to have carried you in safety through a cyclone, in which, as we know, the stoutest ships will sometimes founder. As to the accident on board, it was one of those things that too often occur in a heavy gale, and that cannot be provided against. Of course, I shall hear from the captain all details of that affair. As to your adventure on shore, you must give me a much fuller account when you have had some supper. I shall release you at once from duty, and you had better go down by the coach to-morrow morning to Dover. I know that your father is anxious to see you. He wrote to me about three weeks ago, asking me when I expected the *Tiger* to be home. I know what his reason is, but I think that he would wish to be the first to speak to you about it himself."

"There is nothing wrong, sir, I hope?"

"No, lad, in no way. It is another matter altogether."

Supper was brought up, and Stephen did full justice to it, for the ship had touched nowhere on her way home from

Calcutta, and after feeding so long almost entirely on salt meat, he thoroughly enjoyed the change of fresh provisions. The next morning he started by the seven-o'clock coach for Dover, and arrived there at eight that evening.

"You have grown indeed, Stephen!" his father said after the first delighted greetings were over. "Let me think. You have been away nearly eighteen months. That does make a good deal of difference; still, you have grown more than I should have expected. I used to think that you would be rather short, but now you bid fair to be a good average height, and you have widened out amazingly. Where are your traps, lad? Have you ordered them to be sent up from the coach office?"

"I have not brought any down with me, father. The *Tiger* only got to Gravesend at five o'clock yesterday afternoon, and the captain sent me up by post-chaise to tell Mr. Hewson that she was in. I got to his place at eight, and he told me that I had better start by this morning's coach, as he knew that you were anxious to see me."

"He didn't tell you what for, Stephen?"

"No, sir. He said that he thought that you would prefer to tell me yourself."

"Well, Stephen, I have been anxious for you to get home, for I had a letter from Lord Cochrane about three weeks ago. He told me that he had not forgotten the promise he had made me, to give you a berth if he ever had a chance. He said that the opportunity had come now, for that he had been offered the command of the Chilian navy, and should be shortly starting—as soon, in fact, as he could make his arrangements and get his house off his hands. He said that he thought it would be five or six weeks before he was able to sail, and that he would take you out with him as his flag-midshipman. Of course I wrote to him at once, saying where you were, and that you might be home any day, but that, on the other hand, you might not be back for two or three months. However, if you arrived in time I was sure that you would be delighted at the chance of serving under him; still I said that of course I could not ask him to keep the berth open for you. Well, he wrote in reply that he would, at anyrate, give me a month, but if at the end of that time I had not heard of you, he must appoint some one else; for, as he said, 'I know nothing of the Chilian language, and of course I shall want some one to blow up in English.'"

Stephen laughed. "That would be splendid, father. I have been very happy on board the *Tiger*, and certainly should not like to leave her to sail on any other trading ship. No one could be kinder than the captain and the mates have been. But of course I should like awfully to serve with Lord Cochrane, especially as I have heard so much of him from you. But why have the Chilians appointed a foreigner to command their fleet? Are they fighting with anyone?"

"They are fighting the Spanish, Stephen. They have gone into the war to aid Peru, or rather to free Peru from her oppressors. The Chilians have only just started a navy of their own, and it is altogether outnumbered by the Spanish; but they wisely think that with such a man as Cochrane, who is a host in himself, who has won against much greater odds, they will be able to hold their own, and I have no doubt you will have a stirring time. I only wish that I had been able to go with him. He was good enough to say so in his letter to me. That is unfortunately out of the question. However, Stephen, you must choose for yourself. There is no saying what may come of this business. You know that Lord Cochrane is a hot-headed man, and one who does not mince matters. The Chilians, I believe, are the brightest and most energetic of any of the South American peoples, but that, you know, is not saying a great deal. Cochrane is sure to be maddened by delays and difficulties of all kinds, and if so he will certainly speak out in a way that will ruffle their feelings greatly, and may bring on trouble.

"He is what is called an impracticable man, Stephen. He is himself the soul of honour and generosity, and so is altogether unable to refrain from giving vent to his indignation and disgust when he sees these qualities lacking in others. He has ruined his own career here by his intolerance of wrong, whether the wrong was inflicted upon himself or upon others. He has rather injured than benefited the cause of our seamen by the intemperate zeal with which he pressed his reforms, and by allying himself heart and soul with the ultra-radicals. Such a man as he may get on well with a people like the South Americans, his dashing bravery, his frankness, and his disregard of ceremony will render him popular among the people at large, but will raise up for him enemies innumerable among the governing class. I cannot, therefore, for a minute think that the present arrangement will be a permanent one. I say all this to assure you that you cannot expect to find a permanent career in the service of Chili; but, on the other hand, you will have the advantage of fighting under the bravest officer of modern times.

"You will, I have no doubt, take part in some brilliant feats. And to have served under Cochrane will, as long as you live, be a feather in your cap, just as I feel that it is a great honour for myself, although it has been to my pecuniary disadvantage, to have done so. I have exchanged letters with Mr. Hewson on the subject. He has behaved with the greatest kindness in the matter, and agrees with me that it would in some respects be a great advantage to you. He has offered in the kindest possible way to allow your apprenticeship to run on while you are with Cochrane, just as if you were still serving with his own ships, and whenever you may return to England he will reinstate you in his service, the time you have been away counting just the same as if you had been with him. I expressed a doubt whether your apprenticeship would count; but he said that any master being, from any circumstances, unable to teach a trade to an apprentice, as he covenanted to do, could, with the consent of that apprentice, hand him over to another employer; and that as you will be learning the sea as efficiently on the coast of Chili as elsewhere, he could loan you, as it were, to Lord Cochrane. Besides, of course, there is no real necessity for passing through an apprenticeship in order to become an officer. Large numbers of men do, in fact, become officers without ever having been apprenticed, as it is only necessary to serve so many years at sea, and to pass an examination. Still, there are advantages the other way. All ship-owners prefer a man who has served an apprenticeship in a good line of ships, as he would naturally be better mannered and better educated, and therefore better fitted for the position of an officer in ships carrying passengers. In that way it would be as well that you should obtain your discharge at the end of your term of apprenticeship from Mr. Hewson, although I have some doubts whether your sea-service under a foreign flag would be allowed to count by the examiners if you went up to pass as a mate. Upon the other hand, lad, you are now in a good service, and are certain to get on if you remain in it; and you have less chance of being shot than if you go with Cochrane."

"I don't know that, father. I can tell you I have had just as close a shave under Captain Pinder as I could have under Lord Cochrane. Only three of us out of nine got through; the other six were killed and eaten by the Malays; and if the Spaniards kill a man, at least they will not eat him. Oh, I should certainly like to go with Lord Cochrane!"

"I thought you would. As far as one can see there is no chance of our being engaged in any naval wars for many years to come, for all Europe is in alliance with us, and is likely to continue so; and even if we have trouble with any of them, our fleet is so overpoweringly strong that even a coalition of all the other powers of Europe could not stand against us at sea. It is a good thing no doubt for the nation; but such a peace as this is likely to be, gives no chance for naval men to distinguish themselves. I must say that I consider you are fortunate indeed to have this opportunity of seeing some service under the man who, of all others, is distinguished for dash and bravery. He is the Lord Peterborough of the present day."

"Who was he, father?"

"He was a military man in the days of Queen Anne. He performed extraordinary feats of bravery in Spain, and in many other respects his character bore a strong resemblance to that of Lord Cochrane. Well, Stephen, we had better lose no time, and I propose that we go up to town again to-morrow morning. No doubt he would like to see you, and there is nothing like settling the thing finally; and one interview is worth a dozen letters. Let me see." Mr. Embleton consulted the sailing-list. "As there is no boat sailing to-morrow, we will take the coach. It would be better anyhow, for there is never any saying with certainty when the packets will arrive. With a strong southerly wind they may do it in two tides, though it is only once in a hundred times that they manage it; still, even three tides would be very fair. But we could not risk the chances, and it is a duty to let Lord Cochrane know as early as possible, as no doubt he has many applications, and would be glad to be able to say that the matter was finally settled."

They arrived in town the next evening and called upon

Lord Cochrane the first thing after breakfast next day. On Mr. Embleton sending in his name he was at once admitted.

"I am heartily glad to see you, old friend," Lord Cochrane said as he rose from the table, at which he was writing. "So this is your boy! His appearance saves me asking questions. When did he get back?"

"He arrived in town on Monday evening, came down on Tuesday to Dover, and returned here with me last night."

"You have indeed lost no time. Well, young sir, what do you think of going out with me?"

"I should like it above everything, my lord, and I am deeply grateful to you for offering me the post."

"It is to your father, lad, that you should be grateful, and not to me, for he earned it for you. So you have had eighteen months in the eastern seas?"

"Yes, sir."

"A very good school, I should say, Embleton; one has to keep one's eyes open there."

"Yes indeed. He told me on the way up yesterday of an adventure he had had with the Malays, and as only three out of a boat-load of nine escaped, it must have been a pretty sharp business."

"If only three escaped it must have been sharp indeed," Lord Cochrane said, "and they must have had marvellous luck in getting out of the Malays' hands. He shall tell me all about it on our voyage out. Now, come along with me."

He led the way to the dining-room, where Lady Cochrane was sitting, while her two children, of four and five years old, were playing about.

"My dear," he said, "this is Lieutenant Embleton, whom you have heard me speak of a score of times as a most gallant officer, and a most ill-used man. This is his son, who is, you know, going out with us as my flag-midshipman; he has been eighteen months in the Indian Archipelago. And let me tell you, the Malays are much more serious foes than the Spaniards. You know, youngster, one of the chief duties of an admiral's midshipman is to make himself agreeable to the admiral's wife and family, if there are such incumbrances. He goes errands for her, attends her when she goes shopping, is a sort of head nurse to the children, and in our service he is generally nicknamed the admiral's poodle. However, as soon as I get out there, I hope to find more attractive work for you, and until I do, I am sure my wife and the children will be glad they have someone with them to speak English."

"I shall be very glad to be of any service I can," Stephen said earnestly.

"I am afraid," Lady Cochrane said with a smile, "that we shall have very little opportunity of availing ourselves of your services. When we once get out there you will be carried off by Lord Cochrane, and he will never set foot on shore again unless when absolutely driven to it."

"Is your time for sailing fixed yet, Lord Cochrane?" the lieutenant asked.

"We shall sail on the 15th of August from Boulogne, so that your son will have three weeks to make his preparations."

"Three days would be sufficient," Embleton said, with a smile. "Naval outfitters are not so busy as they used to be, and would furnish an admiral's kit, if necessary, in that time. Is there any particular uniform, sir?"

"No, it is something like our own; and if you rig him out in an ordinary midshipman's uniform that will be good enough. Thank goodness, this weary waiting is over. It is now fourteen months since I accepted the offer of the Chilian government sent me by their agent, Don Jose Alvarez. I was to put off my departure so as to look after the building and equipment of a war steamer for the service, but there have been incessant delays owing to want of money. It has been enough to madden one; and, after all, I have to go without her, and we sail in the *Rose*. She is one of the sloops sold out of the navy, and is now a merchantman. I daresay they would have kept me dawdling about here for months to come if it hadn't been that they have been getting the worst of it out there, and it at length occurred to them that the admiral's place is in command of his fleet, and not to act as a sort of foreman in looking after a single ship being built. We shall embark at Rye, but, of course, it will be more handy for you to send or bring him to Boulogne. I expect that we shall be there on the 13th, so as to have time to shake down before we start. Your son had better be there on that day. I will draw up his commission as my flag-midshipman at once, and will hand it to you when you dine with me, which I trust you and your son will do this evening. It is very fortunate that I am disengaged, for just at present I am going through a painful round of farewell dinners from my political friends."

"I shall be very glad to do so, sir," Mr. Embleton said, "and will not detain you farther now."

As soon as they left Lord Cochrane they went to see Mr Hewson.

"It is all arranged, I suppose?" the latter said as they entered.

"Yes, we have just left Lord Cochrane; but in the first place, Stephen, who is not much accustomed to return thanks, has asked me to say in his name how extremely obliged he is for your most kind offer to allow him to remain on the books of your fleet."

"Say no more about it, Embleton. I am very pleased that I can be of any service to you, and to the lad also. Captain Pinder has spoken most warmly to me of his conduct during the voyage. He behaved in all respects excellently; and although, happily, the captain was not laid up, and was therefore able to attend himself to the details of navigation, he says that had he been disabled he should have felt no uneasiness on that score, Stephen's observations being to the full as accurate as his own. He especially speaks of him in tones of commendation for his conduct in that unfortunate boat affair. Every credit is due to the sailor Wilcox who was with him through it; but the latter himself told the captain that he felt so certain that all those in the boat had been killed, that he should not have undertaken the risk of going near the Malay village had it not been for the lad's insisting. He says, too, that although junior to Joyce—the lad they rescued—Stephen was really the leader; that many of his suggestions were most valuable. Wilcox is particularly strong on the manner in which the lad contrived to kindle a fire by using his watch-glass filled with water as a burning-glass. Altogether, I feel sure that your boy will make an excellent officer as he goes on, and I am glad that he will now have the opportunity of seeing some active service under Cochrane.

"I agree with what you said in your letter, that the berth is by no means likely to be a permanent one. As soon as Cochrane has relieved them from the state in which they now are, they are sure to be jealous of him, and he is the last man in the world to put up with slights, or to hold on to an appointment when he sees that he is no longer wanted. Still, it will do the lad a great deal of good and make a man of him, and his experience will put him outside the general category of mercantile sailors. I have got his chests here; they were sent up yesterday. I shall, of course, try and find out who was the captain of that ship whose chronometers he bought. Captain Pinder has told me all about it, and Stephen is absolutely entitled to the money he got. At the same time his offer to divide it was a generous one, but Captain Pinder and the mates are all dead against accepting it, and I agree with them. The money would be a mere trifle all round, but it will be a comfortable little sum for him. And it will, I am sure, be a satisfaction to him to be able to purchase his outfit now without trenching on your purse, especially as, going out as Cochrane's own midshipman, he must take a much larger outfit than usual, as he will, of course, have to accompany the admiral on all public occasions. Now, I suppose he will like to go down to the dock and say good-bye to them there. The *Tiger* began unloading yesterday, and a good many of the hands will be paid off to-morrow."

Captain Pinder and the first and third officers expressed their sincere regret that Stephen was not going to sail with them on the next voyage, and Joyce was greatly cut up about it.

"I wanted you to go down with me to stay with my father and mother near Oxford," he said. "I wrote to them from Gravesend and I had a letter this morning, in which they told me to make you promise to come down before we sailed again."

"I may be back again in a year," Stephen replied, "and if I am I think Mr. Hewson will appoint me to the *Tiger* again."

The captain undertook to dispose of Stephen's collection of curios and bird skins for him, and also, if no news was obtained as to the lost ship, he would, when he sailed again, hand the chronometers and quadrants over to Mr. Hewson to keep for him.

Mr. Hewson that evening again talked over the question of the bag of money with Lieutenant Embleton, and convinced the latter that Stephen was entitled to keep the money, to which his right was, he declared, unquestionable. Stephen's father was of the same opinion himself, and argued the question only because he felt that the fact that the money was really extremely useful at the present time, might render him unable to judge the matter fairly. He really had no answer to the reasons given by his friend, who, he was well assured, would not urge the matter upon him did he not feel that Stephen was really entitled to keep the money, which had entirely and absolutely passed out of the possession of its former owners, whoever they were.

"I never heard," he said, "that anyone who was lucky enough to recover treasure in an old wreck had his right to retain it questioned, and here not even the wreck remained. So we will keep it and spend it, Hewson; but if you ever discover the owners of that ship let me know, and I shall be prepared to discuss the question with them."

"We shall never discover them, my good sir," Hewson said. "How can any man in the world say that that money belongs to a ship that has disappeared in the Malay Archipelago? The only possible clue is that afforded by the chronometers, and here again it is unlikely in the extreme that the owners of the ship, that has, perhaps, been sailing the seas for thirty or forty years, would be able to swear to her chronometers. Lastly, there is no shadow of proof that the chest in which the money was found came from the same ship as the chronometers; they may be the proceeds of two different acts of piracy. You will never hear anything about it."

CHAPTER VII.

COCHRANE'S CAREER.

"YOU promised, father," Stephen said one evening, "that you would, some time or other, tell me more about the days when you served with Lord Cochrane."

"Well, lad, I will tell you now. The first time I ever saw him was on the day when he joined the *Hind* at Sheerness, in June, 1793. I was a young midshipman on board her, and I can tell you we were all astonished at his appearance, for he was between seventeen and eighteen—a tall, gawky fellow. I believe he had had a commission in the army, but that his taste lay altogether in the direction of the sea, and that he obtained his appointment to us by the influence of his uncle, who was a post-captain at the time. Well, you know we generally entered at the age of fourteen, and you may imagine our surprise and amusement at a fellow arriving to begin, who was as old as the senior mid on board. Lord though he was, there was no nonsense about Cochrane. He was a very pleasant fellow, and I never saw anyone work so hard to learn his profession as he did. He actually satisfied even our first lieutenant, who was a rough, hard-working fellow, who had made his way up after having got his promotion from the main-deck, or having, as we used to call it, come in at the hawse-holes.

"He was an admirable seaman, heart and soul in his work, and ready to take off his coat and put on a suit of slops and work himself. He took rather a dislike at first to Cochrane, first because he was a lord, in the second place because he considered that he had taken to the profession too old to learn, and lastly because he brought a chest on board altogether beyond regulation size. Jack Larmour soon made short work of that. He called up the carpenters, and bade them saw a portion off the chest, cutting it through just on one side of the keyhole, so that the lock was now in the corner. Cochrane only laughed and said nothing, but I have no doubt the lieutenant expected him to say something hasty and so get himself into trouble. However, Jack soon changed his opinion of the new mid. The earnest desire of Cochrane to learn, and his willingness to put on a rough suit and work, showed that he was of the right stuff, and made him at last a prime favourite of the first lieutenant's.

"I was only with him then a couple of months, for I was transferred to another ship, and did not come across him again until he was appointed by Lord Keith to the command of the *Speedy*, lying at Port Mahon. He had done a good deal of knocking about by that time, for the *Hind* was sent out to the coast of Norway, where it was suspected that French privateers used the fiords as hiding-places. On the return of the *Hind* from Norway, Cochrane's uncle was appointed to the *Thetis*, and the *Hind's* crew were transferred to her. The *Thetis* went out with a squadron for the protection of the islands of Nova Scotia, and so well was Cochrane thought of that in January, 1795, he was appointed by the admiral of the station acting third lieutenant of the *Thetis*, and was soon after transferred, with the same rank, to the *Africa*; and in July was confirmed in his rank, though he had been but two years at sea. In the *Africa* he coasted up and down, between Canada and Florida, looking out for ships of the enemy, but in the following January he rejoined the *Thetis*, whose first lieutenant had just been promoted. He then passed as lieutenant, and was afterwards appointed to the *Speedy*.

"The difficulty of his not having served the regulation time had been got over by his uncle in a way which was not uncommon then, and may be still practised for aught I know. His uncle thought that he might one day wish to join the navy, and had therefore entered his name in the books of the various ships he commanded, so that nominally he had formed part of the ship's complement in the *Vesuvius*, *Carolina*, *La Sophie*, and *Hind*, and had therefore belonged to the service for the regulation period. It is a bad practice, lad, but in the case of Cochrane was the means of providing the king's navy with as gallant an officer as ever trod quarter-deck. I went down with him from Gibraltar to Port Mahon with another midshipman who, like myself, had just passed, and was to join the *Speedy*. We were hoping to gain an opportunity for distinguishing ourselves, and getting a step.

"Our first sight of the craft was a grievous disappointment. She was a brig of 158 tons, and as she carried eighty-four men and six officers, you may imagine how we were crowded on board. Her armament consisted of fourteen four-pounders, ridiculous little weapons that were no more good than as many blunderbusses. I remember Cochrane putting fourteen balls into his pockets, and walking up and down the quarter-deck, saying that he was probably the only commander who had ever carried a whole ship's broadsides in his pockets.

"He was awfully disgusted, as you may imagine, with his craft, and he applied for two twelve-pounders, to be used for stern-chasers. When he got them on board he found that there was not room for them to be worked. He had them fired off a few times, but the brig was so weakly built that the timbers would not stand the concussion. He was therefore obliged to send them on shore again. There was only a height of five feet even in the captain's cabin, and I remember that Cochrane used to open the skylight and put his head up through it in order to shave himself, placing the soap-dish in front of him on the quarter-deck. However, we were a pleasant party on board. Cochrane was strict in the performance of duty, but an excellent fellow to sail with, anxious for the comfort of men and officers, and without a shadow of nonsense about him. His first lieutenant had served for a few months in that rank, Rogers and I were acting-lieutenants, and there was a doctor, and one midshipman, Lord Cochrane's brother. Lord Cochrane at that time was twenty-four, or nearly so, his first lieutenant was a year older, Rogers and I twenty-one.

"We had a busy time on board the *Speedy*. We were continually up and down the coast, popping into quiet creeks and little ports in search of French privateers, and overhauling merchantmen, besides bearing what share we could in the general operations.

"Our first prize was a French privateer of six guns and forty-eight men. We had been ordered to convoy fourteen merchantmen from Cagliari to Leghorn, and saw a strange craft take possession of a Danish brig under our escort. We crowded on every inch of canvas, and set off in pursuit. The *Speedy* was not misnamed. Whatever her defects, she was certainly fast, and Cochrane had managed to add to the canvas she carried when he first took the command. The main boom was sprung, and he obtained from the dockyard another spar to replace it. This, however, was a good deal longer than the original, and the dockyard authorities decided that it must be taken down considerably. Instead of doing this Cochrane had about an inch cut off from each end, and had the spar replaced and hoisted. When the dockyard people came on board they did not notice that its length was unaltered, and as soon as we got out some more cloths of canvas were added to the mainsail, and we were thus enabled to carry a considerable spread of canvas for so small a craft. We soon overtook the prize, which surrendered at once, and then set off in chase of the privateer, which we overhauled, the sight of our long row of port-holes and crowded decks no doubt leading the Frenchmen to suppose we were a great deal stronger than he was, though in point of fact his six guns carried a much heavier weight of metal than our fourteen pop-guns together.

"Four days later five armed boats rowed out from Monte Cristo towards the convoy, which was lying becalmed. The brig got out sweeps to endeavour to interpose between them and her charges. Two vessels, however, which were lagging behind the others were boarded and captured. To our delight we soon afterwards saw a dark line on the water, and, directly it reached us, set off in pursuit of the captured merchantmen, which were headed towards Monte Cristo. The breeze soon freshened, and we presently overhauled and recaptured them, and then set off in pursuit of the armed boats. These, however, reached the shelter of the shore battery before we could overtake them; as our duty was to protect the convoy and not to cut out prizes, we hauled our wind and followed our charges, and a week later arrived with them all safely in Leghorn roads, and started to join Lord Keith's squadron off Genoa, which he was blockading at sea while the Austrians beleaguered it on the land side. Here we cruised outside the town for a few days; then Massena surrendered, and the *Speedy* was ordered to cruise off the Spanish coast.

"On our way we captured a native craft off Elba, and a Sardinian vessel laden with oil and wool, which was a prize to a French privateer. We towed her into Leghorn, and again started, and captured the next day a Spanish privateer of ten guns and thirty-three men. Five gun-boats came out from Bastia in chase, but we took the prize in tow, and kept up a running fire with the gun-boats until, after chasing us for some hours, they gave it up. We took several other prizes, and sunk a privateer lying under shelter of a battery. We again took our prizes back into Leghorn, indeed it seemed that we were never to get away from that place, for, starting again, we captured a French privateer, and then fell in with the frigates *Mutine* and *Salamine*, which handed over to us a number of French prisoners that they had taken, and we had to carry them and our prize back to Leghorn. At last we got fairly away, and reached Port Mahon, capturing a Neapolitan vessel with a French prize crew on board.

"As far as I can remember nothing particular happened for

the next three months, except that we got damaged in a storm and were six weeks refitting at Port Mahon. Three days after leaving the port we were off Majorca. There were several strange craft in sight; we picked out the largest and started in chase, when a French craft came out, and we altered our course to meet her. After exchanging fire with us for some time she drew off, but got too close inshore and drove on the rocks. As it was evident that she would become a wreck, we left her and captured one of the other ships.

"The activity of the *Speedy* caused the Spanish authorities to make special efforts to capture her, and she once nearly fell into the hands of a Spanish frigate, which had been painted as a merchantman. However, she opened her ports too soon; and fortunately we were prepared for the situation. Cochrane had had our craft painted in imitation of a Danish brig, which was trading on the coast, and whose appearance was familiar to the Spanish authorities, and a Danish quartermaster had been shipped to answer inconvenient questions.

"Directly we discovered the real nature of the supposed merchant ship, by her opening her ports, we ran up Danish colours, and on the ship's name being demanded gave that of the Danish brig. The Spaniard, however, was not quite satisfied, and lowered a boat, whereupon we ran up the quarantine flag, and the Danish quartermaster, on the boat coming within hail and then stopping at a prudent distance, informed them that he had come from the African coast, where the plague was at that time raging. The boat pulled off to the frigate, which at once made sail and left us in solitude. It was a narrow escape, though possibly we might have made as good a fight of it as we did afterwards.

"Cruising about we took a considerable number of prizes. Our luck, indeed, was extraordinary, and we all anticipated that the prize-money would amount to a large sum. It was on the 4th of May that our first serious adventure began. We had captured some prizes off Barcelona, and a swarm of gun-boats came out to try to retake them. However, we kept them at bay until the prizes had got off, and the following night returned to our station off the town. We found that there was a strict watch being kept ashore, for the gun-boats at once came out, but when we sailed towards them they made for the shore, keeping up a fire at us as they retired.

"Again we drew off and again they came out, and twice during the day they did the same, always returning when we sailed in to meet them. Their fire was exceedingly accurate, and after each skirmish with them we had to draw off and repair damages. It seemed to us that there must be some object in the gun-boats' action, and that they were trying to decoy us to go close inshore, where some larger ship might be ready to come out against us. Just before daybreak on the 6th we again ran in towards Barcelona. As we did so we saw a large ship creeping along under the land, as if making for the port. We at once sailed to cut her off, when, instead of trying to avoid us, she changed her course and sailed towards us, and we saw that she was a Spanish frigate. Two or three of our fellows had expressed an opinion that had we attacked the Spaniard under whose guns we had run three months before, we might have taken her. Lord Cochrane, as soon as she was made out to be a frigate, said to them:

"'You shall now have a fair fight, gentlemen;' and ordered the boatswain to pipe all hands for action.

"I tell you, lad, it seemed to me that our chances were slight indeed, for nearly half our men and two of the officers were away in prizes, and, including officers and boys, we had but fifty-four men on board, so it was probable that the enemy had five or six times that number, while he had thirty-four guns to our fourteen miserable little pieces. I thought it certain we should be blown out of the water, and I fancy everyone else thought the same. However, we held on straight towards her. She fired a gun and hoisted Spanish colours. At that time we were almost abreast of her, and Cochrane, who had the American colours ready, ordered them to be run up. This gave us time to get on to the other tack, and hold on till a little out of her direct line of fire. Then we at once pulled down the stars and stripes and hoisted the British ensign. The Spaniard fired a broadside, to which we made no reply. Our guns were trebly shotted, but Cochrane had given orders that not a shot was to be fired until we were alongside the Spaniard, as our fire would do no damage whatever to the ship. As we headed for her they fired another broadside, but, like the first, this did us no harm, and rounding up under her stern Cochrane ran us alongside.

"Our yards became locked in the Spaniard's rigging, and we then poured in our broadside, which at this distance did considerable damage on her main deck, the first discharge having, as we afterwards learned, killed the Spanish captain and boatswain. Our guns had been elevated to their full extent, for of course she towered high above us. While our shot struck up through her main-deck, the Spanish guns roared overhead, cutting up our rigging, but doing us no harm whatever below, while our fire continued to work havoc among them. We heard the order shouted to board, but were prepared for this, and at once pushed off far enough to prevent them from leaping on to our deck, while the men caught up the muskets that had been ranged in readiness against the bulwark, and poured a volley into them as they appeared at the side in readiness to jump down. Then we gave them another broadside, and closed up again. Twice again they attempted to board, but each time failed, and the fight went on.

"Our fellows were thoroughly excited, and ready for anything, but it was clear that the present state of affairs could not last much longer. Our rigging and sails were cut to pieces, and the masts might at any moment go, and the frigate would then only have to cut herself free, draw off a short distance, and sink us. Cochrane, who was as cool as a cucumber, went along among the men at their quarters, and told them that they had either got to take the frigate or be taken themselves, in which case they would probably get no quarter, as the Spaniards would be maddened at the loss they had suffered from so insignificant a foe. 'It needs,' he said, 'but a few minutes' hard fighting to settle the matter.' All replied that they were ready. Cochrane was always up to fun, and he called a portion of the crew away from the guns, and told them to damp some powder and blacken their faces. You never saw such figures as they were when they came up. Cochrane ordered them to board at the enemy's bow, while the rest of the crew were to board by the waist.

"Guthrie, the doctor, volunteered to take the helm, and when Cochrane gave the order the rest of us, men and boys, sprang on to the deck of the Spaniard. Through the wreaths of smoke they had caught sight of our preparations, and, believing that we intended to board by the bow, the greater portion of their crew were gathered there. The appearance of our fellows' faces as they emerged from the smoke and leapt upon the deck, and with loud shouts rushed at them, struck them with astonishment. I was with this party, and, excited as I was, could scarcely refrain from bursting out laughing at their dismay. Our men certainly were enough to surprise anyone. Bathed in sweat, worked up to a pitch of wild excitement, naked to the waist, with their faces and bodies streaked with the powder, one could understand that the superstitious Spaniards, already depressed by their vain efforts to overpower so puny an assailant, thought that they were attacked by foes straight from the infernal regions. As they stood hesitating and aghast, we went at them, while Cochrane, with the force that had boarded at the waist, fell upon them in rear.

"Recovering themselves, the Spaniards made a rush to the waist, defending themselves stoutly, and for a while it seemed as if their numbers must in the end prevail. The Spanish colours were still flying at her peak, and Cochrane, observing them, told one of the sailors to make his way aft and haul them down. As soon as the Spaniards saw their flag disappear, they thought that the officers must have surrendered, and at once threw down their arms. Without giving them time to think, or for their officers to rally them, they were hurried down into the hold, and cannon were run round, loaded with grape, and pointed down the hatchways in case they should make an effort to retake the ship. As for us, we could hardly believe in our good luck. The fight had lasted an hour and a half, and our loss had been exceedingly small. Our first lieutenant, Parker, had been severely wounded in several places, three sailors were killed, and seventeen wounded. We found that our prize was the *Gamo* frigate, with a crew of three hundred and nineteen men, mounting thirty-two guns, firing a broadside weight of one hundred and ninety pounds, while we had only fourteen small guns.

"She was between six and seven hundred tons, and in the fight had lost her captain, boatswain, and thirteen seamen killed and forty-one wounded, her casualties thus exceeding the whole number of our officers and crew. Even in the annals of our navy there is no instance of so successful an action against such disproportionate odds. We naturally congratulated ourselves upon our fortunes being as good as made. Cochrane would, of course, at once receive post-captain's rank, Parker would receive a step, and I should get at least a second lieutenantship. Cochrane's brother was placed in command of the prize, and we sailed with him to Port Mahon. As I have already told you, the jealousy of Lord Exmouth and the hot temper of Cochrane caused the overthrow of our hopes. Cochrane, after three months' delay, obtained his post rank, of which they could not deprive him, as, having captured a vessel of superior force, he was entitled to it. They refused, however, to promote Parker, which was simply scandalous and altogether in defiance of the usages of the service, and it was some time before I got a berth again. However, after we had repaired damages, matters went on for a time as before.

"After taking some prizes we met the *Kangaroo*, whose captain was senior to Cochrane, and requested him to act with him in an attack upon the fort of Almanara, which we silenced, and brought off a Spanish privateer. The two captains then determined to attack Oropesa, where the forts were supported by a twenty-gun ship and three gun-boats, which had put in there with ten merchantmen under their convoy. Cochrane had fitted out, at his own expense, a Spanish privateer of six guns which he had captured, as a tender to the *Speedy*, and had appointed his brother to command her; and in broad daylight the *Kangaroo*, *Speedy*, and tender sailed in to the attack. The *Kangaroo* engaged the forts, while we and young Cochrane directed our attention to the war-ship and gun-boats. It was as hot an action as any in which I ever took part. For some hours the firing was incessant. At the end of that time the *Kangaroo's* fire was evidently telling on the forts, while the fire of our antagonists was slackening.

"Just as we thought that victory was assured, a twelve-gun felucca and two more gun-boats arrived from Valencia to assist the fort. This reinforcement inspired the Spaniards with fresh spirit, and their cannonade against us again became very heavy. We turned our attention entirely to the new-comers, with such effect that we drove them off, and then hammered away again at our old opponents, and had the satisfaction at last of sinking all four of them, while three of the merchantmen, which had been in the line of fire, had also gone down. The action had lasted nine hours, and both we and the *Kangaroo* had used up nearly all our ammunition. The felucca and the two gun-boats from Valencia had again come up, and we had but a few shot left. We were forced to put a bold face on it; accordingly, the *Kangaroo* weighed her anchor, stood in close to the fort, and again anchored as if to pound it at close quarters, while we headed straight for the felucca and gun-boats. Fortunately they did not await our coming, but turned tail and returned to Valencia.

"The *Kangaroo's* boats and ours were now lowered, and made for the remaining merchantmen. Four of them cut their cables and ran ashore, where they were under the protection of a large body of troops on the beach. We could soon have driven these off had we had any ammunition left, but as it was, we were obliged to content ourselves with the capture of the other three ships. On our return to Port Mahon, after this really successful action, we found to our disgust that instead of the *Gamo* being purchased as usual by government, she had been sold for a mere song to the Algerines, thereby depriving us of the prize-money we had expected to get for her. Cochrane was especially enraged, for had the *Gamo* been purchased, we could have been transferred to her from the *Speedy*, and would have been in a position to do very much more than in that wretched little craft. It was, however, but a piece of the treatment that we had been receiving. The extraordinary number of prizes we had taken excited the jealousy of the senior officers on the station, for indeed we had captured more than all the other cruisers together; and the result was that our prizes were all sold for anything they would fetch, and owing to the ridiculous sums for which they were given away, and the rascality of the prize agents, we did not receive a tithe of the prize-money that should have come to us.

"This ill-will resulted in bringing our career to an end. On our return to Port Mahon we were ordered to escort an extremely slow old mail-packet to Gibraltar. What rendered it more ridiculous was that we were to carry the mail-bags, and only to hand them over to the old tub on her arrival at Gibraltar, and were then to return without communication with the shore. It was supposed that while engaged on this duty we should at least be able to take no further prizes, but we were so much faster than our convoy that while she crawled along we were able to run in and explore bays and creeks. In one several merchantmen were lying. As we bore in towards them they weighed their anchors and ran ashore. As soon as it was dark we sent our boats in and set fire to them, and as one was laden with oil it made a blaze that could be seen fifty miles away. Unfortunately three French line-of-battle ships were within that circle—the *Indomptable*, the *Dessaix*, and the *Formidable*—and they ran in to ascertain the cause of the fire. At daybreak we made out three large ships in the distance, and imagining they were Spanish galleons on their way home from South America, at once prepared to chase them. As the light broadened out we saw our mistake, and made them out to be line-of-battle ships. They at once crowded all sail and bore down towards us.

"'I fear this time, Embleton,' Cochrane said to me, 'it is all up with us. We will do our best to get away, but the chances are small. There is one good thing, they are flying the French flag, and we may expect vastly better treatment at their hands than we should get from the Spaniards, who would as likely as not refuse to acknowledge a surrender, and sink us without mercy.' We got every stitch of sail on her, and as the wind was very light, put out our sweeps. The Frenchmen, however, had more wind than we had, and gained on us fast. We threw our fourteen pop-guns overboard to lighten her, for even Cochrane felt that it was useless to think of fighting now. The three vessels separated so as to ensure that we should not slip past them, and the *Dessaix*, which was nearest to us, began firing broadside after broadside each time she tacked, keeping her bow-chasers going all the time, and cutting up our rigging. For three hours this continued. We threw over all the ammunition and stores, but slowly and gradually the *Dessaix* crept up to us. Just as she was abeam Cochrane put the helm hard down, and we spun round to make a desperate attempt to run between the enemy. We were received with a broadside from the *Formidable*, and the *Dessaix* immediately tacked in pursuit.

"In less than an hour she came up within musket-shot, and yawing to bring all her guns to bear, poured in a broadside that I thought would have annihilated us. Fortunately she had answered her helm so quickly that as she came round her guns bore ahead of us, and the round shot struck the water under our bows. The grape, however, cut up the rigging, riddled the sails, and damaged the masts, and as the next broadside would assuredly have sunk us, Cochrane ordered the flag to be hauled down. Nothing could have been kinder than our treatment. The captain declined to accept Cochrane's sword, begging him to continue to wear it though a prisoner. In our thirteen months' cruise we had taken or retaken upwards of fifty vessels, one hundred and twenty-two guns, and five hundred and thirty-four prisoners. After our capture the French line-of-battle ships took us and our lubberly convoy into Algeciras. It was trying to be lying there almost within range of the guns of Gibraltar. Two or three days later Sir James Saumarez sailed in with a powerful squadron.

The French at once put out boats, carried anchors ashore, and warped in until they grounded, so as to prevent being attacked on both sides. The tide brought the British ships so fast up the bay that in the hurry of the work the French ships still lay head to shore, and were therefore helpless to offer any defence to the expected attack. The greater part of the French sailors were at once sent ashore to the powerful Spanish batteries there, and a very effective fire was opened upon the British ships. Nothing, however, could have prevented the capture of the French vessels had there been any wind.

"There was, however, scarce a breath on the water, and the British, being unwilling to anchor under the heavy fire of the batteries, were swept past by the strong current. Their fire, however, severely damaged the ships of war, and sunk several gun-boats. The *Hannibal* alone managed to tack and made inshore, thinking to place herself inside the Frenchmen, not knowing that they were aground. In so doing she ran ashore, and was there exposed to the broadsides of the French ships and the fire of the batteries and gun-boats. Captain Ferris, who commanded her, continued to reply to their fire until most of his guns were dismounted, and a third of his crew killed or wounded; then, seeing that the efforts of the rest of the squadron to come back to his assistance were vain, he was forced to haul down his flag. The next day a boat with a flag of truce came across from Gibraltar, with propositions for the release of the crews of the *Hannibal* and *Speedy*. There was no regular system of exchange at that time, but as the French did not know what to do with their prisoners, we were all released on giving our parole not to serve again until French prisoners of our own rank were given in exchange for us. This was done a few days afterwards.

"Three days later the Spanish admiral at Cadiz arrived with six ships of the line, several frigates and gun-boats, and the

French men-of-war having been warped off the ground and their damages repaired, the whole sailed away six days after the action, followed by the British squadron, which came up to them at dusk. As soon as it became quite dark, Captain Keith in the *Superb* dashed in between the two sternmost ships—two Spanish men-of-war—each mounting a hundred and twelve guns, poured a broadside into each of them and then shot ahead, and presently engaged a third Spanish man-of-war, the *San Antonio*. In the darkness, aided by the smoke of the *Superb's* guns, she was not seen at all by either of the two Spanish ships between which she had passed, and each concluded that the other was an enemy, and a furious cannonade commenced between them. One of them lost her foretop-mast, the sails of which, falling over her own guns, caught fire; the other, still supposing her to be an enemy, poured broadside after broadside into her, and then approached to board. In the confusion the yards of the two vessels became entangled together, and the second ship also caught fire. Both ships burned until they blew up, nearly all on board perishing, the few survivors being picked up by the boats of the *Superb*, which was at the time engaged in taking possession of the third Spanish ship-of-war, which had struck to her. The officers and men of this ship were released in exchange for those of the *Hannibal* and *Speedy*. We were therefore free to serve again, but were all sent back to England and put on half-pay, and peace having soon after been patched up I remained without a chance of employment.

"Fortunately my parents at that time were alive, and I got on better than some of my comrades. Poor Parker was especially badly treated by the authorities. Cochrane in vain attacked the admiralty, but the hostility to him extended to his officers. He himself had a serious grievance, for the long delay before he had obtained his promotion caused several junior officers to pass over his head, but annoying as this was it affected him less than the cruel treatment of Parker. Some years passed before that officer obtained his promotion. Despairing of getting it, he took a little farm, married, and settled there with his family. Cochrane persevered so strenuously on his behalf that at last he was made commander, and was ordered to join the *Rainbow* sloop in the West Indies. He sold off everything, even his house and furniture, in order to enable him to obtain his outfit, and proceeded to take up his command. On arriving at Barbadoes he reported himself to the admiral, who knew nothing about the *Rainbow*, but supposed that she might be some newly-purchased craft fitting out at the Bermudas. Parker went there, but could hear nothing of her, and then returned to Barbadoes, when it became evident that no such vessel was in existence.

"He returned to England a ruined man. He had expended his whole capital, amounting to upwards of a thousand pounds, in settling his family during his absence, and in providing for his outfit and voyage. The first lord of the admiralty expressed polite surprise that such a mistake should have occurred, and promised compensation for his loss and another command on the first opportunity. Neither promise was kept, and Parker's spirit and health gave way under his misfortunes, and he sank into the grave. Cochrane, finding that he too had small chance of employment, went up to Edinburgh and worked hard at the university there until war broke out again in 1803, when he applied for a ship, and obtained, after a threat to retire altogether from the service, the command of an old brig. That was one of the many old craft purchased from men of influence in exchange for their votes.

"She had been used as a collier, and was unable to sail against the wind. Cochrane was ordered to watch Boulogne, but in a short time he found that if a wind on-shore sprung up nothing could save the ship. He reported this to the admiral, and orders were then sent to him to cruise north of the Orkneys to protect the fisheries. There were no fisheries to protect, and the order was simply a sentence of exile. He remained here for nearly fifteen months, and during the whole of that time not so much as a single ship was ever seen from the masthead. He returned to England on the 1st of December, 1804, and found that Lord St. Vincent had just been compelled to retire from the admiralty. Cochrane's claims were urged by his friends on Lord Melville, his successor, and with such force that he was transferred to the *Pallas*, a new thirty-two gun frigate."

CHAPTER VIII.

THE BASQUE ROADS.

A FEW days afterwards the lieutenant said, "Now, Stephen, as you have nothing to do this evening I will go on with my yarn. Lord Cochrane had not forgotten me, and on the day that he was appointed to the *Pallas* he wrote to me saying that he had applied for me as second lieutenant, and that Lord Melville had promised to appoint me. Two days later I got the official appointment with orders to join at once. I found Cochrane in a very bad temper. He said, 'What do you think, Embleton, that confounded cruise of mine in the *Arab* has ruined me in the opinion of the sailors. Why, if I had been appointed to a hundred-gun ship on the day when we returned together after the loss of the *Speedy*, I could have got volunteers enough for her in twenty-four hours. Now the dismal tale told by the crew of the *Arab* of our exile in the North Sea, and the fear, no doubt, that I am going to be sent off to some similar station, has so frightened them that I have not had half a dozen men apply, and I actually shall have to impress a crew.'

"'I expect, sir,' I said, 'that when we get hold of a few prime seamen, and I tell them that they are as sure of prize-money with you as if it was already divided, they will soon spread the news, and we shall not be long before we fill up.'

"So it turned out; luckily, among the first haul that Cochrane made, there were two or three of the *Speedy's* old crew. I took them in hand, and told them that so far from being in disgrace any longer, Lord Cochrane had a commission to take a month's cruise off the Azores before joining the fleet, and that that job alone was likely to fill every man's pockets. In a very short time we had the pick of the best men in Plymouth, and sailed in the middle of January, 1805, for the Azores. Instead of making straight for the islands, Cochrane ran down the coast of Spain and then worked up towards the Azores, thereby putting us on the track of any Spanish vessels bound from the West Indies to Cadiz. A day or two later we captured a large ship bound from Havana laden with a valuable cargo. Having learned from the prisoners that the ship was part of a large convoy we proceeded on our course, and a week later captured another even more valuable prize, as she contained in addition to the usual cargo some diamonds and ingots of gold and silver.

"Two days later we took another, the richest of the three, having on board a large quantity of dollars; and the next day caught a fine privateer with more dollars on board. These four prizes were sent in to Plymouth. As we only had a month this brought the work to a close, and we returned to Plymouth. We had a serious adventure on the way back, for in heavy weather we fell in with three French line-of-battle ships. They at once made after us, and with half a gale and a heavy sea they gained on us fast. As we had taken out the dollars from the prizes and had them on board the *Pallas*, the thought of losing them was even more vexatious than the idea of seeing the inside of a French prison. The *Pallas* was a very crank vessel, and her lee main-deck guns were under water, and even the quarter-deck carronades were at times immersed. However, the Frenchmen came up so fast that it was necessary, at any cost, to crowd on more sail. Cochrane had all the hawsers brought up, and with these got up preventer stays, and then every sail was spread.

"This drove her bows-under through the seas. Still they came up to us, but they were also plunging so heavily that they too were unable to fire a gun. Presently we had one on each side of us, with less than half a mile interval between us. The third was a quarter of a mile further away. The situation was a very unpleasant one, for now that they were up to us, they would be able to shorten sail a little and occasionally fire at us with their broadside guns. Cochrane gave orders for the whole crew to be ready to shorten sail when he gave the word, and that every sail should come down simultaneously. It was a critical movement, but it was well executed. Cochrane himself shouted the orders, and in a moment down came every sail. The helm at the same moment was put a-weather. Had it not been for the hawsers with which we had stayed the masts, everything must have gone out of her as we wore round, rolling in the trough of the sea. As soon as she was round, up went her sails again, and we went off on the opposite tack to that on which we had before been running.

"The French were altogether unprepared for such a manœuvre in such a heavy gale as was now blowing, and it was a long time before they could shorten sail and get on the opposite tack, indeed they ran on some miles before they could do this, while we were rushing along at the rate of thirteen knots an hour in the opposite direction; so they were a very long distance away before they were fairly after us. By this time darkness was coming on, and when morning broke they were altogether out of sight, and we continued our course to Plymouth. An election was on, and while we were lying two months in Plymouth Cochrane stood as candidate for Honiton, but was defeated. He refused to bribe, and his opponent therefore won hands down, as he paid the usual sum of five pounds for each vote. After the election was over, Cochrane sent ten guineas to each of the men who had voted for him, saying that he had sent it as a reward for their having refused to accept the bribes of his opponent.

"The expenditure was considerable, but, as Cochrane calculated, it ensured his return at the next election whenever that might take place, as each voter naturally calculated that if he had paid ten guineas a vote after he was beaten, there was no saying what he would pay if he were returned. At the end of May we sailed in charge of a convoy for Quebec, and brought one back again. It was dull work, and we were heartily glad when on our return we were ordered to cruise off Boulogne and then to join the squadron of Admiral Thornborough, which was to operate on the French and Spanish coast. There we captured a ship at anchor under the guns of a battery, and also a fast-sailing lugger, and then joined the squadron at Plymouth, and sailed thence on the 24th of March, 1806. We captured some fishing-boats, but let them go, and from information gained from the men brought off two prizes laden with wine, and during the week captured several other ships, and then rejoined the squadron, which we supplied with wine sufficient to last them for some considerable time.

"Leaving the fleet again, we heard that some French corvettes were lying up the Garonne; and after dark we came to an anchor, and the boats, manned by the whole crew—except about forty men—under the command of the first lieutenant, rowed up the river to capture one of them, which was lying a few miles up under the protection of two batteries. About four o'clock in the morning we heard heavy firing. The boats had, after a smart fight, captured a corvette which mounted fourteen guns. No sooner had they taken possession than two other corvettes came up. The guns of the prize were turned upon them and they were beaten off, and the prize was brought safely down the river. In the meantime our position had not been a pleasant one. Soon after daylight three strange craft were seen making for the mouth of the river. They were clearly enemies, and as we had only forty hands on board, things looked very blue.

"'We must make them think that we are strong-handed,' Cochrane said to me; and he ordered the men aloft to fasten up the furled sails with rope-yarn and to cast off the gaskets and other ropes. Then he waited until the enemy approached, while the men remained on the yards knife in hand. When he gave the word they cut the rope-yarns, and the sails all fell together. This naturally produced the impression upon the Frenchmen that we had a very strong crew, and directly the cloud of canvas fell they hauled their wind and made off along the shore. Every hand on board, officers and men, hauled at the sheets, and we were soon in chase. We gained rapidly upon them, divided the crew among the bow-guns, and opened fire. Scarcely had we fired half a dozen shots when the captain of the foremost vessel ran his ship ashore.

"The shock brought down her masts, and the crew landed in her boats. We ran as close as we dared, and fired several broadsides into her to prevent her floating with the rising tide. The other two corvettes came back to assist their comrade, but when we sailed boldly towards them, firing our bow-guns again, the one nearest to us also deliberately ran ashore, and was, like the first, dismasted. The third boat made for the river, but by our superior sailing we cut her off, whereupon she also ran herself ashore, and was abandoned by her crew. I don't know that I ever saw forty men laugh so much as did our fellows at seeing three strong corvettes thus deliberately run ashore and destroy themselves, when, if any one of the three had attacked us single-handed, we could have made no real resistance. The prize captured by the boats now came down, and the *Pallas* rejoined the squadron. Admiral Thornborough wrote a very warm despatch as to the gallantry of the affair, but no notice was taken of it at the admiralty, and the first lieutenant did not receive the promotion that he deserved. After two or three other affairs we were ordered to sail into the Basque Roads to reconnoitre a French squadron lying there. This, after a brush with a French frigate and three brigs, we succeeded in doing, and discovered that there were five men-of-war, two heavy frigates, three smaller frigates, and three brigs. A few days later we sailed inshore, and the boats landed and destroyed two of the French signal stations and carried the battery and spiked its guns.

"A day or two afterwards we had a sharp fight in the Basque Roads. A frigate and three brigs came out to meet us. We disabled one of the brigs, drove the frigate on to a shoal, and were on the point of capturing it when two other frigates came out to her assistance, and as we had lost several spars when we ran aboard the first frigate we were obliged to make off. After this we returned to England. Another election was coming on. Cochrane stood again for Honiton, and was returned to parliament without spending a penny. On the 23rd of August he was appointed to the command of the *Impérieuse*, and the crew of the *Pallas* were turned over to her, and on the 29th of November we joined the fleet again. We took several prizes, and returned to Plymouth in February. While we were there another election came on. As Honiton was sick of Lord Cochrane and Cochrane was sick of Honiton, he stood this time for Westminster, and was returned. He presently brought forward in the House of Commons a motion with reference to the abuses in the navy, the only result of which was that he was at once ordered to join the *Impérieuse*.

"In September we sailed to join Lord Collingwood's fleet in the Mediterranean. I need not go through all the events of that cruise. We took a great many prizes, and had a good many actions with batteries. Spain joined France, and we had a brisk time of it and gained an immense amount of credit, and should have gained a very large amount of prize-money had it not been for the rascality of the prize-court at Malta, which had, I believe, been instigated by some one in London to adopt as hostile an attitude as possible towards Lord Cochrane. The most important and exciting affair that we had was our defence of Fort Trinidad, close to the town of Rosas. Lord Cochrane's orders had been to assist the Spaniards against the French, and he had done a great deal that way by landing strong parties, who blew up roads, blocked communications, and rendered the passage of bodies of French troops difficult if not impossible. When we arrived off Rosas the French had already invested the town. The marines of the *Excellent* had been holding Fort Trinidad; but had suffered severely from a battery erected by the French upon a hill commanding it. They were withdrawn on the arrival of the *Impérieuse*, and their place taken by our marines.

"It was a rum place that fort. The side towards the sea sloped gradually but steeply, and two. forts were placed one above another, like big steps. Above these stood a tall tower, very strongly built. The forts had no guns; but had they had them they could not have used them against the enemy's battery on the high cliff, for the tower stood in their way and so protected them from the French fire. We defended the place for a long time, even after the town of Rosas had itself fallen. Several

COCHRANE SCATTERS THE FRENCH FLEET

Page 156

attempts at assault were made, but all were repulsed. The last was the most serious. The enemy had made a breach at the foot of the tower, but to reach it they would have to scale the cliff on which it stood, by means of ladders. Cochrane prepared for the assault in a very curious way. Just below the breach was a sort of vault, some forty feet deep, under the tower. Cochrane knocked away a portion of the arched roof of this vault, so that on reaching the top of the breach the French would see a great gulf in front of them. With timbers and planks he erected a sort of slide from the breach down into this vault, and covered it with grease, so that those trying to descend would shoot down to the bottom and remain there prisoners until released.

"When he had completed this he laid trains to blow up the magazines in case it was necessary to evacuate the fort. Being thus prepared, he waited for the assault. Commanded as the tower was by the batteries on the cliff, nothing could be done to prevent their making this breach, and for the same reason there were no means of preventing the scaling parties placing their ladders and climbing up. Interior barricades were, however, formed, and when they made an attack before daybreak we repulsed them with ease. Forty of the enemy who got on to the top of the breach were destroyed by our musketry fire as soon as they reached it; shells were dropped down upon those waiting below, hand-grenades thrown, and after suffering severe loss they drew off. The French erected fresh batteries, and at last the place became absolutely untenable; so we took to the boats, blew up the castle, and got safely on board the *Impérieuse*. After capturing some more prizes and doing other service the *Impérieuse* returned to Plymouth, and Cochrane was appointed to go out and take the command of some fire-ships, and to attack the French fleet in the Basque Roads.

"Admiral Gambier, who was in command of our fleet on that coast, was in strong opposition to the plan, and had denounced the effort as desperate; but the ministry were extremely unpopular, and they desired to strike a blow that would excite enthusiasm. They themselves did not believe in success, but offered Cochrane the command in order that, should it fail, the blame could be thrown wholly on his shoulders. He at first declined altogether to have anything to do with it, and drew up a memorandum showing the number of batteries that would have to be encountered, and the extreme improbability of their ever arriving near enough to the French squadron to do them any harm. His objections were overruled, and he was ordered to sail for the Basque Roads, where six transports prepared as fire-ships were to join him. This appointment caused, as was natural, very great dissatisfaction among the captains commanding the ships in Gambier's squadron. They were all senior to Cochrane, and regarded his appointment on such a service as being a slur, and indeed an insult on themselves personally, their anger however being excited rather against Lord Gambier than against Cochrane himself. The fleet, indeed, was in a state of general disorganization approaching mutiny, at the inactivity in which they had been kept and at various measures that had been carried out by the admiral. As he might have had to wait for a long time before the fire-ships arrived from England, Cochrane obtained from Gambier several craft which he fitted up as fire-ships. The others, however, arrived from England, and Cochrane wanted to make the attack on the night they joined, before the French could gain any knowledge of the nature of the attempt that was going to be made against them. But Lord Gambier refused to consent, and the result was that the French did get notice of our intentions and were prepared.

"In order to avoid the danger, the enemy's ten men-of-war

struck their topmasts and got all their sails on deck, his four frigates alone remaining in sailing order. These were placed half a mile in front of the men-of-war, and lay in shelter of an immense boom, specially designed to arrest the approach of an enemy at night. In addition to the fire-ships, Cochrane had prepared two or three vessels as what he called explosion-ships. These were intended not so much to damage the enemy as to terrify them, and to prevent their sending boats to divert the course of the fire-ships. A solid foundation of logs had been first laid on the keel, so as to form an extremely solid floor and to give the explosion an upward tendency. On these were placed a large number of empty spirit and water casks set on end. Into these fifteen hundred barrels of powder were emptied; the space around them was filled in with timber and sand, so as to form a solid mass, and over the powder casks were laid several hundred shells and some three thousand hand-grenades.

"The French deemed their position impregnable. Their men-of-war were ranged close together in two lines, and the frigates and guard-boats they considered would be sufficient to divert any fire-ships that might make their way round the boom. Half a gale was blowing on shore. Cochrane himself went in the explosion-ship that led the advance.

"The night was dark, and when Cochrane reached what he thought was the vicinity of the advanced ships of the French he lit the fuse, and with the officer and four men with him took to the boat and rowed away. They made but little way against the wind and sea, and the fuse, instead of burning for fifteen minutes as intended, only burned half that time. This, however, was really the means of saving the lives of those on board the boat. She was nearly swamped by the effect of the explosion; but as its force, as intended, took place upwards, the shells and grenades exploded far overhead, scattering their contents over a wide area, and the boat itself lay inside the circle of destruction. We on board the *Impérieuse*, which was anchored three miles away, felt the shock as if the ship had struck heavily on a rock. For a moment the sky seemed a sheet of fire. Then came the crash of the exploding shells and the rattle of the grenades, and then a roar as the fragments and pieces of wreck fell into the sea.

"The fire-ships were very badly handled. Many of them were lighted over four miles from the enemy, some were put on the wrong tack before they were left by the crews; and although there were upwards of twenty in number only four reached the enemy's position, and not one did any damage whatever. Nevertheless, the desired effect was produced—the explosion-vessel was alongside the boom when she blew up and completely shattered it. The enemy were so appalled by the explosion that, believing the fire-ships were equally formidable, they not only made no attempt to divert their course, but with one exception all the French ships cut their cables; and when morning dawned, the whole of their fleet except two ships were helplessly ashore. The tide had ebbed, and they all lay over on their side, with their bottoms exposed to fire, and had Lord Gambier sent but two or three ships in to complete the work of destruction not one of the powerful French squadron would have escaped.

"The forts had begun to open upon us, therefore we sailed away towards the fleet that was lying ten miles off, and on getting within signalling distance, Cochrane signalled that all the enemy's ships except two were on shore, and that the frigates alone could destroy them. Beyond acknowledging the signals no notice was taken, and it was not until eleven o'clock that the fleet got up anchor, and then, sailing in to within three miles and a half of the road, anchored again. By this time the tide had risen, and most of the enemy's ships were already afloat. Furious at seeing the result of this attack absolutely thrown away, Cochrane ordered the anchor to be weighed, and allowed his vessel to drift towards the enemy. He could not get up sail, as he knew that he should be at once recalled if he did so, he therefore drifted until but a short distance from the enemy. Then at half-past one he suddenly made sail and ran towards them, hoisting at the same time the signal 'in want of assistance', and engaged three line-of-battle ships. On seeing this several ships were sent to our assistance, but before they came up, one of the men-of-war hauled down her colours and was taken possession of by us. The ships that came up engaged and captured the two other French men-of-war, while another was deserted by her crew and set on fire.

"The signal for our recall was now hoisted by the admiral, and was obeyed by most of the other ships, a frigate and four brigs, however, taking upon themselves to remain with the *Impérieuse*. However, they were prevented from destroying the vessels that still lay at their mercy by another peremptory order of recall. That brought the service of the *Impérieuse* and my service to an end, and the service of Cochrane also. We were ordered back to England, and Lord Gambier's despatch as to the affair was so scandalously untrue that Cochrane denounced it in parliament. Gambier demanded a court-martial, and as he had the support of an utterly unscrupulous government, a scandalously partial judge, and false witnesses backed by forged charts, the result was a certainty. The public indignation was excited to the highest pitch by the shameless manner in which the trial was conducted, and although Cochrane's career in the service was ruined, he became perhaps the most popular character in the country.

"He was, as you know, afterwards imprisoned and expelled the house, and has suffered persecutions of all kinds. Westminster, however, has remained faithful to him, and has returned him at every election, and he has never relaxed his strenuous efforts to obtain naval reforms and to vindicate his own character. On both points I need hardly say that I am heart and soul with him, and so terrible is the persecution to which he has been in a variety of ways exposed, that I cannot blame him if his zeal has at times outrun his discretion. Most other men would, like poor Parker, have sunk under such treatment as he has received. As I told you, we did not get anything like a tithe of the prize-money we should have received for our captures, and his share of it was more than spent in his litigation with dishonest officials. Fortunately, I laid out a portion of my share of the prize-money in buying this house, and invested the remainder in the funds, and it has enabled me to live in comfort, which I certainly could not have done had I been wholly dependent upon my half-pay. Although it has been most annoying remaining for so many years unemployed, I do not regret having served with Cochrane in the *Speedy*, the *Pallas*, and the *Impérieuse*, for indeed no three ships of their size ever inflicted such damage upon the enemy's commerce, captured so many ships, or performed more gallant exploits. When I am dead I shall leave instructions that the words, 'He served with Cochrane in the *Speedy*, the *Pallas*, and the *Impérieuse*', shall be placed on my tombstone. They will be by far the most striking testimony that could be written as to my career as a sailor."

CHAPTER IX.

IN CHILI.

SEEING that a boat was advertised to sail from Dover to Calais on the 11th of August, Lieutenant Embleton and Stephen went over there on the evening before; going on board at seven in the morning, they arrived at Calais at mid-day. Mr. Hewson had obtained passports for them, and they went on next morning by diligence to Boulogne. Stephen's chest was at once taken on board the *Rose*. Making inquiries at the *mairie* they learned that Lord Cochrane had arrived with his family on the previous day from England, and had put up at the Cheval Blanc Hotel. They therefore went there and engaged rooms, and then called upon Lord Cochrane.

"You have arrived in good time, Embleton," he said as they entered. "When did you come?"

"Two hours ago we got in from Calais, and I have just been on board the *Rose* and left my lad's traps there; then I found out at the *mairie* that you had arrived and had put up here, and we have also taken up our quarters in the house."

"We laugh at these French official regulations," Lord Cochrane said, "but they have their advantages. If this had been an English town you might have spent half the day in looking for me. I have not been on board the *Rose* yet; in fact, she only arrived here last night, and as the cabins have been engaged for some time there was no occasion to hurry about it. In fact, this morning I have been engaged in laying in a good stock of wine, not for the voyage but for use in Chili. Of course one gets it here a good deal cheaper than in England, as one saves the duty; and besides, I might have had some trouble with the custom-house here if it had been sent over. I don't suppose they would admit their own wine and brandy without charging some duty upon it. Are you ready to enter upon your duties, Mr. Embleton?"

"Quite ready, my lord."

"Well, I have nothing for you to do, and as far as I am concerned your duties will be a sinecure until the day we arrive in Chili. Katherine, you must take this young gentleman in hand."

Lady Cochrane smiled. "I am new to command, Mr. Embleton. Lord Cochrane has not been to sea since our marriage six years ago, and consequently I am altogether in ignorance of the powers of an admiral's wife. Are you fond of children?"

"I don't know anything about them, Lady Cochrane; I have never had any little brothers and sisters. Of course some of my school-fellows had them, and it always seemed to me that they were jolly little things when they were in a good temper."

"But not at other times, Mr. Embleton?"

"Well, no," he said honestly, "they did not seem particularly nice when they got in a passion."

"My children don't get into passions," Lady Cochrane said with a laugh, "at least very very seldom."

"Don't praise them up too much, Katherine," her husband said. "Children are naturally plagues; and though unfortunately I have been so busy a man that I have not had time to do more than make their casual acquaintance, I don't expect that they differ much from others; and besides, even I fly into passions occasionally—"

"Occasionally?"

"Well, pretty often, if you like—I certainly shall not be surprised if I find that they take after me."

The next two days were spent by Mr. Embleton and Stephen in exploring Boulogne.

"I have often looked at the place from the sea," the lieutenant said, "as we were cruising backwards and forwards, keeping a bright look-out to see that Bonaparte's boat flotilla did not put to sea, but I did not expect that I should some day be walking quietly about the streets."

"Lady Cochrane seems very nice, father," Stephen said presently, as they strolled along the wharves watching the French fishing-boats come in.

"She is very nice; and so she ought to be, for she has cost Lord Cochrane a fortune. She was a Miss Barnes, and was an orphan of a family of good standing in the Midlands; she was under the guardianship of her cousin, who was high sheriff of Kent when Cochrane first met her. He fell in love with her and was accepted; he was at that time living with his uncle, the Hon. Basil Cochrane, who had realized a large fortune in the East Indies, and was anxious that Cochrane should marry the only daughter of an official of the admiralty court. Even had he not been attached to Miss Barnes the proposal was one that was signally distasteful to Cochrane. He had been engaged in exposing the serious malpractices by which the officials of the admiralty court amassed great fortunes at the expense of the seamen, and for him to have benefited by these very malpractices would have seemed a contradiction of all his principles. His uncle in vain pointed out to him that the fortune he himself would leave him, and that which he would obtain by the marriage, would suffice to reinstate the Earls of Dundonald in their former position as large landowners.

"Cochrane's determination was unshaken and he married Miss Barnes, so his uncle cut him out from his will entirely and broke off all acquaintance with him. I am sure, however, he has never for a moment regretted his choice. I believe that she makes him as perfectly happy as it is possible for a man of his restless disposition to be."

On the 15th of August, 1818, the *Rose* sailed from Boulogne, and Lieutenant Embleton, who had remained on board with his son until she got under way, returned to England.

"Do you know anything about this Chilian business?" Lord Cochrane asked Stephen as they walked up and down the deck together on the following morning.

"My father told me a little about it, sir, but he said that he had not paid much attention to the matter until he received your kind offer to take me."

"Well, lad, it is well you should know something about the rights and wrongs of the struggle in which you are going to take part. You know that the Spaniards obtained their possessions in South America partly by right of discovery, and partly by the papal bull that settled the matter. The Portuguese were given the east coast, while to Spain were handed, besides the islands, the vast territories of Mexico and Central America and the whole of the western portion of South America. In extent it considerably surpassed that of Europe, and its natural wealth, had it been properly administered, would have been fabulous. The Spaniards, however, thought but of two things: one was to force the natives to embrace their religion, the other to wring all they possessed from them. The first caused the death of great numbers of the Indians; the second brought about the virtual enslavement of the whole of the native races.

"The tyranny practised by the Spaniards upon these poor people was inconceivable. Tens of thousands, I may say hundreds of thousands, perished from the labour exacted from them in the mines, and the whole people were kept in a state of poverty that the Spanish officials might be enriched, and that the annual amount of gold and silver sent to Spain might be obtained. No doubt it was the successful revolt of the North American colonies against us that first inspired these down-trodden people with the hope of shaking off the intolerable yoke under which they suffered. The first leader they found was Francesco Miranda, a creole of Venezuela, that is to say, he belonged to a Spanish family long settled there. He came over to Europe in 1790, and two years later took part in the French Revolution. Hearing that revolutionary movements had taken place in Mexico and New Granada against Spain he obtained a promise of assistance from Pitt, who naturally embraced the opportunity of crippling Spain, which was hostile to us, and in 1794 went out and threw himself into the struggle, which continued with but doubtful success for some years.

"In 1806 Miranda obtained some valuable aid from my uncle, Sir Alexander Cochrane, who was then in command of the West Indian station, and things looked much brighter for the cause of independence. But unfortunately a few months later Pitt died, the Whigs came into power, and as usual a feeble policy succeeded a strong one, and all aid was withdrawn from Miranda. The result was that, for a time, the Spaniards were able to crush the insurgents. In 1810 Miranda again organized a revolt in Venezuela; but he was unable to cope with the power of Spain, and two years later he was taken a prisoner and sent to Madrid, where he died in prison. However, his work had not been without result, for the same year that he commenced his unfortunate venture in Venezuela a revolt broke out in Mexico headed by a priest named Miguel Hidalgo. This was conducted in a barbarous fashion and was speedily crushed. Two leaders of a better type, Morelos and Rayon, still continued to carry on the war, but their forces were defeated in 1815, and though I believe there has been occasional fighting since then, matters have been comparatively quiet.

"In South America things went better. In 1809 a revolt broke out at Quito; it was headed by a man named Narenno. His force, however, was never strong enough to seriously menace the power of Spain. However, for five years he maintained a guerrilla warfare, fighting with desperate bravery until he was captured and sent to Spain, where I believe he also died in prison. So far a great deal of blood had been shed, great destruction of property effected, and Spain had been put to a vast expense, but the situation was practically unaltered. A change was, however, at hand. Bolivar, a native of Caracas, had been brought up in Europe, but, stirred by the news of the struggle that his countrymen were maintaining, he went out in 1810 to join Miranda in Venezuela. When the latter was defeated and taken prisoner Bolivar crossed into New Granada, where an insurrection had broken out, and his knowledge of European methods of warfare and discipline soon placed him at the head of the movement there, and two years after his arrival he was appointed Captain-general of New Granada and Venezuela.

"The title was an empty one, and in a very short time he was defeated and forced to fly from the country by a formidable Spanish army, which was sent out in 1815 to crush the rebellion. Bolivar fled to Jamaica, where he remained but a few months. He organized a considerable force in Trinidad in 1816, and landed again on the mainland. The cruelties perpetrated by the conquering Spaniards upon the population, had stirred up so intense a feeling of hatred against them that Bolivar was speedily joined by great numbers of men. He gained success after success, swept the northern provinces clear of the Spaniards, founded the republic of Colombia, of which he was elected president, drove the tyrants out of New Granada, and marching south freed the province of La Plata from the Spanish yoke. While these events had been taking place in the northern and western provinces the national movement had extended to Chili. Here in 1810 the people rose, deposed the Spanish Captain-general Carrasco, and set up a native government, of which the Count De La Conquista was at the head.

"The movement here was not so much against Spain, whose sovereignty was still recognized, as against the Spanish governor, and to obtain a series of reforms that would mitigate the tyranny that had been exercised. Naturally, however, these reforms were obnoxious in the extreme to the Spanish authorities, and in 1811 the Spanish troops attempted to overthrow the new government. They were, however, unsuccessful; the revolution triumphed, and the rule of Spain was formally thrown off, and Chili declared an independent state. This was a good beginning, but troubles set in almost directly. Three brothers, of the family of Carrera, set to work to turn the popular movement to their own benefit, and by their intrigues overthrew the National Congress, and established a new government with the elder of them as its head. So much dissatisfaction was caused by the corruption and misgovernment of the Carreras, that the Spaniards endeavoured to reconquer Chili.

"When the danger was imminent a new actor came to the front. General O'Higgins, a man of Irish descent, whose father had been a Spanish viceroy of Peru, was put at the head of affairs in November, 1813, and the Spaniards, who had won their way to the capital, were forced by his good generalship to retire again. The intrigues of the Carreras, however, still divided the forces of Chili, and the Spaniards again advanced from Peru. O'Higgins, seeing the danger, effected a junction with the forces of the Carreras, and offered to give them his support, and to resign his position in their favour, if they would co-operate with him. The Carreras, however, held aloof with their bands from the battle, and left O'Higgins and his little body of 900 men to oppose 4000 Spanish troops. The natural result was the defeat of the Chilians. On the 1st of October O'Higgins, with his little party, were attacked at Rancagua by the Spaniards, and for thirty-six hours resisted their continuous attacks. The Carreras' force was but a short distance away, and both sides expected them to attack the Spaniards in rear. They preferred, however, that their rival, as they regarded him, should be destroyed, and held aloof.

"At last O'Higgins, with but 200 men—all that now survived of his force—was driven into the great square of the town, and surrounded on all sides. He still resisted, however, until half his force had fallen, and then, although seriously wounded, he placed himself at the head of the survivors, cut his way through the enemy, and effected his retreat. The extraordinary valour displayed by the Chilians in this battle stirred our English blood, and we felt that here was a people who had not, like the rest of the South American races, become absolutely demoralized by centuries of misgovernment by the Spaniards. At the time, however, their cause seemed lost. The Carreras submitted without trying to strike another blow, and O'Higgins, with the handful of survivors from Rancagua, and some hundreds of fugitives, crossed the Andes into La Plata, where they remained for two and a half years in exile. General San Martin, who fought under Bolivar, and had taken the leading part in aiding La Plata to obtain its freedom, felt himself strong enough at the beginning of 1817 to aid O'Higgins to recover Chili from the Spaniards, who had been carrying out wholesale confiscations and persecutions among all who had taken any part in the revolution.

"In February they crossed the Andes with 5000 men, fell upon the main Spanish army, of about the same strength, which was encamped on the heights of Chacabuco, a position from which they overawed all the large towns. Having the advantage of surprise, they completely defeated the Spaniards, and in a very short time drove them altogether out of Chili. The republic was again established, and the presidency offered to San Martin. He declined the honour, however, and it was then conferred upon O'Higgins. He and his council saw that it was impossible to hope for permanent peace so long as the Spaniards were able to gather armies in Peru, and pour them down into Chili whenever they chose, so he lost no time in sending Don Jose Alvarez over here to endeavour to raise money in the name of the republic to build war-ships, and enlist public sympathy on their behalf.

"Among other things he was commissioned to offer me the command of the Chilian fleet as soon as one should be created; and as my sympathies were very strongly with the brave people who were struggling against tyranny, I at once accepted, but have been detained in England upwards of a year trying to get the war-steamer that we have been building completed. At last the Chilians have concluded that as they cannot get the steamer they may as well get me, and so you see I am on my way out."

"Thank you, sir," Stephen said; "I shall feel a great interest now in the cause of the Chilians. My father told me they were fighting against the Spaniards, but I did not interest myself much in the matter, and thought much more of the honour of serving under you than of the Chilian cause. Now that I know that they are really a brave people, struggling to maintain their freedom, I shall feel proud of fighting in so good a cause."

"How old are you, Mr. Embleton?"

"I was sixteen some months ago, sir."

The admiral nodded: "A very useful age for work; you are old enough to hold your own in a fight, not old enough to begin to think that you know all about everything. Now, tell me all about that affair of yours when you lost your ship. Tell me everything you can think of, just as it happened. Don't exaggerate your own share in it, but, on the other hand, let me know what you did and what you said. You see I know very little about you as yet; but if you will tell me all the details of the business I shall be able to form some idea as to how far I shall be able to entrust the carrying out of my orders to you, and to confide in your ability to discharge any special missions on which I may employ you. You see, Mr. Embleton, the conduct of the Chilians in that matter of the Carreras shows that, however bravely they may fight, as yet they have not much idea of subordination. They know nothing of sea-service, and the chances are that interest and family will go further in obtaining the appointment of officers to ships than any question of abilities; and it will be very useful for me to have some one I can trust—even if only a junior officer—to see that my orders are carried out when I cannot be present myself; therefore, I want to gather from your story exactly how you would be likely to behave under difficult circumstances. We will sit down in these two deck-chairs; and you shall tell me the story exactly as you would tell it to your father. Remember that I am in no hurry. This voyage is going to last a good many weeks. The more you tell the story in detail the better I shall be pleased."

So closely did the admiral question Stephen as to every detail that it took many hours to tell the story. Even when he mentioned about the idea that by putting some water in his watch-glass he could, when the sun was overhead, use it as a burning-glass, the admiral stopped him to inquire about the watch.

"Is it the one you are carrying now?"

"Yes."

"Then let me look at it. Handsome watch, youngster; did your father give it to you?" And then Stephen had to break off from his story, and to tell exactly how it came into his possession—the whole history of his trading, and its result. The story was not brought to a conclusion until the following afternoon.

"Very good, Mr. Embleton," Lord Cochrane said; "now I know a great deal more about you than I did before, and feel that I can employ you without hesitation in matters in which brain as well as courage is required. If I had heard your story before I would have taken out that sailor as my coxswain. Between you, you showed a great deal of resource, and, as far as I can see, the credit of the matter may be divided between you. Your getting your fellow-midshipman out of the hands of the Malays was well managed. You took every precaution possible to throw them off the scent. You acted very wisely in deciding to make for that wreck when you discovered its position; and you showed good powers of resource in your arrangements there, especially in the matter of getting fire. I hear from your father that you are well up in navigation, and altogether I congratulate myself on having a young officer with me whom I can trust. It was, of course, a mere matter of chance I appointed you—simply in order to oblige your father, who is a gallant officer, and who has suffered in his profession owing to having served under me. Among the many applications made to me were some for young officers who possessed very high testimonials of conduct and good service, and I may say frankly that I was more than a little tempted to regret that I had selected one of whose conduct I knew nothing, although I felt sure that your father's son would assuredly have no lack of courage and ability. However, I am now well content that I made the choice I did, indeed I feel sure that I could not have made a better one."

It was a long voyage, for the *Rose* met with such bad weather off the Cape that she was at first unable to weather it, and it was ten weeks from the date of her sailing before she entered the harbour of Valparaiso. The voyage had been of advantage to Stephen. In the rough weather off the coast he had volunteered for duty, and had shown activity and courage, going aloft to reef or furl sails in the worst weather. He had, too, by his readiness at all times to take the children off Lady Cochrane's hands, to play with them, and to tell them stories, gained the warm approbation of their parents, and, before they arrived at Valparaiso, the admiral treated him with a kindness and cordiality such as he might have shown to a young nephew acting as his flag-midshipman. Lord Cochrane was received at Valparaiso, and at Santiago, the capital, with enthusiasm—dinners, fêtes, and balls were given in his honour; and although he cared but little for such things, it could not but be gratifying to him, after the cruel treatment he had met with from those for whom he had performed such brilliant services, to find that elsewhere his reputation stood at the highest point.

Stephen, who of course accompanied the admiral on all occasions, enjoyed these festivities very much more than did Lord Cochrane. To him it was all quite new, and very pleasant. He shone in the reflected light of the admiral, and was made a great deal of by the young Chilian ladies, the only drawback being his ignorance of the language. He had, however, on the way out, picked up a little from some Chilian passengers on board the *Rose*, and it was not long before he was able to talk to a certain extent to his partners in the dances. Nevertheless, much as he enjoyed himself, he was by no means sorry when, on the 22nd of December, Lord Cochrane, who had received his commission as Vice-admiral of Chili, and Commander-in-chief of its naval forces, hoisted his flag on board the principal ship of the Chilian navy.

He had arrived none too soon. A large Spanish force was advancing from Peru against Santiago, their formidable fleet were masters of the sea, and they were fitting out a naval expedition for an attack on Valparaiso. The Chilian admiral, Blanco Encalada, had succeeded in capturing a Spanish fifty-gun frigate, which had been renamed the *O'Higgins*; but this was only a temporary success; and with his undisciplined and badly-equipped fleet he was quite unable to withstand the threatened attack of the Spaniards. Lord Cochrane had to encounter troubles from the outset. Among the Chilian fleet was the *Hecate*, an eighteen-gun sloop that had been sold out of the British navy, and purchased by two men, Captains Guise and Spry, as a speculation. They at first attempted to sell her at Buenos Ayres, but, failing to do so, had brought her on to Chili, where the government had bought the ship, and had appointed them to command her. They, and an American captain named Worcester, had obtained a considerable influence over Admiral Encalada, and seeing that this influence would be shaken by Lord Cochrane's ascendency, they formed an intrigue to persuade the Chilian admiral to insist upon retaining the chief command, or upon dividing it with Lord Cochrane.

Admiral Encalada, however, refused to allow himself to be made their tool, saying that he would wish for no greater honour than that of serving under so distinguished an officer as Lord Cochrane; for a time, therefore, their intrigue was defeated. No sooner had he hoisted his flag on board the *O'Higgins* than Lord Cochrane set to work with his usual energy to complete the outfit of his little fleet. This consisted, in addition to the *O'Higgins*, of the *San Martin* and *Lautaro*—both of which had been East Indiamen: the former carried 56 guns, the latter 44— the *Hecate*, now called the *Galvarino*, of 18 guns; the *Chacabuco*, of 20; the *Aracano*, of 16; the *Puyrredon*, of 14. The Spanish fleet consisted of three frigates: the *Esmeralda*, of 44 guns; the *Bengenza*, of 42; and the *Sebastian*, of 28; and four brigs: one of 22 guns, and three of 18. There was also a schooner carrying one heavy gun and 20 small ones; the rest were armed merchantmen: the *Resolution*, of 36 guns; the *Cleopatra*, of 28; the *Fernando*, of 26; the *La Focha*, of 20; and the *Guarmey* and *San Antonio*, of 18 each.

On the 16th of January, leaving Admiral Blanco to complete the equipment of the *Galvarino*, the *Aracano*, and the *Puyrredon*, Lord Cochrane sailed with the *O'Higgins*, *San Martin*, *Lautaro*, and *Chacabuco*. From the day the admiral's flag was hoisted to that upon which he sailed, Stephen's life had undergone a sudden and complete change. From morning until night he was engaged in rowing from the flagship to the other vessels, and in carrying orders, ascertaining how certain portions of the work were getting on, and reporting to the admiral, or going on shore to the dockyard with urgent requisitions for stores required. Lord Cochrane himself was equally busy. He went from ship to ship, and stood by the captains while the crews were put through their exercises in making and shortening sails, practising the drill and cutlass exercise on the deck, or working the guns. Hard as was the work imposed upon them by the constant drills, the enthusiasm and energy of the admiral so communicated itself to most of the officers and seamen that astonishing progress was made in the four weeks that elapsed before sailing. Though it could hardly be said that the smartness of the crews equalled that which would be shown by British men-of-war's men, the work was very fairly done, and the admiral felt convinced that his ships would be worked and manœuvred far more rapidly than those of the Spaniards.

Stephen had from the first messed with the ship's officers. Lord Cochrane had said to him on the day when he hoisted his flag: "As my flag-midshipman, Mr. Embleton, I could very well have you, as well as my flag lieutenant, at my table, but I think that it would be better for you to mess with the officers. I find that in the Chilian service the midshipmen do not mess by themselves, as is the case with us, but have a common mess with the lieutenants. There are certainly considerable advantages in this arrangement; though it might not work well in our navy, where boys are much more mischievous and given to pranks than are those of southern people. They do not enter so young into the service, and the six midshipmen on board are none of them younger than yourself. They are all members of good old families here, and there is therefore no need for so strict a line of distinction between midshipmen and lieutenants as there is with us. The system is more like that which prevails in our army, where the youngest ensigns associate when off duty on terms of equality with their elders. Mingling with them you will acquire the language far more rapidly than you would do were you to take your meals at my table. Moreover, I think that it will be a more pleasant and natural life for you, while it will avoid any appearance of favouritism and be altogether better."

Stephen bowed. Fond as he was of the admiral, he felt himself that it would be more pleasant to associate with lads of his own age, than to be always on his best behaviour. He already knew all the officers, having met them at the various entertainments at Valparaiso. He had found them pleasant young fellows, though their airs of manliness and gravity had amused him a good deal, but he wished that he had in addition his old friend Joyce, with whom he could occasionally skylark, quarrel, and make it up again, after the manner of boys. The wardroom was large and airy, and there was ample space for the party. At meals they consisted of the three lieutenants, the surgeon, purser, and seven midshipmen. As he had never been accustomed to a rough life in the cock-pit of a British man-of-war, the contrast to his former condition was not so strong as it would have been to a midshipman in the royal service; but the somewhat stiff courtesy that prevailed among the Chilian officers in their relations to each other differed widely from the frank heartiness at Captain Pinder's table. When the meals were over, however, the air of restraint softened a little, and Stephen soon became on intimate terms with the other midshipmen, three or four of whom had never been to sea before.

"Is this like life on board your ships?" one of them asked him a few days after he had joined.

"Not a bit, Don Enriques. To begin with, the midshipmen never dine with the lieutenants, and they don't live half as well as we do. In the next place, you are a great deal more serious, and a great deal more dignified that English midshipmen are. With us they are always playing tricks with each other. We may be officers on board the ship, but when we are among ourselves we are just like other boys of the same age."

"But you do not consider yourself a boy, Don Estevan?"

"I do indeed," Stephen laughed; "and no one thinks himself a man until he is quite a senior midshipman."

"But if you play tricks on each other you must quarrel sometimes?"

"Oh, yes, we quarrel, and then we have a fight, and then we are good friends again."

"Ah! Do you fight with swords or pistols?"

Stephen laughed. "We fight with our fists."

"What, like common people!" the young Chilian said, greatly shocked.

"Just the same, except that we fight a little better. That is the way we always settle quarrels among boys in England, and a very good way it is. One gets a black eye or something of that sort, and there is an end of it. As for fighting with swords or pistols, I do not know what would happen if two midshipmen were to fight a duel. In the first place they would get into a frightful row, and in the second place they would be the laughing-stock of the whole fleet. Of course, in a country like this, where a blow is considered as the deadliest of insults, things are different; but in England it is not viewed in the same light. Everyone knows something of boxing, that is, of the proper way of using the fists, and it has come to be the national way of fighting among the common people and among boys of all classes."

"And would you, for example, Don Estevan, consent to fight with a boy or with a man of the peasant class if he injured you?"

"Certainly I would," Stephen said. "I don't know that I would fight a big man, because evidently I should have very little chance with him; but if I quarrelled with a fellow my own age, we should of course pitch into each other without any question of rank."

Exclamations of surprise broke from the other midshipmen as Stephen made these statements in very broken Spanish. He was questioned over and over again by them to make sure that they had not misunderstood him.

"You seem to think it terrible," Stephen said; "but you don't stand on rank yourselves when you fight. When you board an enemy's ship you fight with a sailor who attacks you, and don't stop to discuss with him whether he is one of gentle blood, like yourself, or a mere peasant. For the time being you put yourself on an equality with him, and it is a pure matter of strength and skill. It is just the same with us in most matters. We stand on our rank the same as you do, but when our blood is up we put all that aside and fight without caring whether our opponent is a nobleman or a peasant, and when it is all over we shake hands and don't feel that there is any bad blood between us."

CHAPTER X.

WRECKED.

ON the fifth morning when the ships got up anchor there were no signs of movement on board the *Chacabuco*, nor was any attention paid to the admiral's signals.

"Mr. Embleton, take one of the gigs, row on board, and report what is the matter there."

Stephen did so. The approach of the boat was apparently unobserved, and the companion-ladder was not lowered. He therefore ordered the men to cease rowing; presently an officer appeared at the side.

"The admiral wishes to know what is the matter, and why you do not obey his signals," Stephen said sharply, standing up in the stern-sheets.

"The crew are in a state of mutiny," the officer said, "and they refuse to get up the anchor."

Stephen returned with the message. The admiral at once gave orders for the frigate to bear down on the *Chacabuco*, and the crew were mustered at quarters. When she came within a cable's length of the *Chacabuco* the frigate was thrown up into the wind, and the admiral shouted: "Unless the anchor is a-peak in five minutes we will blow you out of the water."

There was no mistaking the earnestness of the tone, and many of the men sprang at once to the capstan bars, and the anchor was soon out of the water. "Make sail," Lord Cochrane again ordered, "and keep along close beside us."

A few minutes later the fleet were all under sail, and that afternoon entered the port of Coquimbo. As soon as the anchors were let go the admiral's gig was lowered, and he went on board the *Chacabuco*.

"What is all this about?" he asked the captain, who received him at the gangway.

"The men say that they are overworked, your excellency; that they are kept hard at it all day making and taking off sail, and that they want to leave the ship."

"Muster the crew, sir," Lord Cochrane said briefly. The crew silently assembled. The port-holes of the *O'Higgins* were all opened, and the men could be seen standing at the guns.

"Now, men," Lord Cochrane said, "I give you five minutes to pick out the twelve men who have been the ringleaders in this mutiny. You will iron them and bring them on board the flag-ship, where they will be tried and punished for their offence. What! is there a ship's crew of Chilians so regardless of their duty, so careless of the honour of their country, that they are ready to disgrace themselves by turning into a pack of mutineers, merely because they are required to do extra work to fit them for fighting the enemies of their country? I am willing to believe that you have suffered yourselves to be misled, and that you did not understand the magnitude of the crime that you were committing. There, six bells are striking. You have five minutes to put your ringleaders into a boat. See that you do not exceed that time, for as soon as my watch tells me that five minutes have gone, I give the order to fire. One broadside will be sufficient to send the *Chacabuco* to the bottom. Gentlemen," he said, turning to the officers, "at the end of the five minutes, if my orders have not been carried out, you will take to the boats and leave the ship, and as soon as you have done so we shall open fire."

He then turned on his heel, went down the ladder, and rowed back to his ship. As he left he saw there was a great uproar on board the *Chacabuco* as the sailors disputed among themselves who had been their leaders in the matter. Two boats were lowered at once, and just before the expiration of the given time twelve men were put on board them ironed, and were then rowed to the flag-ship. A signal was made for the first lieutenant of each of the other ships of the squadron to come on board, and a court-martial was at once held upon the mutineers. The man who was shown to have been at the bottom of the whole affair, was sentenced to be hung, and the rest to terms of imprisonment. The admiral remitted the death sentence and changed it to ten years in jail, and the culprit and the other prisoners were taken on shore and handed over to the civil authorities. Having thus given a wholesome lesson, Lord Cochrane proceeded northward to Callao Bay, where he intended to attack a considerable naval force gathered there.

They were protected by the batteries of Callao and of San Lorenzo, a little island in the bay, mounting in all one hundred and sixty guns, in addition to those on board the Spanish war-ships, which consisted of a few frigates, two brigs, and eight gun-boats. To attack such a force lying under the guns of their batteries was too perilous an enterprise for even Cochrane to undertake. He determined, however, to make an attempt to do them at least some damage. He knew that two American men-of-war were expected to arrive in Callao, and he made some slight changes in his flag-ship and the *Lautaro*, hoisted the American flag, and sailed toward the harbour. The Carnival was at the time being carried on, and there was the less chance that a vigilant watch would be kept up by the forts and ships. Unfortunately a dense fog came on, and for eight days the Chilians were forced to remain inactive. At the end of that time, hearing a heavy firing, and believing that one of his ships must have gone into the bay and had been attacked by the enemy, Cochrane stood in the direction of the sound. The other ships did the same, when the fog clearing up in a moment, they discovered each other, and found a small gunboat lying close to them.

This they captured at once, and learned that the firing was a salute in honour of the viceroy, who had been paying a visit to the batteries, and was now returning to the town in a brig-of-war which was crowding all sail. The fog again closed in, and hoping the capture of the gun-boat had not been noticed, Lord Cochrane determined to risk a partial engagement rather than withdraw without firing a shot, as a retreat now would raise the spirits of the Spaniards and depress those of the Chilians. Accordingly the *O'Higgins* and the *Lautaro* stood on, each having a boat ahead sounding. The wind fell very light, and instead of going in and engaging the Spanish ships as he intended, Lord Cochrane was forced to anchor at some distance from them. The moment that the two Chilian vessels were made out through the fog the ships and batteries opened fire upon them, showing that the capture of the gun-boat had been observed and the sailors and garrison called to the guns.

For two hours the ships were exposed to a heavy fire from the batteries and ships. They replied steadily, their aim being chiefly directed against the northern angle of one of the principal forts, whose fire especially annoyed them. As soon as a little breeze sprang up, anchors were weighed, and the two ships sailed to and fro in front of the batteries returning their fire, until Captain Guise, who commanded the *Lautaro*, was severely wounded, and his ship at once retired from action. Neither of the other Chilian vessels ventured within range from first to last. The flag-ship being thus left alone exposed to the whole fire of the enemy, Lord Cochrane was ultimately obliged to relinquish the attack. He retired to an island three miles distant from the port, and for five weeks blockaded Callao.

"This is dull work, Mr. Embleton," the admiral said one day, as he paced up and down the quarter-deck. "What can one do with four badly-equipped ships, one of which has lost its commander, who though not friendly to me was at least an officer of courage, the other two commanded by men who are afraid to bring their ships within range of the enemy's guns, and all badly manned, badly provisioned, and by no means in fighting trim. If the Spaniards would but sail out to engage us, we might do something, but they have dismantled their frigates, and nothing will tempt the gun-boats to move out from the forts. The only consolation is that the spectacle of our blockading the place successfully cannot but rouse the spirit of the Chilians, and induce them, I hope, to make an effort to put a force on the sea capable of completely crippling the Spaniards."

At the end of five weeks the little fleet proceeded to Huacho, a short distance north of Callao. The bulk of its inhabitants were secretly in sympathy with the Chilians, and the Spanish garrison evacuated the place and fled almost immediately the ships opened fire. The order was given for boats to be lowered, and Lord Cochrane himself landed to see that there was no scramble for the property of the government. Of this a large quantity was found in the stores, together with a considerable amount of money, which was of even more importance to the Chilians, whose treasury was empty, and who were crippled in all their operations by want of specie. During April and May Lord Cochrane cruised up and down the Peruvian coast. Several landings were effected, and valuable captures made of money and stores.

The property of the Peruvians was always respected, and the admiral spared no pains to convince the inhabitants that the Chilians were their friends and were hostile only to the Spaniards their oppressors. Several ships laden with stores for the Spanish troops also fell into their hands. Towards the end of the cruise a sail was observed at some distance in the offing. As, at the moment, the boats were about to effect a landing to capture a fort from which the Spaniards had been driven by the fire of the ships, the admiral turned to Stephen and said:

"Mr. Embleton, please to take command of the second cutter. She is a fast sailer, and I have no doubt that you can overhaul that brig in a couple of hours. The boat's crew are already on board and armed, but I don't suppose you will meet with any resistance. When you have boarded her you will take command of her and navigate her to Valparaiso. I shall be returning there in the course of two or three days."

Stephen touched his hat and ran below. He was delighted at the prospect of his first command, though it was not a very important one. He had brought the best of his chronometers with him, and snatching up this, his quadrant, and a pocket compass, he at once descended the ladder to the boat, which had been hailed by the admiral and ordered to lie there, the petty officer who commanded being transferred to another boat. The crew consisted of twelve men. As the breeze was off shore Stephen ordered the masts to be stepped at once, and the two lug-sails hoisted. The crew were glad to escape the labour of carrying down stores from the fort and transporting them to the ship, and sat down contentedly in the bottom of the boat, while Stephen himself took the tiller. The brig was hull-down when seen from the boat, and Stephen calculated that she was six or seven miles out. She was steering south and had evidently less wind than that which was taking the cutter fast through the water. He made his course to a point some four miles south of the brig, so as to cut her off, and it was not long before it was evident to him that he should succeed in doing so.

They were within two miles of the ship when he saw the sailors talking earnestly together and looking towards the shore. Glancing round he saw that the tops of the hills were enveloped in clouds, a sign, as experience had already taught him, of the approach of a gale. The brig, which had evidently not noticed the boat, had also observed the threatening aspect of the clouds, and as Stephen again looked ahead, began to shorten sail.

"Had we not better return?" one of the Chilians asked.

"Certainly not," Stephen said. "The wind is against us, and the storm will burst before we could get back, so that we should be much better off in that brig than we should be in this open boat. Get out oars, men, and help her along. The wind is freshening already. If it rises much more the brig will run away from us."

The wind indeed got up rapidly, and the oars had to be laid in while the cutter was still a mile off from the brig. She had evidently been observed, and an attempt was being made to hoist some of the upper sails that had been lowered; but the boat was now flying through the water, and in a quarter of an hour ran up on the leeward side of the brig. The sails were dropped, the bow man caught hold of the chains with his boat-hook, and Stephen and the rest of the crew at once scrambled on board cutlass in hand.

There was, however, no resistance. The crew of the brig were as numerous as the boarders, but the successes of the Chilians had created such an effect that the captain cried out, as they leaped on board, that they surrendered. Stephen's first order was to get the cutter up, and tackles were soon hooked on to her, and she was raised from the water and laid bottom upwards on deck. While this was being done the Peruvian crew were ordered to shorten sail.

It was none too soon, for the brig was heeling far over, and the wind momentarily increasing in strength. The Chilians gave a cheer as soon as the boat was safely on board, and in a very short time the sail was reduced to double-reefed top-sails.

Under these and a storm-jib she was laid head to wind. The sky was now entirely obscured, the land was no longer visible, and the sea was beginning to rise.

"Is it going to be a heavy gale, do you think?" Stephen asked the Peruvian captain.

"Very heavy, I think. I have seen it coming on since daybreak, but I hoped to get to Callao before it burst. We are heavily laden, and in no state for facing a great gale."

"What have you on board?"

"Military stores and ammunition."

"Any money?"

"I believe so, señor. There are twenty boxes sealed up in the lazarette."

"Now, tell me what you would have done if we had not captured you? You know your ship better than I do. Would you lie-to or let her run?"

"I should put her before the wind, señor, and at once; it will be dangerous to do so when the sea gets up."

"Well, put two of your best men at the helm, captain, and give them the necessary orders. I know what ought to be done, but I do not know enough of your language to make sure that I shall not make a mistake. Man the braces, all hands," he shouted. "Now, obey the captain's orders as if they were mine."

The manœuvre was safely executed, and the brig brought before the wind. She felt the relief at once, and sped rapidly before the storm on an even keel.

"How far will this gale extend beyond the coast?"

"There is no saying, señor. An ordinary gale will seldom be felt above a hundred or a hundred and fifty miles; but a big one, as this will I think be, may take us a thousand miles before we can get on our course again."

"Are there any dangers to be feared?"

"If we go far enough we may get among some islands; but on the course that we are steering we shall run some hundreds of miles before we reach them."

"You have got a chart, I suppose?"

"I have a chart of the coast, señor, but nothing beyond. We only do a coasting trade."

"Then the look-out is a bad one if the wind holds like this," Stephen said. "However, there is nothing to do now."

The gale continued to increase in violence, and in a couple of hours Stephen ordered the main topsail to be lowered on to the cap and there secured. It was a dangerous service, and was undertaken by the Chilians, who are far more handy sailors than the Peruvians. Stephen felt grateful when the last of them stepped on to the deck again. Small as was the amount of sail that was now spread, the brig flew before the wind with alarming rapidity, the sea seeming to stand up on each side of her. The foremast bent so much under the pressure that Stephen had to order preventer-stays to be rove. These were with great difficulty and risk fastened above the hounds and taken well aft, where they were tightened by tackles, and the strain on the mast considerably relieved.

"I wish we could get down that upper spar," he shouted to the captain; "its pressure helps to keep her head down."

After watching it for some minutes he ordered the stays and runners to be cut, at the same time calling all hands aft. Scarcely had the men gathered there than the vessel plunged her head into the sea. There was a loud report, and the top-gallant mast fell over her bows with a crash. Two of the Chilians with axes crawled out along the bowsprit and cut away the gear that held the spar alongside, and the wreckage at once floated away. The jib-boom was then got in, and the vessel felt the relief and lifted her head more buoyantly over the seas. For four days the gale continued, her bulwarks were carried away, and the waves swept her decks continually. One tremendous roller carried away the boats, the caboose, and all the deck fittings, together with four of the Chilians and six of the Peruvian sailors. The straining had opened her seams, and although the pumps had been kept going as long as the crew had been able to work at them, the water had been gaining steadily, and even the Chilians, who had kept on doggedly long after the Peruvians had thrown themselves down exhausted and hopeless, now ceased what was evidently a useless labour.

The mainmast had been cut away, and was towed by a long hawser from the stern, thereby aiding to keep the vessel dead before the wind. Stephen felt that there was nothing to be done but to wait for the end. There were no materials for making a raft, and indeed the constant wash of the seas would have rendered the task an almost impossible one, even had there been spars at hand; but a raft, could one have been manufactured, would have prolonged life but for a few hours. They were now, he calculated, fully a thousand miles from the land, and there was no chance whatever of any vessel coming across them in these unfrequented seas. From the time the gale burst upon them he had but twice thrown himself down for a short sleep, and had eaten no food save a dry biscuit or two. The Peruvian captain agreed with him that the vessel would float but a few hours longer. She rose but sluggishly upon the seas, and several times she had plunged her head so deeply into them that Stephen thought that she was going to dive bodily down.

Night fell. He and the captain lay down on two of the sofas aft, while the crew were all in the forecastle. None expected to see the morning light; but Stephen left the door open, saying to the captain:

"It will make no difference; but I should rather make a

struggle for my life before I die, than be drowned like a rat in a hole."

The Peruvian, who had shown much cool courage during the storm, shrugged his shoulders.

"It makes no difference," he said, as he rolled a cigarette and lighted it; "we have done all that we could. As for me, I would as lief be drowned here as outside. But I don't think that there will be much choice; we shall have no warning when she goes; she will plunge down head-foremost."

Stephen was too worn-out to reply, but he felt that what the captain said was true. But even the thought that when he woke it would be but for a short struggle for life was insufficient to keep him awake, and in a minute or two he dropped off to sleep. How long he slept he could not tell; he was awakened suddenly by a tremendous crash that threw him on to the floor. He struggled to his feet and rushed out almost instinctively, in obedience to his train of thought before sleeping. As he issued out of the poop a wave poured down from above, and for a moment he shrunk back. He was conscious that the ship was fast. There was no longer any movement; but the sea struck against the stern with a force that made the vessel quiver. As to going forward it was out of the question, for each wave swept right over her. The Peruvian had joined him at the door.

"Our voyage has ended, señor."

"Yes, as far as the ship is concerned; but if she holds together until morning there will be a chance of getting ashore."

As he spoke a great wave struck the vessel. She rose on it, moved a few yards further forward, and then fell again with a crash that threw them both off their feet.

"There is not much chance of that," the Peruvian said as he rose again, taking up the conversation at the point at which it had been broken; "an hour or two will see the end of her, perhaps even less."

"It felt to me as if she struck all over," Stephen said, "and I should think she is on a flat ledge of rock. I don't think that the wind is blowing as hard as it was when we lay down. There are some stars shining. At anyrate we may as well go in again and wait. We should only be swept overboard if we tried to go forward."

He turned to re-enter the cabin, but was nearly carried off his feet by a torrent of water that swept along the passage.

"That last wave has smashed her stern in," he said to the Peruvian; "we must stand outside."

They seated themselves on the deck, with their backs to the poop. The cataract of water which from time to time swept over them from above, fell beyond them and rushed forward.

"Her head is lower than her stern," the Peruvian remarked. "I begin to think she may hold together until morning; she has not lifted again."

It seemed, indeed, as if the storm had made its last effort in the great surge that had shifted the vessel forward. For although the waves still struck her with tremendous force, and they could hear an occasional rending and splintering of the timbers astern, she no longer moved, although she quivered from end to end under each blow, and worked as if at any moment she would break into fragments.

"The foremast has gone," Stephen said presently. "I suppose it went over her bows when she struck. I am afraid none of the men have escaped. I can't make out the head of the vessel at all."

"They may have been washed ashore; but it is probable that the fall of the mast imprisoned them," the captain said; "and as the stern is raised a good many feet, they must have been drowned at once. Poor fellows, there were some good men among them."

"I wish we had had them all aft," Steve exclaimed in a tone of deep regret. "Of course, we never thought of this; and indeed there was but small room for them in your little cabin. It seemed that death would come to us all together, and that their chances in the fo'c's'le were as hopeless as ours in the stern cabin."

"It is the will of God," the Peruvian said philosophically; "and it is probable their turn has come only a few hours before ours."

They sat silently for a long time. At last Stephen said: "The sea is certainly going down, and I can make out the outlines of the land. I think day will soon be breaking. We must have slept a good many hours before she struck."

He took out his watch, but it was too dark to see the face. He opened the case and felt the position of the hands: "It is half-past three," he said. "In another half-hour we shall have light enough to see where we are."

Gradually the dawn spread over the sky, and they could make out that the shore was some three hundred yards away, and that trees came down almost to the water's edge. They lay at the mouth of a small bay. As the captain had supposed, the ship's bows were under water, and only a few inches of the top-gallant fo'c's'le were to be seen. Another half-hour and the sun was up. Long before this Stephen had explored the wreck astern. Several feet had been torn off, and the water flowed freely in and out of the cabin. It was evident that the ship had been carried on the crest of the great wave beyond the highest point of the reef across the mouth of the bay, and to this fact she in some degree owed her preservation, as the waves broke some twenty yards astern of her, and so spent a considerable portion of their force before they struck her. Looking astern, the sea was still extremely heavy, but it no longer presented the angry appearance it had done on the previous day. The wind had almost dropped, the waves were no longer crested with white foam.

"In an hour or two we shall be able to get ashore," Stephen said. "We have been saved well-nigh by a miracle, captain."

"Saved so far," the captain said; "but we cannot say yet what is in store for us. These islands are, for the most part, inhabited by savage natives, who will make short work of us if we fall into their hands."

"Well, we must hope for the best," Stephen said. "We have been preserved so far, and we may trust we shall be preserved through other dangers. As soon as the sea goes down we must haul the foremast alongside, cut away the ropes, and drift ashore on it. It would be no great distance to swim now, but there is no hurry, and we had best find out whether we cannot get hold of some provisions. I see there are some boxes and casks on the shore, I suppose they have been washed out of the stern. One of the first things will be to get some arms."

"There are several cases of muskets down in the hold," the captain said, "and a large quantity of ammunition, but it will be a difficult business to get at it."

"We shall have plenty of time," Stephen said, "that is, if the natives do not interfere with us. However, the first thing is to find something to eat, for I am half famished."

"I have no doubt we shall find something in the steward's cabin," the captain said. "Fortunately it is the first inside the door, and has not shared the fate of the stern cabin. If Jacopo had slept there last night, instead of going forward with the crew, he would have been saved also."

They opened the door of the cabin, and uttered an exclamation of surprise as they saw the steward quietly asleep in his bunk.

"Why, Jacopo, you lazy rascal," the captain shouted, "I have just been mourning for you, and here you are, sleeping as quietly as if you were safe in port."

The man sat up with an air of bewilderment. "Why, what has happened, captain?" he asked. "The sun is shining, and there is no motion. I did not think to see the morning."

"Oh, you rascal!" the captain said, pointing to an empty bottle lying in the bunk, "you thought that it was all over, and so you emptied one of my bottles of aguardiente, and have slept like a hog all night."

"Pardon me, captain," the man said, with a shamefaced expression; "everyone said that the ship could not live until morning, so I thought I would take a good drink so as to know nothing about it."

"And you did not feel even the crash when we were wrecked?"

"Wrecked!" the man repeated, as he ran to the door; "are we wrecked after all?" He uttered a cry of horror as he looked round.

"It might have been worse," the captain said; "at least we three have been saved, though, in your case, you are far from deserving it. Now, look about and do your duty. We want breakfast; see you get it, and quickly, and I will say nothing more about that bottle of spirits you stole. Now, what have you got here?"

"Two fine hams, captain, and some bunches of onions, and half a barrel of flour, and some salt beef and a skin of wine."

"Not so bad," the captain said. "Well, make a fire and do us some slices of ham; are there any biscuits left?"

"Yes, captain, there is half a barrel."

"Then we will make shift with a biscuit and the ham; but

see that you are quick about it, for this English officer and I are both famished."

"Where am I to make a fire, captain? the caboose is gone."

"Never mind about that; the iron plate is still fixed to the deck, make up your fire on that. Look about in the other cabins and break up anything that will supply you with wood. Now, señor, we will get off the after hatch while this rascal is cooking breakfast, and have a look at the state of things below."

"I am afraid we shall find most of the cargo cleared out," Stephen said.

"No, I do not think so. There is a strong bulkhead just below where we are standing. The things you see on shore were in the small hold under the cabin that was used for the ship's stores, while the main contains the cargo. We got at the lazarette from a hatch under the table of the cabin. It was not convenient, but it was an advantage having a separate place when we were loaded up with hides, and there was no fear of the sailors getting at the things. We did not carry a great store—five or six barrels of flour, a few sacks of potatoes and onions, a barrel or two of biscuits, and a couple of casks of salted meat, a barrel of coffee and one of sugar."

"Well, then, in that case the sea has saved us the trouble of getting them on shore, captain, for there are at least a dozen casks of one kind or another on the beach. Now, really the principal things are the arms. If we get up a case of a dozen muskets and a barrel of ammunition we shall do. Of course, they will be at the bottom."

"Yes, above them are bales of soldiers' clothes. They will be too heavy for us to lift out. They were heavy enough when they were dry, and the three of us could not lift them out, sodden as they must be with water."

"Then we must get up a sort of derrick. There are plenty of blocks and ropes on that foremast. The difficulty will be about light spars. We shall have to go ashore and cut down two or three young trees to make our tripod with.

"I think, captain, we had better make up our minds to live on board until we have got this job done. There is less fear of our being attacked by natives, and we could do nothing in the way of searching for game until we get something to shoot it with. We must make a raft of some sort for coming backwards and forwards with. There are plenty of bits of timber on the beach that will do for that."

Breakfast was greatly enjoyed, and it was not until an hour afterwards that the sea was sufficiently smooth for them to begin their preparations for landing. The foremast was dragged alongside, the shrouds cut away, and the running rigging unrove and coiled on deck ready for future use. A couple of coils were fastened to the mast, and late in the afternoon the captain and Stephen swam ashore, taking with them the end of one of the coils, while Jacopo remained on board to pay out the other, so that until the main raft was made the mast could be towed backwards and forwards. As soon as they were on shore they hauled at their rope and brought the mast to the beach. Then they set to work examining the casks. As the captain had predicted, most of the contents of the lazarette had been cast up, and they found that they had an ample supply of food to last them for some months. The mast had towed so easily that they agreed that it would be the best way to use it as the main portion of their raft. They dragged pieces of timber close to the mast and lashed them side by side there, so as to form a platform some three feet wide on each side of it, the length varying from four to twelve feet, according to that of the pieces of timber.

Having accomplished this, after two or three hours' hard

work, they took their places on it, and shouted to Jacopo, who hauled them back to the side of the wreck. They had fastened one end of the other rope to a tree, and at daylight next morning they again landed, and proceeded with their knives to cut down three young trees of some four inches in diameter. This took them the best part of the day. The heads were then cut off, leaving three stout poles of some fourteen feet in length, and with these they returned to the ship, taking with them a bag of coffee-berries and a supply of sugar. They had found on breaking open the cask that the sugar was somewhat damaged by the sea-water, but this had not penetrated far, and by drying and repounding that touched by the water, no great harm would have been done. The next morning the shears were erected, and they set to work. It took them two days' labour before they could clear enough of the cargo out to get at the cases. They were not troubled much by water, for at the stern-post there was but a depth of four feet on the reef, while at her bows there was nearly twenty. Working as they did at the after-hatchway, there were but five feet of water below, and the uppermost tier of cases was consequently above the water-level. The barrels of cartridges were still further on, and it was the fourth day before they were reached.

Three of these barrels were got up, and when two cases of muskets had been opened, the weapons cleaned, and made ready for service, they felt a sense of security to which they had been strangers since they arrived at the island. There was now an urgent matter to be attended to. Hitherto they had drunk wine at their meals, but the contents of the skins were getting very low, and it had become absolutely necessary that they should without delay search for water. As there were hills of some size in the interior, they felt confident that there must be plenty to be found. The great point was whether it would be in the neighbourhood, or at a distance from the ship.

This was a vital question, for useful as their raft was for coming and going between the wreck and the shore, it was far too heavy and clumsy for transporting their valuables any distance; and without hatchets or carpenters' tools they could not construct a raft by breaking up the deck, and the cutting down of trees with their pocket-knives was not to be thought of.

Accordingly the three set out on foot one morning, each carrying a musket and a store of ammunition, a portion of cooked ham, and some biscuits, together with a bottle containing the last of their stock of wine. When they rounded the point of the little bay they gave a shout of satisfaction, for but fifty yards away a small stream flowed from the forest across the sand into the sea.

"What a pity we did not search for this before," Stephen said, as throwing themselves down each scooped a hole in the sand, and took a long drink of the fresh water. "We could have saved our wine for some special occasion."

They agreed at once to follow the stream up, as by this means they would leave no trace of footmarks, and might be able to find some suitable spot for an encampment.

CHAPTER XI.

A DANGEROUS COMPANION.

THEY had gone but a few hundred yards up the stream when they heard the sound of a waterfall, and presently they came upon a perpendicular cliff some eighty feet high, over the edge of which the water fell unbrokenly.

"It would be a splendid place to camp at the edge of this pool," the captain said. "We should have our bath always ready at hand, and even on the hottest days it would be cool in the shade of the trees."

"It would not be a nice place to be caught by the natives," Stephen said. "Even if we fortified ourselves, they would only have to get up above and throw rocks down at us."

The Peruvian regarded this risk as trifling in comparison with the advantages of the situation. Stephen, however, determined to climb to the top of the cliff, and examine the position there, so leaving the others lying in indolent enjoyment by the pool, he set to work to find a way up. He had to go fully a quarter of a mile along the foot of the cliff before he could find a place where it could be ascended. Once on the crest, he followed the edge back until he came to the top of the waterfall. To his surprise he found that this flowed almost directly from a little lake of some three hundred yards in diameter. For about fifteen yards from the fall on either side the rock was bare; and although the level of the little lake was some three feet below it, Stephen had no doubt that in the case of a heavy tropical rain the water would rush down from the hills faster than the gap through which it fell below could carry it off, and that at such a time it would sweep over the rock on either side, and fall in a torrent thirty yards wide down into the pool.

The view, as he stood on the patch of bare rock, was a striking one. The tree-tops of the forest between the cliff and the shore were almost level with his feet, some of the taller trees indeed rising considerably higher than the ground on which he stood. Beyond, a wide semicircle of sea extended, broken by several islands, some small, others of considerable size. Behind him the ground rose, in an apparently unbroken ascent, to a hill, which he judged to be some three or four miles away.

"This would be a grand place for a hut," he said to himself.

"Of course we could not put it on the rock, for we might be swept away by a sudden flood, and besides there would be no shade. But just inside the edge of trees we should do splendidly."

He found, in fact, that at a distance of twenty yards from the edge of the bare rock it was but the same distance from the edge of the pool to the brow of the cliff.

"We could only be attacked on one side here," he said. "And though we could not cut down the trees, we might make a defence with creepers twined in and out among the trunks that would be quite sufficient against a sudden attack; and with such a store of muskets as we have got we might keep a whole tribe at bay. The question is how to get the casks and things up here."

Going to the edge he found that one of the trees had a large arm overhanging the cliff.

"By fixing a block there," he said, "we might bring them up from below without difficulty."

Looking over, he shouted to the two men below.

"I have found a place here," he said, "where we can make ourselves very comfortable, and with a little labour defend ourselves from any number of savages."

"How can we get the things up?" the captain shouted back.

"Easily enough. We have but to fix a block to the arm of this tree over my head, and we can then run them up without difficulty. Come up, captain. You will see at once the advantages of the position."

In a quarter of an hour the Peruvian captain joined him, and, when Stephen explained his plan, agreed that it was a good one.

"As you say," he said, "we can only be attacked along this narrow place, and we could strengthen it so that they would hardly venture to try it." He broke off suddenly. "There are two cases of swords in the hold. I never thought of them before. They might not be much good for cutting trees, but they would do for chopping down bushes, and especially those long creepers, which, being as tough as cables, would blunt our knives in no time. If I remember rightly, the cases were stowed just under the barrels of ammunition we got out, so there won't be much trouble in getting at them."

"That would be first-rate," Stephen said. "As there is nothing to do now, we had better go back to the ship, and get one of the cases out at once. When we have done that we can begin the work of rolling the barrels along the sand to the stream."

"It will be terrible work getting them to the foot of the cliff," the captain said.

"Yes, too heavy altogether. We must knock the heads in on the shore, fill the contents into the sacking that holds the clothes, carry them on our backs to the foot of the falls, and then sling them up. There are any number of bales, so that they can remain up here until we get the empty barrels up, and fill in the stuff again. It will be time enough to set to work at our fence when we have got everything up."

A week later they were established in their new camp. The sugar, coffee, and other articles were all repacked in the casks, which were headed up again to protect them from the weather and the assaults of insects, portions sufficient for a week's consumption only being left out. The labour had been great, but the Peruvian captain seconded Stephen's efforts well. The steward, however, grumbled frequently, and had many times to be spoken to sharply by the captain. Another week was spent in fortifying the position. Young trees were cut down and stuck in the earth two feet apart in the intervals between the trees. A wattle-work of the tough thorny creepers was interwoven across the little promontory, eight feet high. This was painful work, for, however careful they were, they frequently tore their hands with the spikes.

When this was done a similar defence was made along at the edge of the water to within a short distance of the falls. This was carried to the height of five feet only. A tent had been erected with canvas brought from the wreck, thrown over a pole, fixed between two trees, and in a smaller one by its side the barrels were stowed.

"Now, captain," Stephen said, as they spent a day in absolute rest after their labours, "there is one more thing to be done."

"What is that, señor?"

"It is that gold. You said there were five hundred thousand dollars, which comes to a hundred thousand pounds in our money. That, as we know, is lying safely in the stern, for we looked the day after the wreck. So long as it is there it is safe enough, but the next storm that comes will certainly smash up the wreck altogether, and the boxes may be swept into the deep water between her and the shore. Now at the present moment we may consider that gold to be common property. If a Spanish ship ever comes here she will, of course, capture it; if, on the other hand, an English or a Chilian vessel arrives, I shall hand it over to them as their lawful prize. If neither of them come, which is most likely by far, it is worth nothing to anyone. I think we ought to get it ashore, and bury it in the sand above high-water mark."

"I think that that would be a very good plan," the captain agreed. "We may manage in time to get away somehow, and even if we cannot take it all, we might take some of it. There will be no great trouble in getting it ashore. The boxes weigh a hundred pounds each. There are twenty of them, and the raft would take them in three or four journeys.

If we make an early start, we ought to get the job done easily enough in a day. The gold is of no use to us now; but we may be here for years, and if it is long before we get away, the Spaniards may be driven out of Peru as they have been out of Chili. Your admiral will have gone home. There will be no one to claim the treasure; the Spanish government has lost it, the Chilian has never gained it, and it will be a sort of windfall that we can with a clear conscience divide between ourselves."

"If you don't mind, captain, I think that it would be a very good plan to say nothing whatever to Jacopo about this business of the gold. I own I don't like the fellow. In the first place, he is abominably lazy, and never does anything like his share of the work; in the second place, to my mind he is an evil-looking scoundrel. I don't want to deprive him of a share of the money if the time ever comes when we may talk of dividing it, but in the meantime there is no reason why he should know it has been moved. That day when we examined it and found it was safe, I noticed an evil look come into his eyes, and, unless I am greatly mistaken, the idea struck him that if he were to rid himself of us, he would be master of all that treasure. There will be no difficulty in carrying out the matter without his knowing it. When we were moving the stores he often remained behind under the pretence of cooking, and we have only to say that we are going to overhaul the cargo and see if we can find anything else that may be useful to us some day, and he will be glad enough to be left in charge here."

"I think that you are right," the captain agreed. "I have no reason to doubt Jacopo's honesty, still the thought of so much wealth, although it is of no more value here than so much sand, may excite his avarice. Many a man's throat has been cut in Peru for a score of dollars or less, and it is just as well not to put any temptation in the fellow's way. You and I at the present moment would exchange all that gold for a stout twenty-feet boat, well provisioned; but to him it would be simply wealth beyond his dreams, and it is just as well not to put any ideas into his mind by ever mentioning the stuff before him."

The gold was brought on shore and buried in the sand at the foot of a tall tree standing just beyond the highest watermark. The work took them two days, as some time was spent in making a further search in the cargo, from which was fished up a bale of linen trousers and coats, which formed the undress uniform during the heat of summer. Some shoes were also found, and Stephen and the captain returned to the fort, each laden with a large bundle. Stephen was especially glad at the discovery of the light clothes. Those in which he had started on the chase of the brig were so shrunk with sea water as to be almost unwearable, and he had been going about in Spanish uniform, which he found most uncomfortably hot. He was almost barefooted, and the shoes were even more highly prized than the light clothing. The captain had also lost all his effects, but Jacopo had saved his scanty wardrobe.

"We are now prepared for everything," Stephen said. "I don't think shipwrecked mariners were ever better set up. We have clothes sufficient for a lifetime, a great stock of weapons and ammunition, and provisions enough for a couple of months at least. The last is our weakest point, I admit. But there is the whole island as a hunting-ground. We must begin and set to work to explore, captain. The ham has gone long ago, and I have been longing for some time for a change from salt meat; besides, we want some fruit or vegetables badly. We have stuck to work well, and deserve a holiday. The first thing to do will be to climb to the top of the hill and get some idea of the size of the island. I begin to think that it cannot be inhabited, for if it had been they would surely have discovered the wreck before now."

"That is not certain," the captain replied. "It may be a large island, and the villages may lie on the other side. However, we have certainly grounds for hope that we have got it all to ourselves. One thing I am anxious to find is some sheltered spot or cave where we can pass the rainy season. The place where we now are is charming in such weather as this, that is for ten months in the year; but it is not a perch I should choose in such a gale as that which cast us ashore."

"No; it would certainly be unpleasant. I should not think there is much chance of our finding a cave except on the seashore—caves are by no means common articles. However, we shall no doubt be able to light on some sheltered place where we can take up our abode during the rain. But, first of all, we must find out whether the island is really uninhabited; there will be all sorts of things to do as soon as we can assure ourselves of that.

"I should be rather glad of one good gale, captain—a gale strong enough to break up the vessel altogether. Of course, it has been a perfect treasure-house to us, but I never go on board without a shudder at the thought of the fo'c's'le just below the level of the water."

"It is no more than standing at the edge of a graveyard," the captain said philosophically.

"Yes, that is true, and I know that even if we could have got at them the first day, taken them ashore and buried them, it would have been an unpleasant business."

"Very," the Peruvian agreed; "things have turned out for the best—they are buried at sea instead of being buried on land. For myself, my regret that the ship did not lie on an even keel was not because we could have got at the bodies and buried them, but because in there we should have found many things that would have been useful. We should probably have got an axe or two, some tools, canvas, needles, and twine, all of which would have been very valuable to us."

"Well, all the same, captain, I shall be glad when a gale knocks the ship to pieces. Besides, as long as she is there she would be seen at once by any canoe coming along on this side of the island, and on going on board the natives would see that some of the crew must have survived, and that things have been brought up and taken ashore; then there would be sure to be a search after us."

"Yes, you are right there, señor; I had not thought of that. No doubt it is desirable that she should disappear."

"Do you think that we could blow her up, captain? There is plenty of powder on board."

The Peruvian shook his head. "We could shatter her, but portions would still remain sticking up above water, and the explosion would be heard fifty miles round, and the cloud of smoke be seen from all the islands within that distance, and there would soon be canoes coming to see what had caused it. No; it will be best to let her remain as she is until she breaks up with the first gale."

The next morning they started, taking Jacopo with them. The captain proposed leaving him behind, but Stephen pointed out that if left alone for a long day the man might not improbably swim off to the ship to assure himself that the gold was still in its position.

"He might do that," the captain agreed; "but, like most of his class, he is superstitious, and I doubt whether he would go on board the wreck alone. Still, it will be better to take him with us. It is certain that there is no fear of our hut being disturbed during our absence, and if we should come upon natives three of us are better than two."

It took them four hours to reach the summit of the hill,

the undergrowth of creepers being so dense that they were often compelled to cut a way through it. At last they reached the summit; as they did so they stopped in surprise. Before them was a cup-shaped depression some two hundred yards across, the centre being a hundred feet below the edges.

"It is the crater of an old volcano," the Peruvian said; "it is ages since it was active, so that we need have no fear or uneasiness on that score."

The interior was clothed with verdure. Here and there black crags showed through the foliage, but elsewhere all was smooth and smiling. The slope was regular, and it was evident that, as the captain said, long ages had gone by since there had been any disturbance. Vegetation had grown up and died, until a soil thick enough to conceal all the rocks, that had at one time no doubt thickly strewn the bottom, had been buried.

"What is that down in the centre?" Stephen said. "There seems to be a patch clear of trees, and there are some figures of some kind there. See, on the other side what looks like a regular path has been cut through the trees and bushes. Perhaps it is a burying-place; at any rate we will go and see."

They walked round to the other side of the crater. From there they could obtain a view of the side of the island opposite to that on which they had landed. It was far less extensive than they had expected, the hill sloping steeply down, and the sea was but a quarter of a mile away. A great number of islands studded the ocean, and some of those at a distance appeared considerably larger than that upon which they had been cast.

"Thank goodness," Stephen exclaimed, "the island is evidently uninhabited; now we can wander about freely."

"Yes; we might have saved ourselves all the trouble of fortifying that position," the captain said.

"It gave us something to do, captain, and did us good in

that way. Besides, parties of natives from the other islands may land here sometimes. Now let us go down and explore the crater."

They descended the path and soon stood in the bottom of the crater. This they saw was a veritable graveyard. In the centre was a rough structure built of large stones sloping inwards, and forming a rough representation of a hut. They had evidently been placed there centuries before, for they were green with age; lichens and mosses grew upon them, and here and there small shrubs sprang up in the crevices. What had once been an entrance was closed with a great flat slab of rock. Round this central cairn were some eight or ten smaller ones.

These were evidently of comparatively recent origin, and one of them was surrounded by a hedge of spears, on some of which hung pieces of tattered cloth of native manufacture. Round the central hut were arranged four figureheads of ships; while in a circle stood a number of the hideous idols carried by many of the South Sea Islanders in their war-canoes.

"I should say that this accounts for the island being uninhabited," Stephen said. "I suppose there are still traditions of this having been a volcano, and that the mountain and perhaps the whole island is sacred, and only used as a burial-place for some very great chiefs."

He went across to the grave surrounded by spears.

"Here," he said, "are a dozen skeletons piled together—sacrifices, I suppose, on the tomb of a chief. If it had not been for these spears and skeletons, I should have said, from the appearance of the cairns, that they must all be at least a hundred years old, perhaps a great deal more."

"All the better," the Peruvian said. "I hope it will be a hundred years before they come to bury anyone else here."

"They must come here a good deal oftener than that,"

Stephen said. "These gods of theirs are all new, or at any rate freshly painted. Besides, the place is evidently kept with some care; and I should think very likely the people of the other islands make pilgrimages here once a year or so to offer sacrifices to the god supposed to reside in that central cairn, and to keep his house in order. I think that we cannot do better than follow this path back and sees where it goes to. It may not extend beyond the crater; but if it continues through the forest down to the shore it will be evident that it has recently been visited, for things grow so fast in a climate like this that in a year a path would be completely blocked up by vegetation. Where is Jacopo?"

"There he is at the top of the crater; he did not come down with us, and no doubt considered that the place was likely to be haunted by spirits."

They ascended the path to the top of the crater. The ground here was bare for a short distance, and Stephen saw that two lines of stones marked the course of the path to the trees. It did not lead down towards the sea, but was carried obliquely round the top of the hill until it reached the edge of the forest on the side of the island on which they had landed. Two rude images marked the spot where it entered the forest. It now led down in a direct path six feet wide. This was completely clear of shrubs, and not the smallest shoot of brushwood showed above the soil. Wherever the ground descended steeply rude steps had been cut; the trees on each side of the path had been barked on the side facing it. Here and there sticks, some ten feet high, with pieces of coloured cloth hanging from them, stood along the side of the path. The path itself was almost like a trough, the centre being fully two feet lower than the general level.

"It must be used very frequently," the Peruvian said, "and has probably been used for ages. No doubt in the rainy season the water helps to hollow it out, but the work must have been begun by human feet."

Jacopo kept closely behind the others, crossing himself frequently and muttering invocations to the saints. They followed the path until it came out at the head of a deep inlet.

"It is a useful road to the top of the hill," Stephen said. "It has not taken us more than three-quarters of an hour coming down, while we were six times as long in going up, and hard at work all the time. Look there; there is no mistake as to the numbers who come here," and he pointed to the patches of ashes and charred wood scattered thickly on the sand above the water-line, all along the edge of the inlet."

"There can be no doubt about that," the Peruvian said; "the place must be constantly visited, or at any rate by a great number at a time. However, I don't know whether that need disturb us. They evidently go straight up to worship or sacrifice and come straight down again, and all that we have got to do is not to fire a gun when they are on the island. However, we may as well look along the shore to see if there are any further paths into the forest."

They examined carefully, but could see no signs that the natives had gone inland at any other point.

"We may as well go along the shore now," Stephen said, "then we shall see how far this inlet is from our bay."

They were turning to start when there was a rustle among the undergrowth, followed by a short deep sound. Jacopo dropped his musket and fell on his knees. The captain crossed himself hastily; but Stephen dashed forward towards the spot where the sound had come, shouting:

"Come along, captain, it is a pig."

There was a rush as he entered the bushes, and a dozen pigs dashed off. He levelled his musket and fired at the hindmost, and gave a shout of delight as it rolled over.

"Fresh meat, captain," he exclaimed as the Peruvian joined him; "and there are at least a dozen others who have made off. Hurrah! there is no fear of starving; we may be sure that this is not the only herd on the island."

The pig was dragged out on to the sea-shore; it was a young animal, although nearly full grown. Jacopo was now in his element; he cut the pig open, eviscerated it, carried it down to the edge of the water, washed it, tied the legs together, and with his sword cut down a sapling and thrust it through them.

"We will carry the pig, señor, as you shot him. That is but a fair division of labour," the captain said, raising one end of the pole on his shoulder, while Jacopo took the other. They had gone but a hundred yards further when the trees near the beach grew less densely, and the ground beneath them was covered by a plant with large leaves and yellow flowers. Stephen, who was walking ahead, went up to examine them.

"Hurrah, captain!" he shouted, "they are wild melons."

The others laid down the pig and ran up to him. The patch extended as far as they could see; the plants covered the ground and climbed the trees by means of the rattans, festooning them with their bright leaves and flowers and fruit of all degree of ripeness. On the ground they found no ripe fruit. There were evident signs that this was a favourite resort of the pigs, and that they devoured the fruit as fast as it ripened.

"We will fence in a large patch of this," Stephen said; "there will be plenty for the pigs and us too. I never felt thankful that a pig could not climb before," he laughed, as he cut a melon hanging overhead. Although somewhat wanting in flavour the fruit seemed to the three men, after their privation for upwards of a month from green vegetables or fruit, to be delicious. "How do you suppose that it got here, captain?"

"The seed may have been carried by birds from some place where melons are cultivated," the captain said, "possibly even from the mainland. I have heard that seeds are carried immense distances in that way. It may be that some seeds were washed overboard from a passing ship and some were cast ashore here. I do not care how they came here, I am well contented to find them."

"We will carry away the seeds of those we eat and plant them near our camp," said Stephen; "we shall soon get a supply without having to come here to fetch them. Besides, these will attract the pigs and enable us to get fresh meat without having the trouble of scrambling through the forest, and tearing ourselves and our clothes to pieces with thorns."

They cut as many melons as they could carry in addition to the pig, and then proceeded on their way. They followed the shore but a quarter of a mile further, when to their satisfaction they found themselves at the bay at the mouth of which the wreck was lying, and in another half-hour they were at home.

"We are certain to see boats coming," Stephen said, as he stood at the edge of the cliff and looked out over the sea, "unless they come from some of the islands on the other side and coast round to their landing-place. But on the other hand, there is the disadvantage that as they come in to the inlet they can hardly help seeing the wreck. We must make it a rule when we go down, to walk in the stream until we get to the edge of the sea, and then to keep along on the wet sand where our footprints will disappear directly. In that way they would have no clue whatever to the direction in which to look for us."

"Yes, it would be as well to observe that precaution," the Peruvian said. "When we once get a melon patch here we shall not have any reason to go down there very often. We have got everything we want from the wreck, and we have all the coast along to the left to explore, where we may make some useful discoveries."

Two days later they again went to the sea-shore and followed it to the left, leaving Jacopo this time behind. They had gone but a mile when they came upon a thorny bush covered with fruit, which the Peruvian pronounced to be guavas; they eat some of these and then proceeded on their way, and before long came upon a group of trees bearing a fruit considerably larger than an orange. Stephen had seen these when cruising on his first voyage among the islands, and pronounced them to be bread-fruit.

"Let us go no further," the Peruvian said; "we have found enough good things for one day, let us leave the rest for to-morrow."

Stephen laughed. "At any rate it is a good excuse for getting back again; and indeed I am quite ready to do so, for I have a strong desire to see what Jacopo has been up to in our absence, and would be willing to make a wager with you that we don't find him at the hut."

They gathered a quantity of the bread-fruit and passed the guava bush reluctantly.

"We must set to work to make a basket, captain," Stephen said, "we want such a thing badly. We can each make a good-sized bag out of sacking, which will do very well for melons and bread-fruit, but we want something that we can carry things like guavas in without crushing them."

On their return to the camp they found, as Stephen expected, that Jacopo was absent, and at once set out along the edge of the cliff until they reached the point at which they obtained a view into the bay. The wreck lay apparently deserted.

"Let us sit down and watch," Stephen said, "he may not

have reached it yet. No, there he is." As he spoke, a figure came out from the door of the poop. "Just as I thought, captain. He has gone down to see if the gold is there. Look at him." Jacopo was evidently furious; they could see him waving his arms and stamping angrily on the deck, and then he went to the side and shook his fist in the direction of the tent.

"That fellow is dangerous, captain," Stephen said gravely.

The captain nodded.

"The safest plan will be to shoot him at once."

"No, we cannot do that; we had better tell him frankly to-night that we have moved the gold and buried it, lest the vessel should go to pieces in a storm, that we intend to give it up to any Spanish or Chilian ship that may come here; but that if it is a long time before we are rescued we shall then divide the gold between us, and that he will get a fair share of it."

"It would be better to shoot him," the captain said. "You were right, it is evident that he has been thinking over that money, and that as likely as not he has determined to possess the whole of it. However, we shall see how he behaves. I may as well tell him as soon as he arrives; when he sees that we mean fair by him he may possibly be content, at any rate for a time, especially as he must know as well as we do how small is the chance of a ship coming along. We are altogether out of the line of traffic. Ships going round the Horn keep far south of this on their way to China, while those for Peru and Chili keep up the coast; and there is no traffic at all from Peru or Chili to China or India."

"Now that we have everything we want here, captain, and know that we can hold on for a long time, we ought to begin to think over our plans for the future. If we had tools we could certainly build a craft that would carry us to Chili; but it would be a terrible business to build one with nothing but our swords to cut down trees, hew out the timbers, and shape planks. Still, if there is nothing else to be done we must do that. It is only a matter of time and patience, and we shall find that the hours hang very heavy on our hands when all our necessary work is done here. I should think that we ought to be able to build a craft of twenty tons in a couple of years at the outside; at any rate, I can think of no other plan for getting away."

"I have been thinking that we might steal a canoe when the natives come here," the Peruvian said.

"I daresay we might, captain; but if, as is probable, they come in large canoes, three of us would make but very little speed with one of them, and we should be pursued and overtaken in no time. You may be sure that they don't spend the night up on the hill, and probably when they go up they will leave some of their number on the beach to look after the canoes, and cook. But even if we did get away we could do nothing with such a canoe."

"I don't know," the captain said; "we might land with her on some small island, fit a deep keel on to her, and get up a couple of masts and lug-sails, which, of course, we should make beforehand."

"Yes, we might do that," Stephen agreed; "but the difficulty of carrying off the boat would be immense. And besides, she would have to be victualled; we should have to take food and water for a long journey. And to get our barrels filled with fresh water on board would be a long task, and utterly impossible to carry out in the short time that we should have to spare, even if the beach was entirely deserted."

"Yes, I see it is very difficult," the captain agreed; "but I would not mind running the risk rather than undertake two years' hard labour."

"I would not mind running the risk either, captain, if I saw any probability of success, but I own that this seems an impossibility. However, it may be that sometimes a small party comes alone, and that we could get possession of a canoe of manageable size. At any rate, we may as well prepare for such a chance before setting to work to build. We have plenty of canvas from the fore-topgallant sail and head-sails of the brig, and can make a couple of lug-sails fit for a large canoe and a couple for a smaller one, and get the spars ready; that would not take us a great deal of time, and if a bit of luck does fall in our way we should be ready to avail ourselves of it. That fellow has swam ashore now, so we had better be going back to the hut."

A quarter of an hour after they reached it Jacopo appeared. He stopped in surprise when he saw them.

"So you have been off to the wreck, Jacopo," the captain said. "We found as much fruit as we could carry, and have brought it straight back again; and finding that you had gone we went along the cliff and saw you on the deck. I suppose you went off to see if the gold was all safe. We have seen to that; we did not like to leave it there, for the ship will break up in the first gale, and the boxes might be swept into the deep water and be lost, so we carried it ashore. The gold, you know, is not ours, it is the property either of the Spanish or the Chilian government, and we shall hand it over to the first ship of either of these nations that may come along. If, however, as is likely enough, no ship comes near the island for years, and the Spanish, as may well be, have by that time lost their possessions on the west coast altogether, we may then consider it to be ours, and if we get away we propose to divide it into three equal shares. As officers we have a right to a larger share than you; but we have agreed that if you do your work here with us willingly and cheerfully we shall not stand on our rights, but shall give you an equal portion of it with ourselves. At present the gold is of no more value to any of us than so much sand, beyond the fact that if we build a craft, as the señor and I have been talking of doing, the boxes will be found excellent ballast, otherwise it is not worth a thought either way."

"You are very good, señor," Jacopo said humbly, "and I can promise that you shall have no reason to complain of me;" and without another word he turned, cut off a portion of the pig that was hanging from a bough near, and proceeded to prepare a meal.

"I hope that that has made the matter all right," the Peruvian said in a low voice to Stephen; "but we must watch him closely for a short time and see how he goes on. If he looks at the matter sensibly he must see that, as I said, the gold is of no value to any of us at present."

"He spoke too humbly altogether in my opinion," said Stephen; "but as it is evident that so long as we are here our interests are all alike, and that the three of us will have a better chance of escape than one would alone, he may give up all thought of the gold until the time approaches for us to make a start."

The next day they went down, unlaced the fore-topgallant sail from its yard where it lay on the beach, upon which it had been washed up after they had stripped the mast, and proceeded to cut from it two lug-sails, so as to save themselves the trouble of carrying the entire canvas up to the tent.

CHAPTER XII.

DEATH OF THE CAPTAIN.

THE work of making up the sails occupied the next three days. Some of the canvas was unravelled for use as twine, and holes were made with long sharp thorns. Jacopo, when not engaged in cooking, worked diligently, seldom joining in the conversation between the captain and Stephen, a conversation which turned principally upon the best method of building and launching the proposed boat. Stephen's proposal was that they should, if possible, first get up the deck planks, which could be done by driving wedges between them and the beams, and after one was taken up, the work of the wedges could be aided by poles used as levers. When all the planks had been taken up as far forward as the water would permit them to work, he proposed to blow up the after-part of the ship, by which means they would obtain a large amount of beams and timbers that could be utilized for the boat, at much less cost of labour than would be entailed by the cutting down of trees. He proposed that the explosion should take place at night, as the roar and flash would be supposed by the natives of the islands near, to be something supernatural connected with the spot evidently held in such veneration.

"Even were they to row across to see if anything had taken place," he said, "which is about the last thing that they would be likely to do, they would no doubt make for their usual landing-place; and as the greater portion of the ship above water would have disappeared, anything that remained would not be likely to catch their eye."

He calculated that if the plan succeeded they ought to be

able to build a boat of the required size in six months at the outside. The preparation of the planking had been the most arduous portion of the plan they had first laid out, and this would be done away with altogether; and as the nails would doubtless draw out of the planks, and they would obtain plenty of bolts and fastenings from the fragments of the wreck, the building of their boat was now comparatively simple, and Stephen even fancied that they might complete it in four months. No word was spoken as to the gold, but Stephen felt that a difficulty might finally arise out of it. He himself considered it as a lawful prize for the Chilian government; but the Peruvians were two to one against him, and although they might have no desire to return it to the Spaniards, who were detested by the great majority of Peruvians, they might set up a claim to it on their own account. However, he dismissed the idea from his mind as one that must be left to be determined by circumstances.

For a month they laboured assiduously. The planks were successfully taken up, and then, after much consideration, preparations were made for blowing up the vessel. The powder barrels were brought up, fuses were made, each six feet long, passing from barrel to barrel, and the chain of barrels was laid from the stern to the point where the deck was level with the water. This plan was adopted in order that the whole fabric should be shaken and broken up, while, had the whole force of the explosion taken place at one point, it would have entirely destroyed the timber there, while perhaps leaving a considerable portion still standing above the water.

The success of the explosion was complete, and in the morning there was no sign of the ship above water, while the bay was covered with floating wreckage. It took some time to collect this and bring it to shore, and then to tow it to the spot they had decided upon as being best suited for the launch.

It was near the point of the bay, and the beach here sloped more steeply than elsewhere.

Their first work was to erect a platform sloping still more steeply, and covered with pieces of timber too short for other work. The craft would thus be built at an angle which would ensure her sliding down into the water, and during the progress of building she could be retained in her place by ropes fastened to a tree behind, and by blocks of wood under her stern-post. Among the timbers, one was found long enough to serve as the keel, and when this was laid down, and the stern-post and stem were fitted to it and securely bolted, they felt that the most difficult part of the work was done. Great labour was required to get out the copper bolts from the timbers, and in some cases the wood had to be split up before they could be extracted. The work of getting out the ribs, and fastening them in their places, was much less arduous than they had expected, for the greater portion of the timbers of the brig had come on shore, and among these they were able to find many with curves fairly suited to their requirements. Some required hacking off with cutlasses, while on to others pieces of planks were nailed to get the required curve. By the end of five months the hull was planked and decked, and all felt very proud of the work. It was caulked with oakum obtained from some of the least serviceable of the ropes of the brig, dipped in a resin that they found oozing from some trees.

The fore-topmast of the brig furnished a suitable mast, and was stepped and stayed; a bowsprit, boom, and gaff were constructed from the light spars; a mainsail, a foresail, and jib had been manufactured during the long evenings; and when the boat was completely rigged, the timbers down which she was to glide were smeared with lard, and carried down as far as possible under water, being kept in their places by heavy stones placed on the ends. It was a great day when the shores were knocked away, the ropes that held her stern being previously cast off, and she at once moved rapidly down into the water amid a shout of triumph from her constructors. She drew about three feet of water, and they calculated that when they had got the ballast, stores, and water on board she would sink another foot, and would then have three feet of free-board.

They had already laid in a large stock of pork, which they had salted, obtaining the salt by filling pools in the rock with salt water, which was replenished as fast as it evaporated. A great stock of melons had also been cut. The barrels had been carefully examined, and placed in the lake to swell and become water-tight. Now that the boat was once in the water they were anxious to be off without the smallest possible delay, for were the natives to appear just at this moment all their labours would be thrown away. As soon, therefore, as they had gone on board, and found that the craft was perfectly water-tight, they hauled her towards the spot where they had buried the gold, dug up the boxes, and carried them down to the water's edge. The boat was then hauled in until she was in four feet of water. Stephen and Jacopo waded out, carrying the boxes on their heads, then the captain lifted them on board, and, taking them below, packed them along her keel.

By this time it was late in the afternoon, and they calculated that by beginning at daybreak, they would get the greater portion of their stores and water on board next day. It was a moonlight night, and, after indulging in supper and a long talk over the next day's work, they lay down to sleep.

It was some time before Stephen fell into a light sleep, being too excited at the thought of their approaching deliverance to compose himself to a sound slumber. He was awakened by a slight movement, and, turning round, saw in the moonlight Jacopo kneeling by the captain with a knife uplifted. With a shout Stephen sprung up, grasped his sword, which he had, ever since the gold was hidden, placed by his side when he lay down, and rushed at the Peruvian. The knife had, however, descended twice, and the assassin gained his feet just as Stephen fell upon him. So quick had been the latter's movement that the edge of his sword fell on the side of the murderer's face before he had time to place himself on guard. With a howl of pain and rage he sprang out from the end of the tent, and rushed to the narrow opening left in their barricade.

Stephen pursued him hotly, but the Peruvian was quicker footed, and, dodging among the trees, presently left him behind. Stephen returned to the tent, stirred up the fire to a blaze, and then bent over the captain. He saw at once that the latter was dead, the knife having twice struck him in the region of the heart. Stephen took up one of the loaded muskets and sat down at the entrance of the barricade. He felt completely crushed at the blow. His early suspicions of Jacopo had gradually died out, for the man had worked willingly and steadily; he had seemed perfectly contented with the prospect, and entered as keenly into the building of the cutter as Stephen and the captain had done. But it was evident now that he had all along meditated the murder, and had only delayed until the craft was built and fitted, the gold in its place, and everything ready for sailing save putting the stores on board, which he could manage by himself.

An hour before everything seemed clear, now Stephen blamed himself that he had prevented the captain from shooting the villain, on the day when the latter discovered that the gold had gone. And yet the act would have been murder, for there was no proof that Jacopo intended to play them false. What, Stephen asked himself, was he to do now? He was certain that the murderer would not permit him, without an effort, to sail away, and that he would be able to hide among the trees, and to spring out at any moment upon him as he came past laden with barrel or sack. It was not even clear how he could get a wink of sleep, for at any moment the assassin might crawl up and stab him.

So Stephen passed the night. He watched attentively for the slightest sound, but he did not think that the fellow was likely to return that night, for he was certain that he had wounded him very severely; and besides, the scoundrel would feel sure that he would keep a vigilant watch. As soon as day broke he got up, and went to the tent to verify a thought that had struck him during his watch. He counted the muskets; there were but twenty-two. A cold perspiration broke out on his forehead; his worst fears were realized. Jacopo had managed during the last day or two to take two of the muskets and carry them away with him, so that should his intentions to murder his two companions miscarry, he would be able to wage war against them. He would certainly have provided himself with a good store of ammunition. Difficult as the position had seemed before, the difficulties and dangers were increased tenfold now he knew that the Peruvian was provided with firearms.

There would be no occasion for an open attack. The fellow would only have to hide up in the undergrowth and shoot him down as he passed. It was a danger against which there was no providing; at any moment from the time he left the tent he would be liable to be shot down by the invisible foe. Moving about almost mechanically, Stephen boiled some water in a very thin-skinned gourd, which they had found the best substitute for a kettle. It was necessary to use a fresh one frequently, but they were plentiful in the woods, and a supply was always kept on hand. As soon as it boiled, he threw in a handful of coffee that had been roasted and pounded a day or two before, laid a chop cut from the pig on the embers, and put biscuits on to toast beside it. He had no thought of being in danger, for he felt sure that Jacopo would not run the risk of approaching the tent. After the meal was cooked and eaten, he sat for a long time pondering over what had best be done.

His first impulse had been to take to the woods, carrying a couple of muskets and a store of provisions sufficient for a day or two, and to hunt the Peruvian down. In this case each would be ignorant of the other's position and movements, and neither would have any advantage over the other; but, on the other hand, while he was hunting Jacopo, the latter might be putting a sufficient store of melons and perhaps the carcase of a pig on board the boat, and making off with it. The gold was there, and the assassin would be ready to run any risk to get away with it. He would doubtless prefer to silence the only voice that could give evidence against him, but he would know that the chance of Stephen's ever making his escape by himself would be so small that it might be disregarded. Stephen thought that, at any rate, the risk of the Peruvian's attempting to set sail that day was small. He would be suffering intense pain from the wound, and would probably be incapable of making any great exertion; but most of all he trusted to Jacopo's thirst for vengeance to keep him for a while on the island. Eager as he might be to sail away with the gold, he might well postpone his departure for a few days, until he had avenged himself for the wound that had been inflicted on him.

Jacopo had one advantage over him. He could select a spot where he would at once command the path down to the shore and keep his eye upon the cutter, while from the camp Stephen was unable to obtain a view into the bay.

As he was thinking the matter over, Stephen's eye fell upon the block and rope by which the barrels had been hoisted up. It had for a long time been disused, for they had found it much shorter to clear a path from the spot where they descended from the cliff direct to the little bay, thereby saving at least two-thirds of the distance, a matter of importance while they were engaged upon their boat-building. The idea at once presented itself that he might leave the spot by this means without the knowledge of the Peruvian, and would thereby turn the tables on him. He was about to put the loop at the end of the rope around his body, and swing himself over, when he hesitated. He might be driven to adopt the same plan that he credited Jacopo with the intention of following. After some thought, he took some seventy pounds of salt pork from the barrel and put it in a sack, round which he fastened the rope in such a manner that as soon as the strain on it was relieved it could be shaken off. Then he climbed out on to the bough, and poured a little melted lard on the sheave of the block to prevent it from creaking. Then he lowered the barrel down, shook off the fastening, and drew up the rope again.

Then he sent down a large sack full of melons; this done, there was nothing to do but to wait until dusk. He kept up a good fire all day, thinking it probable that Jacopo would have placed himself where he could see the smoke rising. He calculated that the man would suppose that he would be likely to attempt to leave his post after dark, and would then place himself somewhere on the path to shoot him as he went past. As soon as it was dark, he lowered four of the muskets, with a bag of ammunition, and then followed himself. He first carried the muskets and ammunition down to the shore, and then made two trips with the pork and melons. Then he rolled one of the water-casks, that had already been filled, down the sand into the sea, and, entering the water breast-deep, pushed it before him until he came to the rope from the stern of the craft to the shore. Returning, he fetched the pork, melons, muskets, and ammunition. Then he waded and swam out to the cutter, holding his sword in his teeth, pulled himself noiselessly up, and then, sword in hand, descended into the cabin, where he thought it was just possible that the Peruvian might be sleeping. The light of the moon was sufficient to show him that it was empty.

Ascending to the deck again, he slackened out the headrope attached to a heavy stone that served as an anchor; then he hauled on the rope ashore until he felt the stern touch the sand. Making fast the rope, he lowered himself down and waded to shore. Then he brought off the muskets and ammunition, pork and melons on his head, and lastly got the barrel of water alongside, put a sling round it, fastened the main halliards to it, and hoisted it on board. He was now in a position to make off, but still altogether inadequately provisioned for such a voyage as he meditated, and after some thought he determined to return on shore.

He had at first thought of remaining on board and hoisting the sail. This would attract the attention of Jacopo as soon as it was light enough for him to see it, and probably in his fury at being outwitted the man would rush frantically down, and try to get on board; but in that case Stephen should have to shoot him in cold blood, which he felt he could not bring himself to do.

He decided finally upon going on shore, where he could meet the man on equal terms. He accordingly hoisted the sail, and then landed with a couple of loaded muskets, taking his place behind a tree a short distance up the path, and waiting until morning. The various journeys had taken him some time, and it was now, he judged, about three o'clock. As soon as it was light his watch began in earnest. Contrary to his expectations, it was fully an hour before he heard any sign of Jacopo coming. He accounted for the delay on the supposition that the Peruvian would think perhaps that although he had outwitted him and got on board, he must be altogether unprovided with stores, and unable, therefore, to put to sea. He would suppose then that he had returned to shore, especially as there were no signs of him on board the craft.

At last he saw him coming down the path with a stealthy, crouching step, with one musket slung behind him, and the other in his hand ready for instant action. He was a dreadful sight. His face was bound up with a sleeve cut from his shirt. His forehead was encrusted and his hair matted with dried blood, with which also his linen jacket and trousers were thickly stained. Stephen had chosen a tree round whose foot was a thick growth of bush, and he now proceeded to put into execution the plan that he had decided upon. Stooping behind the trunk of the tree, he thrust up from among the bushes his cap on the top of a ramrod, taking care that the upper part only just showed above the leaves. Almost instantly Jacopo levelled his rifle and fired. Stephen gave a loud cry and dropped the cap. The Peruvian, with a yell of exultation, threw away the gun, drew his knife, and bounded forward. As he came up, Stephen sprang out, and brought the butt end of his gun down with all his strength on the Peruvian's head, striking him senseless to the ground. Stephen picked up the murderer's knife and placed it in his belt, took the musket from his shoulder, and then with a cord he had brought with him bound his feet, and turning him over fastened his wrists tightly together.

Then he raised him, and placed him in a sitting position against the tree, passed the cord several times round him and the trunk, knotting it firmly behind the tree. Then he went away to the stream and cut a couple of gourds, filled them with water, and returned. Jacopo had now opened his eyes, and was looking round him in a dazed condition. When he saw Stephen approaching he made a struggle to rise.

"It is of no use, Jacopo," Stephen said quietly; "your power of mischief is at an end. You have murdered your captain, and you would have murdered me, so now your life is justly forfeited. Did I give you the fate you deserve, I would bring down the body of your victim, tie it to you, and leave you to die of thirst. Fortunately for you I am a British officer, and I cannot be both judge and executioner."

The Peruvian's reply was a volley of curses and execrations.

"Will you drink some water?" Stephen asked, without paying any attention to his words.

The Peruvian's only reply was to spit furiously at him. Stephen placed one of the gourds on the ground close to him, saying: "You will think better of it presently", poured the contents of the other over Jacopo's head; and then returning to the boat, brought off another coil of rope with which he still more securely fastened Jacopo to the tree, and then went up to the tent. He spent the day in carrying down the store of provisions, arms, and ammunition, asking Jacopo each time he passed him whether he would have some water. For some time the prisoner refused; but the agony of thirst caused by the fever of his wounds at last overcame his resolution, and he cried loudly, as Stephen approached him, for water. Stephen held the gourd to his lips until he drank off the whole of its contents, then he went and refilled both gourds, poured one over the man's head, set the other down beside him, and continued his work.

By nightfall he had carried everything on board, and there remained but to take the other water-casks alongside. Jacopo had drunk several gourds full of water during the day, but by evening he became delirious from fury and the fever of his wounds; Stephen therefore undid all his fastenings save those round his ankles, and took up his post near him. All night the man raved incessantly. From time to time Stephen got up and poured water between his lips, and in the morning cut a very

STEPHEN BEATS OFF THE GREAT WAR-CANOE

Page 228

ripe melon, squeezed the juice from the pulp, and gave it to him to drink. Then he went down and towed the other waterbarrels to the cutter and got them on board, and afterwards returned to his prisoner. For three days the delirium continued. Stephen kept the bandages round his head constantly moistened with water, and gave him melon juice to drink. The third night the ravings sank to a whisper, and presently became silent, and Stephen thought that all would soon be over. However, the man's breathing became quiet and regular, and in the morning he opened his eyes with consciousness in them.

"You here still!" he murmured, as Stephen bent over him.

"Yes, Jacopo; villain as you are, I could not leave you to die."

"How long have I been here?" the man murmured after a long pause.

"It is four days since you attacked me. Now that you are sensible I shall set sail, but I will first carry you to the side of the stream. Now that you have got through the fever you will recover. I have left at the tent one of the muskets and a store of ammunition, so that you will be able to shoot pigs; and there is, as you know, an abundance of melons, bread-fruit, and guavas, and I daresay you will discover other things ere long. I trust that in the time that is before you, you will repent of your sins, and try and make your peace with God. I have buried the body of the man you murdered."

With some difficulty Stephen got Jacopo on to his back, carried him to the stream, and laid him down at its edge in the shade of the trees; then he placed within reach of him a number of melons, bread-fruit, and some biscuits. He had long since taken the rope off his ankles.

"I do not understand why you have done all this for me. I would have killed you if I could; you have treated me as if

I were your brother. I know that it is of no use my asking you to take me with you, but will you do me one last favour?"

"Certainly, if it is in my power, Jacopo."

"Will you bring the musket and ammunition down here? I could not go near there again."

Stephen nodded. "I will get them for you," he said, and at once started for the tent. He first pulled this and the store-tent down, rolled them together, and lowered them to the side of the pool, climbed out and cut the fastening of the block, and let it and the rope fall beside them. He then threw over the case of swords which he had not thought worth taking away, and then getting the gun and ammunition, he returned to Jacopo.

"There they are," he said. "Here are three hundred rounds of ammunition; by the side of the pool under the cliff you will find the two tents, the rope, and ten spare swords, which may prove useful to you. Here are three gourds full of water close to your hand, and by reaching over you can fill them as often as you like. In a week I have no doubt that you will be strong enough to walk. Is there anything else I can do?"

"There is nothing, señor. May God bless you for your kindness!"

"And may God pardon you!" Stephen said; adding as he turned away, "It may be that some day a passing ship may carry you off."

Then turning he walked slowly back to the shore. Wretch as this man was, he felt a pang at leaving him behind. But he was sure that even if he could overcome his repugnance to him as the murderer of the captain, he could not take him with him, for he would never be safe for a moment. With returning health and strength would come afresh the lust for the gold, which might soon overcome any feeling of gratitude for the treatment that he had received.

DEATH OF THE CAPTAIN.

When he reached the shore near the boat, he cast off the stern rope and then swam on board, hoisted the jib and foresail, pulled up the anchor, and took his place at the tiller.

The breeze was a very light one, and for a time the cutter moved along but slowly, but as it got beyond the shelter of the land it felt the wind, and began to spin fast through the water. Stephen's spirits, which had been greatly depressed for the last few days, rose as the little craft heeled to the breeze. Nearly six months had been spent on the island, but at last he was free. As to his course, he had but the sun by day and the stars by night to guide him; but he knew that the vessel had been blown almost due west, and that by heading east he should make the coast either of Chili or Peru. He found to his satisfaction that the boat would keep her course very near the wind, that she came about easily and rapidly, and was certainly swift under her canvas.

She carried no topmast, as they had agreed that, with only three hands, it would be better to avoid all complications of gear. In the middle of the day the wind fell a good deal. At the time he was abreast of a large island, and he presently saw a war canoe shoot out from the shore. Lashing the tiller, he ran down below, brought up the twenty-three muskets, loaded them all, and laid them against the bulwark astern. Then he took his place at the helm again, and looked anxiously across the water in the hope of seeing a dark line that would tell of the breeze freshening again. He knew enough, however, of the winds prevalent among the islands to be sure that it would not strengthen much for the next two or three hours. From the number of paddles going on each side of the canoe he calculated that she must carry from forty to fifty men. His hope was that they would be unacquainted with firearms, and would draw off when he began to fire.

When they came within about four hundred yards he took

up a musket and fired, taking aim at some little distance from the side of the boat. At the report the paddles ceased instantly, and for a time it was evident that great confusion reigned among the rowers. While this was going on Stephen reloaded his piece. After some five minutes' delay the men recommenced paddling, but at a pace that contrasted strongly with the rapid and eager stroke which they had before rowed. Stephen waited this time until they were within two hundred and fifty yards, and then lying down on the deck and resting the barrel on the bulwarks he took a steady aim and fired. One of the men standing up in the bow fell overboard. The paddling ceased again, and a hubbub of voices was heard. As she lay motionless Stephen fired shot after shot. One or two of these hit the canoe, two or three others went wide, but the rest did execution among the crowded mass. By the noise it was evident that some wished to go on, others to retire, and after discharging twelve shots Stephen began to hastily reload the pieces he had fired.

The cessation of fire apparently reassured the war party, for when he had reloaded six of them the paddles again began to work. Stephen at once recommenced firing, and his eighth shot brought down a chief who was standing prominently in the stern, and was evidently in command. His fall had an instantaneous effect. With a yell of terror the natives ceased paddling. Then some began to back and others to row, and the canoe turned slowly round and then sped away at a rate as fast as it had come up, although the number of paddlers was markedly decreased. Satisfied that they would not return, Stephen reloaded all the muskets and then went below for his first meal on board. The cabin would have seemed a poor place to yachtsmen, with its rough beams and timbers and its discoloured planking, but no yachtsman ever felt prouder of a craft than Stephen did of the boat in whose building he had taken a share. There were no bulk-heads, the hull being open from end to end. The water-cask and provisions had been stowed aft the mast.

One of the barrels served as a table, the iron plate that had been taken from the floor of the ship's galley had been placed forward of the mast on a layer of sand three inches thick, and a forecastle hatch had been placed above it to serve as an exit for the smoke. A store of wood, the result of their ship-building operations, was piled in the bow. Stephen did not trouble to cook, but boiled some water over some chips of wood, made himself a cup of coffee, or rather the half of a small gourd of coffee, ate a melon and a biscuit, and presently went up on deck again. At three o'clock a light breeze sprung up, and this, an hour later, strengthened to a heavy blow. Stephen sailed on until midnight, then reefed the mainsail and fastened the boom amidships, lowered the foresail and hauled the jib to weather, and having thus laid the cutter head to wind lay down on the deck and slept soundly until daybreak. The next day he passed two or three islands, but all at a considerable distance. Beyond these no land was visible, and he hoped that he was fairly beyond the Archipelago with its hostile natives.

Day after day passed without incident. Stephen always lay to at night for a few hours, and calculated that the rate at which he sailed during the remaining eighteen was, allowing for calms, some four knots an hour. On the sixth day the appearance of the sky changed, and Stephen prepared for bad weather by fully reefing his mainsail. The clouds banked up rapidly and the wind rose. It was southerly, and the boat tore rapidly through the water. Two hours later Stephen let the foresail run down, and under the reduced sail the boat went more lightly and easily over the rising sea. By evening he had stowed the mainsail altogether, and slackening the jib sheet held on his course. By midnight it was blowing a gale. He raised the gaff four or five feet, put lashings round the sail to prevent its blowing out, and then hauling on the weather sheet let her lay to, taking now his place at the tiller, so as to be able to bring her head up did she pay off the wind.

It was an anxious night, but the little craft was lightly ballasted and buoyant, and rose to the seas without taking any great quantity of water over the bows. For two days the storm continued. Stephen never left the tiller during that time save to run below at intervals and snatch a mouthful of food. After the first two or three hours he had felt no fear whatever as to the ability of the craft to weather the gale, but it was a long strain, and he was deeply thankful when the wind abated sufficiently for him to be able to hoist the reefed mainsail again and to lie to comfortably. As soon as this was done he went below, and slept for twelve hours. The sun was shining brightly when he awoke, a light breeze was blowing, and save for a long swell the sea had gone down. He indulged in a hearty breakfast before proceeding on his way. Then he shook out the reefs in the mainsail, hoisted it, got up the foresail, slacked off the weather sheet of the jib, and again headed east.

One morning ten days later he saw the sun rise behind a broken outline instead of the line of the horizon, and knew that this could be nothing but the hills of the mainland. Lofty as these were he might be still a hundred and fifty miles from them, but the weather was fair, the wind fresh, the boat travelling at six knots an hour, and by mid-day to-morrow he would be close to land. Whether it was Chili or Peru that lay ahead of him he had no means of knowing, but he believed it was the former, for he had headed rather to the south of east and felt sure that he should strike the coast somewhere on the long seaboard of Chili. He was the more convinced of this as two days before he had seen an island far to the north of him and guessed it to be either San Felix or San Ambrose, and had shaped his course rather more to the south in consequence. That night he was too excited to turn in as usual, but held on his course. By morning the land lay little more than twenty miles away, and he recognized at once the outline of the hills that he had passed when sailing north, and knew where Valparaiso lay, some fifty miles further south. He changed his course accordingly, and at four o'clock in the afternoon dropped his stone anchor a hundred yards off the quay of the Chilian port.

CHAPTER XIII.

PRIZE-MONEY.

STEPHEN busied himself in stowing away his sails. By the time he had done so a small crowd had collected on the quay looking with surprise and wonder at the little craft with its unpainted sides and rough appearance. In a short time a boat with a port official rowed alongside, and stepping on deck the officer looked round in surprise at seeing only one person on board. Stephen had, before arriving at the port, donned a clean suit of linen trousers and jacket; his cap was out of all shape, and the badge on its front had faded into a blur; he was barefooted, and his hair had grown almost to his shoulders. The aspect of the boat was almost as surprising as that of its solitary occupant. There were no signs of paint visible, the work was rough, the stanchions of various sizes, some new in appearance, and some blackened with age and sea-water

"Who are you, señor?" the official asked, "and what craft is this?"

"The craft has no name, señor, though we who built her thought of naming her the *Deliverer*. I myself am Stephen Embleton, flag-midshipman to Admiral Lord Cochrane. May I ask if the admiral is now in port?"

"He is," the official replied.

"May I beg you to send off a shore boat by which I may despatch a message to the admiral?"

"Your story is a strange one," the official said gravely. "I myself have seen the young officer, you state yourself to be, in company with the admiral, but I am bound to say that I do not recognize you."

"I am not surprised at that," Stephen said with a smile. "In the first place, I should imagine that my face is the colour of mahogany from wind and sun; in the second, my hair has not been cut for six months; and lastly, this suit of clothes, though excellent in its way, is scarcely in accordance with my rank."

"I will myself row off to the admiral's ship," the official said, "and convey your message to him. What shall I tell him?"

"I thank you, sir. Will you please say that Stephen Embleton is on board this craft, that I am alone, and for certain reasons cannot leave it, and pray him either to come himself or to send a trusted officer with a party of sailors to take charge of it."

The official saluted him gravely. He was by no means sure of the sanity of this young fellow, but his curiosity had been aroused by his appearance and that of his craft, and he therefore condescended to undertake a mission that at ordinary times he would have scorned. Stephen watched the boat row alongside a frigate anchored a mile away. Shortly afterwards he saw a stir. A boat was pulled up to the accommodation ladder. A party of sailors then took their places in her, and two figures came down the gangway and the boat pushed off. A few minutes later it reached the side of the cutter. Stephen saluted as Lord Cochrane sprang nimbly on board.

"My dear lad!" the admiral exclaimed, grasping his hand, "I gave you up for lost many months ago, and we have all mourned for you deeply. Where have you been? what have you been doing? what on earth have you done to yourself? and where did you get this extraordinary craft?"

"I have been cast away on an island some twelve hundred miles to the west. Only three of us were saved. We built this craft between us. One of my comrades is dead, the other remains on the island, and I have sailed her back single-handed. I think this, sir, will account for my somewhat strange appearance."

"Fully, fully, lad. Well, you must tell me all about it afterwards. Why did you not come direct in the boat to my ship instead of sending for me?"

"Because I was afraid of anyone else coming on board until you had sent someone you could trust to take possession of her?"

"Why, bless me!" Lord Cochrane said with a laugh, "I should not have taken her to be as valuable as all that. She is most creditable as a specimen of the work of three shipwrecked men, and I should say from her appearance as I rowed up to her that she was fairly fast. She might be worth a good deal as an exhibition if you had her in the Thames, but she would not fetch many hundred dollars here; though I have no doubt that, when properly painted up and in trim, she would make an excellent little coaster."

"It is the cargo and not the ship, sir, that is valuable."

"What does it consist of?"

"It consists of gold, sir. There are five hundred thousand dollars stowed in boxes."

The admiral looked at him in astonishment.

"Five hundred thousand dollars, Mr. Embleton! Are you in earnest?"

"Quite so, sir; the ship you sent me off to with twelve hands was laden with military stores and money for the payment of the Spanish troops. I was fortunate enough to get on board and capture her just before the storm burst. When she was wrecked, on an island of whose name I am ignorant, her stern, where the gold was stowed, was fortunately in only four feet of water, and we had, therefore, no difficulty in getting at the boxes and carrying them on shore, where we buried them until we had built this craft."

The admiral ran down the companion into the cabin and saw the boxes lying side by side along the length of the keel.

"I congratulate you heartily," he said to Stephen, "this is by far the richest prize that has fallen into our hands. You did perfectly right in sending for me, for, in faith, I would not trust this treasure out of my sight on any consideration, until I handed it over to the Chilian government, after taking care to deduct the fleet's share of the prize-money. It will be welcome, I can tell you, for the pay of the fleet is terribly in arrear. The treasury is empty, and there are no means of refilling it. Properly speaking, the whole of the fleet's share of the money should go to you, but the rules of the service are arbitrary."

The conversation had been in English, and the admiral going on deck ordered the officer, who had remained sitting in his gig, to tow the cutter alongside the flag-ship. The officer at once gave the necessary orders. Two of the men jumped on board and hauled up the anchor, and nothing but the presence of the admiral prevented a burst of laughter among the boat's crew as the stone came to the surface. As it was, there was a broad grin on their faces. The two men resumed their places in the boat, and the cutter was towed to the side of the flag-ship. Lord Cochrane ordered a whip to be sent down with slings, and himself superintended the bringing up of the boxes, whose weight in comparison to their size excited lively surprise among the sailors who brought them up to the deck. The slings were placed round them one by one, and they were hoisted to the deck of the frigate, and carried into the admiral's cabin.

After the last box had been swung up, the admiral and Stephen went up the accommodation ladder to the deck. The officers were gathered round the boxes wondering at their weight.

"What should you say they have in them, gentlemen?" Lord Cochrane asked.

"I should say that they contained specie," the captain said, "had it not been out of the question that so great an amount could be collected in Chili."

"I am happy to inform you, gentlemen, that those boxes contain Spanish gold, and that they are a lawful prize captured from the enemy by a boat's crew from this ship, under the command of my flag-midshipman, Mr. Embleton. Every man on board, therefore, in proportion to his rank, will come in for a share of prize-money, and for this you will have to thank your fellow-officer here."

Hitherto none of them had recognized Stephen, but had been wondering who the strange figure was, that had come on board with the admiral. They still looked almost incredulous, until Stephen stepped forward and held out his hand to his special friends and addressed them by name.

"Why, is it really you, Don Estevan? We had all given you up for lost. We are glad indeed to see you again."

The other officers all came round and heartily greeted Stephen, all asking questions together about his long absence and the wonderful prize of which the admiral had spoken.

"I will answer as many questions as I can presently," Stephen protested; "but, in the first place, I must have a bath, and change my clothes, and have my hair cut. Are my things still on board, and is anyone else in my cabin?"

He learned to his great satisfaction that his cabin was as he had left it.

"For weeks the admiral hoped that you would return. There was, indeed, much anxiety about the boat when we saw the storm coming on. Whether you had gained the brig before it burst, of course none of us knew. We could only hope that you had done so. The storm was a terrible one here. While some thought that the brig might have foundered at once when it struck her, it was certain that if she weathered the first blow she would have to run for it. It was one of the worst storms, people here say, that has been experienced on the coast for many years, alike in its fury and in its duration, and all agreed that she would have been blown at least a thousand miles off the land before the gale spent its force. As the wind continued in the same quarter for a long time it would have taken the brig weeks to beat back against it, but when two months passed without your return, all concluded that you had either sunk before gaining the ship, or that she had gone down in the gale, or been wrecked among some of the islands into whose neighbourhood she must have been blown. However, the admiral continued to hope long after the rest of us had given you up. At the end of two months he appointed me his flag-midshipman to fill your place, as he especially said, until your return. This being the case, I have not shifted my berth, and your cabin has remained unoccupied."

One of the officers gave orders that a tub should be at once taken to Stephen's cabin filled with water, and that the ship's barber should hold himself in readiness when called upon.

When Stephen came out, an hour later, dressed in uniform, and with his hair a reasonable length, he was told that the admiral had requested his presence in his cabin as soon as he was dressed, but had ordered the message not to be given to him until he came on deck.

"Now, lad, let me hear the whole story," he said; "but first fill your glass from that bottle. I should imagine that you have almost forgotten the taste of wine."

"I have not touched it since two days after we were wrecked, sir; but on the whole we have not done at all badly with regard to food."

"In the first place, what has become of your boat's crew?"

"They are all dead, sir. Some were killed or washed overboard during the storm; the rest were drowned at the time of the wreck."

"That is a bad business. However, begin at the beginning, and tell the story your own way. I have plenty of time to listen to it, and the fuller you make it the better."

Stephen related the story, from the time of his leaving the ship until he had anchored in the bay. As he saw that the admiral wished to have full details, he told the story at length, and the sun was setting by the time he brought it to a conclusion.

"You have done wonderfully well, lad," Lord Cochrane said warmly when he had ceased speaking, "wonderfully well indeed; no one could have done better. The arrangements throughout were excellent, and you showed a noble spirit in delaying your departure for four days in order to assist the poor wretch who had murdered your companion, and would have murdered yourself in his greed for gold. I do not praise you for bringing the treasure back here; it is the conduct that I should expect from every British officer; but, at the same time, it is clear that you had it in your power to leave it buried on that island, so that you could have gone back in some craft, and brought it away with you. I shall represent your conduct in the strongest light to the government. By the rules of the service, of course, you are entitled only to a junior officer's share of the ship's portion of the prize-money, but I shall certainly suggest that your case shall be specially considered. Now, I will take you ashore with me. I am going to a dinner given by the president, and I shall create a sensation when I state that I have, after deducting a fifth for the fleet's share of the prize-money, four hundred thousand dollars to hand over to them.

"I shall take you first to my wife. She will be delighted to see you again, and so will the children. You can give her an outline of your story. If you had been three days later you would not have found me here. For the last four months I have been endeavouring to get my ships fitted out, but in vain, and I am putting to sea no stronger than when I came back, and there can be no doubt that, profiting by their last lesson, the Spaniards will have made Callao stronger than before. However, we will do something which shall be worthy of us, though I fear that it will not be the capture of Callao."

A few minutes later the admiral's gig was alongside, and the admiral, his captain, and Stephen went ashore. Lady Cochrane greeted Stephen as warmly and kindly as her husband had done, and the children were exuberant in their delight at the return of their friend.

"He has a wonderful story to tell you, my dear," Lord Cochrane said. "It has taken him more than three hours to give me the details, and you will have a greater treat listening to them this evening than I shall have at this state dinner."

"It was too bad, Don Estevan," one of his friends said to

Stephen next morning, "that the admiral should have taken you on shore with him yesterday after you had been with him all the afternoon. We had been looking forward to having you all to ourselves, and hearing your story. You may imagine that we are all burning with curiosity to hear how it is that you came back all alone in that curious craft astern, and, above all, how you have brought with you this prize-money. All we have heard at present is that the whole of the boat's crew that went with you are dead. I promised the others that I would not ask any questions until our morning's work was over, so that we could hear your story together."

"It is just as well not to tell it by driblets," Stephen said. "It is really a long story, as it consists of a number of small things, and not of any one special incident. It can hardly be cut as short as I should like to cut it, for I am but a poor hand at a yarn."

After the usual work of exercising the men at making sail, preparing for action, and gun and cutlass exercise had been performed, anchor again cast, ropes coiled up, and everything in apple-pie order, the Chilian officers rallied round Stephen, and, taking his seat on the breech of a gun, he told them the story, but with a good deal less detail than he had given to Lord Cochrane. This relation elicited the greatest admiration on the part of his hearers. The fact that he and two others alone, and without any tools save swords, should have built the stout little craft astern, and that he should, single-handed, have sailed her some thirteen or fourteen hundred miles was to them nothing short of marvellous. All had, the afternoon before, gone on board of her, and had seen that she only wanted paint to be a handsome little boat. Unaccustomed to manual labour, it seemed wonderful that three men —two of whom were officers—should have even attempted such work with only the materials from a wreck to build with.

Stephen had passed very lightly over his four days' nursing of Jacopo, but this incident surprised them more than anything else, save the construction of the cutter. That, after the man had murdered the captain and attempted to shoot Stephen, with the intention of obtaining possession of the whole of the gold, the latter should have nursed him back to life instead of finishing him at once, seemed to them an incomprehensible piece of folly.

"But the man was a murderer, señor; he deserved death. Why should you have troubled about him, especially when, as you say, the natives might have come at any moment and taken the craft that had cost you so much pains and labour, and carried off the treasure."

"You see, when he became powerless, he was no longer an enemy," Stephen replied. "He was a criminal, it is true; but the temptation had been great. The man saw a chance of possessing himself of what to him was a fabulous treasure; better men than he have yielded to such a temptation; and though I do not say that he did not deserve death, the punishment of seeing the failure of his plans, and of being left, probably for life, a prisoner on that island was a severe one indeed. He will, at any rate, have time to repent of his sins, and some day he may be picked up by a passing vessel, and thus be able to retrieve his errors. At any rate, he will do no harm there."

"Well, no ill came from it," one of the officers said; "but I own that, for my part, as soon as I had knocked him down, I should have put my musket to his head and blown out his brains, and should never have repented the action afterwards."

"I might have done so," Stephen said, "had I overtaken him directly after he had murdered my companion; but, you see, twenty-four hours had passed, and I had had time to think how great had been the temptation to which he had yielded.

Besides, everything had gone well; I had obtained possession of the cutter, and had partially victualled her; I had completely turned the tables on him, and instead of his lying in wait for me I was lying in wait for him. He was practically at my mercy, as I could have shot him down without giving him any chance whatever. When one has got things all his own way one can afford to be lenient. The man had been already very severely wounded, and his power for doing harm was at an end. At any rate, I am very glad now that I did not kill him. And you must remember that I owed him something for his work upon the cutter, from which he was not now to profit, but which was to afford me the means of returning here and bringing back the treasure from which we shall all obtain some benefit."

"That is all true, Don Estevan; but the real reason of all was that you pitied the poor wretch, and so were ready to run a great risk to succour him. We might not have acted as you did, but at least we shall all love you the better for it. As to the prize-money, it is ridiculous that our share of it should be as large as yours, and I hope the government will see that, under the circumstances, you have a right to a handsome slice of it, for indeed, after the wreck of the vessel, it seems to me that their claim to it was fairly lost."

"I cannot see that. It was never out of my possession."

"I don't know," the other laughed. "They were two to one against you, and probably held the opinion that they had as much right to its possession as you."

"If they had been Spaniards it might have been so," Stephen agreed; "but you see the treasure had never been theirs, and from the moment that the ship surrendered they had nothing whatever to do with it."

"Nothing except to take possession of it, and I grant that the temptation to do so must have been strong."

"I felt that," Stephen replied; "but until the vessel was completed and victualled and a means of escape open, the gold was absolutely useless, and therefore the question as to its possession would not really arise until we neared land. I did think it probable that the two Peruvians might then put in a claim to at least one of the boxes of money each; and I had made up my mind that if they would content themselves with this, I should be willing for them to land somewhere along the coast with it, rather than run the risk of a fight, especially as I could not possibly have kept awake night and day, and they must therefore have had me in their power. I am sure that the captain meant honestly, and under the circumstances his claim to a portion of the money, that he and his companion had done as much as I had to save, would not have been an unfair one."

"It would have been terrible had the natives arrived when you were building the boat, Don Estevan."

"It would have been terrible for them," Stephen said, "but it would have hurt us but little, for had they discovered our fort they could never have taken it. With our twenty-four muskets we could have held it against any number of savages, while as for the boat it would have been useless to them, and they could scarcely have injured it. Even when it was finished there was nothing on board to attract them. They might have knocked away the props and tumbled her over, but they would have had to blockade us in our fort while they did anything to her; for otherwise we could have moved along the cliff to a point where we should have commanded the boat, and could there have kept up a fire that would have speedily driven them from her.

"No; we had no fear whatever of the natives from the time we had once finished our wattle-work of thorny creepers until the day when we got her into the water. After that we were certainly horribly anxious, for they might have taken it into their heads to tow her away with them, for the purpose of breaking her up at their leisure for the sake of the bolts and nails."

In the afternoon Lord Cochrane took Stephen ashore with him. "The president and the council desire to thank you personally, Mr. Embleton, as I told you last night as we came off. After dinner I gave them a brief recital of your adventure, and said publicly that I considered you were entitled to a handsome share of the prize-money which you had almost miraculously brought back, and the president thoroughly endorsed my views. The money is of the greatest consequence to them at the present moment, for they are absolutely crippled, so much so that I deemed it right, some time back, to offer to hand over to them my share of the prize-money for the captures we had effected. They declined the offer, to my regret, for though I am far from being a rich man, I would willingly have given the money in order to get to sea again."

Stephen was warmly thanked by President O'Higgins for his great service to the republic, and highly complimented on his conduct. He announced to him that he and the council had decided to present him with the sum of twenty-five thousand dollars as a recognition of his services.

"We consider," he said, "that you deserve a much larger sum, but the circumstances of the state are such that we feel it is impossible for us to do more than the barest justice at the present time. We have, however, decided upon raising you at once to the rank of lieutenant. Lord Cochrane told me last night that such promotion, before you had served your full time, was quite contrary to the rules of the service; but we considered this an altogether exceptional case, and that you have amply proved yourself to be fully capable of carrying out the duties of any rank to which you may attain."

Stephen in a few words thanked the president and the council very heartily, and then retired with the admiral.

"That is a nice little nest-egg for you, Stephen," the latter said. "I consider that it ought to have been fifty thousand, but their necessities are so great that they cannot afford to be generous."

"I consider that it is immense, sir," Stephen replied, "and had never any thought of a reward for doing my duty."

"You will not want the money out here, lad," the admiral went on; "at any rate, your share of the ship's prize-money will be ample for anything that you may require. If you like, therefore, I will hand over your box along with my own share of the prize-money to the firm here who act as my bankers, and they will give you an order on their bankers in London, which you can send to your father to draw and invest in your name or otherwise, as you may prefer."

"Thank you very much, sir. You will, I hope, be kind enough to let me continue to perform the duties of your flag-midshipman."

"You will become my flag-lieutenant, Stephen. The post is vacant, for Don Valdes was yesterday appointed to the command of the *Independencia*, an American-built corvette of twenty-eight guns that has been purchased and fitted out."

On the 12th of September, 1819, the fleet set sail from Valparaiso. It consisted of the *O'Higgins*, *San Martin*, *Lautaro*, *Independencia*, *Galvarino*, *Araucano*, and *Puyrredon*, mounting in all two hundred and twenty guns. There were also two old merchant ships to be used as fire-vessels. On the 29th they entered the Callao roads. The next day Lord Cochrane sent in a boat with a flag of truce, and challenged the Viceroy to come out for a fair fight. The challenge was rejected, although the Spanish fleet was nearly twice as strong as that of Chili.

On the night of the 2nd an attack was made, but failed, owing to the rockets, from which much had been hoped, turning out useless. They had been manufactured in Chili by Spanish prisoners, and had been so badly constructed that they inflicted far more damage upon the men who fired them than upon those against whom they were aimed. On the 5th a fire-ship was despatched with the intention of destroying the booms that protected the harbour; but a sudden calm came on, and the ship was riddled with shot from the Spanish guns and was fast sinking when she was exploded, but was too far distant from the booms to injure either them or the shipping. Finding himself thus unable to get at the enemy, Lord Cochrane was obliged to abandon for a time his project of taking Callao.

The fresh supply of provisions promised from Chili had not arrived, and sickness broke out on board the fleet. The admiral continued to watch the port for some weeks, despatching an expedition which captured the town of Pisco, and obtaining the much-needed provisions. On the 21st of November the sick were sent off to Valparaiso in charge of the *San Martin*, the *Independencia*, and the *Araucano*, while with the remainder of the fleet Lord Cochrane sailed to the mouth of the river Guayaquil, where he captured two large Spanish vessels, mounting together thirty-six guns and laden with timber. After a delay of a fortnight, occasioned by a mutiny attempted by Captains Guise and Spry, he sent one of his ships with the prizes to Valparaiso, left two others to watch the Peruvian coast, and started alone in his flag-ship with the intention of undertaking the capture of Valdivia; for at that time the southern portion of what is now Chili remained in the hands of the Spaniards.

Valdivia was a very strongly fortified place, and was regarded as impregnable by the Spaniards; and it was from this port that they directed their attacks upon Chili from the south, just as they did on the north from Callao. To reach it he therefore had to sail south from the Guayaquil along the coast of Peru and then past that of Chili. On approaching the fortress he hoisted Spanish colours and made a signal for a pilot. The Spaniards, having no idea that there was a Chilian war-ship on that coast, at once sent one off, together with an officer and four men. These were promptly made prisoners. The pilot was ordered to take the ship through the channels leading to the port, and much information was obtained from the other prisoners as to the fortifications of the place. As they sailed up the channel, the idea that the stranger was an enemy occurred to the commander of the fortress, and the non-return of the boat with the officer confirming this suspicion, a heavy fire was opened upon the *O'Higgins*; she did not reply, but continued her work of investigating the channel, and then withdrew out of range.

Two days were spent in further reconnaisances of the approaches, and on the third day a brig was captured entering the port. She carried some important despatches, and twenty thousand dollars for the payment of the troops. Having ascertained the nature of the difficulties to be encountered, Lord Cochrane sailed away to Concepcion, two hundred miles distant, and obtained from the Chilian governor a force of two hundred and fifty soldiers under Major Beauchef, a French officer in their service. He there found a Chilian schooner, which he attached to his service, and a Brazilian brig, which volunteered its aid; with them he sailed for Valdivia. On the night of the 29th they were off the island of Quiriquina. Owing to the incompetence of his officers the admiral had been obliged to personally superintend everything that was done on board, and when the ship was becalmed lay down for a few minutes' sleep, leaving orders that he was to be called at once if a breeze sprung up. A breeze did spring up; the officer of the watch was asleep, and a sudden gust carried the vessel on to a sharp rock, where she hung beating heavily.

They were then forty miles from the mainland, and the

brig and schooner were both out of sight. For a short time a panic took place among the crew, and officers and men made for the boats. The admiral, followed by Stephen, rushed on deck, pistol in hand, and the former soon succeeded in calming the panic, his authority among the men being unbounded. He pointed out that the boats would carry but a hundred and fifty men, and that there were six hundred on board, so that were a rush to take place to the boats, they would assuredly be overcrowded and perhaps sink, while, should any gain the shore, the occupants would be made prisoners, and would certainly be put to death by the Spaniards. Their only hope, therefore, was to get the ship off.

On sounding the well it was found that there were five feet of water in the hold. The pumps were out of order, the carpenter utterly inefficient, and Lord Cochrane, taking off his coat, himself set to work to repair them, ordering Stephen to keep the men at work baling with buckets; the captain being under arrest for disobedience to orders, and the one other lieutenant absolutely incompetent. When the pumps were got to work it was found that they and the buckets sufficed to prevent the water from rising, and preparations were at once made to get the vessel off the rock. There was danger that when this was done she might sink, but Lord Cochrane pointed out that the leak was not likely to increase, and declared he had no doubt that she would swim as far as Valdivia. The anchors were got out astern, the crew set to heave on them, and it was not long before she floated off. But it was found that the water had entered the magazine, and that the whole of the ammunition, except a little on deck and in the cartridge-boxes of the soldiers, was rendered unserviceable.

This accident would, with a less determined commander, have put an end to their enterprise; but Lord Cochrane relied, not upon the ship's guns but upon the men, and considered that as these could not fire they would be obliged to trust to their bayonets, and that the chances of success would not therefore be diminished. In the morning they were joined by the schooner and brig, and on approaching Valdivia as many men as possible were transferred to the two small vessels. The admiral went on board the schooner, and ordered the *O'Higgins* to stand out to sea, as he intended she should be used only in case of necessity. The channel leading up to the town was three-quarters of a mile in width, and was commanded by six large forts on the western shore, two on the eastern, and a very large fort on an island, with six minor forts well situated for defence. The position was all but impregnable, and, indeed, the surf was so heavy that it was impossible for a landing to be effected save at a spot close to Fort Ingles.

Having made all his preparations, Lord Cochrane sailed on to the port, and boldly entered the channel. The troops were all sent below, while the two little vessels entered, and anchored boldly off Fort Ingles. The swell was so heavy that even the landing-place was unapproachable. The boats had been towed on the lee side of the ships, and when shouted to to send a boat ashore an answer was given that these had been lost in a storm. The Spaniards, however, were not satisfied, and alarm-guns were fired and troops brought up from the other forts. No hostile steps were taken, however, until, some time later, one of the boats drifted astern. The Spaniards had no longer any doubt as to the nature of the two vessels, and Fort Ingles at once opened fire upon them, the first shot passing through the brig and killing two men. It became necessary, therefore, to land at once, in spite of the surf. They had but two launches and a gig altogether; Lord Cochrane took charge of the gig, while Major Miller, who commanded the marines of the *O'Higgins*, embarked on board one of the launches.

They got safely through the swell, and in spite of a heavy fire from the Spanish troops effected a landing. They at once rushed upon the Spaniards, who came down from the forts to oppose them, and drove them back at the point of the bayonet. The second boat quickly arrived from the brig, both returning to the ships, and in less than an hour three hundred men had landed. From the spot where they had obtained a footing, the only approach to Fort Ingles was by a precipitous path which could only be passed in single file. The fort itself was only accessible by a ladder that had been drawn up, as soon as the party driven back from the landing-place had returned. An attack seemed well-nigh hopeless; but the Chilians' confidence in their leader was unbounded, and none doubted but that success would attend their efforts. It was already late in the afternoon when they landed, and while waiting for darkness to cover the operations, they were sheltered by the nature of the ground from the fire of the large body of troops which had assembled in the fort.

CHAPTER XIV.

A PRISONER.

AS soon as it was dark the admiral prepared for the attack. From the prisoners he had learned all details as to the fort, and found that while almost impregnable from the river face, the flank of the fort was defended chiefly by a strong palisading. He detached a small party of marines, under Ensign Vidal, to endeavour to enter at that point. Another party then silently moved forward to the direct attack of the fort, and as soon as it had taken up its position under the wall, the main body advanced, cheering and firing. The enemy at once opened a heavy fire of artillery and musketry, but in the dark they were unable to take aim, and but little damage was caused by their fire. The movement had the result intended—of occupying the whole attention of the eight hundred men in the fort, and of drowning any noise that might be made by those tearing down the palisades.

With great exertions Ensign Vidal succeeded in getting up a couple of the beams; he and his men passed through the opening, used the beams as a bridge across a wet ditch inside the palisade, and then advanced noiselessly until near the Spaniards, into whom they fired a volley. The Spaniards were seized with a sudden panic at finding themselves thus unexpectedly taken in flank, and instantly took to flight. The moment the fire of the marines told the admiral that the flank attack had succeeded, he led the main body round to the rear of the fort. The Spaniards, as they poured out there, communicated their panic to a body of three hundred troops drawn up behind in reserve, and the whole fled toward the next fort, followed hotly by the Chilians, who bayoneted numbers of them, and pressed so closely on their heels that they entered the works, one after the other, with them, driving them from fort to fort, together with two hundred men who had been placed with a battery of guns on rising ground to sweep the rear of the forts.

The last of these, the castle of Coral, was stormed with scarcely any opposition, the enemy thinking only of escape. Numbers of them got away in boats to Valdivia, while the rest plunged into the forests behind the forts. Little over a hundred prisoners were taken, and a like number of men were killed, their panic having been too great for anything like resistance to be offered. On the Chilian side the loss was seven men killed and nine wounded. The fall of all the western forts practically entailed that of Valdivia, for while preparations were being made to attack the eastern forts, the *O'Higgins* appeared off the mouth of the river, and the Spaniards, seeing this reinforcement to their foes, at once abandoned the remaining forts and the town, and retreated into the interior. The booty taken by the Chilians included fifty tons of gunpowder and ten thousand cannon-shot. One hundred and seventy thousand musket cartridges, a large number of muskets, and one hundred and twenty-eight cannon also fell into the hands of the victors. A large ship with valuable stores, together with a quantity of plate taken by the Spaniards from Chilian churches, also were captured.

The value of the conquest was not, however, to be reckoned by the amount of spoil taken. Its effect on the struggle was enormous. It raised the spirits of the Chilians to the highest pitch, whilst it brought home to the mind of the Spanish government the hopelessness of continuing a struggle against an enemy so well led, and capable of carrying out the most desperate enterprises.

Although Lord Cochrane was received with unbounded enthusiasm by the population at large on his return to Valparaiso, his success had excited the jealousy of the minister of marine and other officials, and by them he was treated with the grossest ingratitude. They even proposed to bring him to court-martial for having exceeded his orders; and although the indignation the proposal excited compelled them to abandon this, it was but to resort to other measures hostile to him.

It was months before the fleet received their share of the prize-money of the capture of Valdivia, in spite of the admiral's earnest efforts on their behalf. His own share, which was sixty-seven thousand dollars, he never received at all. He failed altogether in his endeavour to obtain a fleet of sufficient force to attempt the capture of Callao, and for many months was kept in a state of inactivity. So irritating was the persecution to which he was subjected, that on the 14th of May he tendered his resignation.

The resignation was refused, but nothing was done. O'Higgins, who was an honest man, was practically powerless, as the entire government was in the hands of a senate of five members, which assumed dictatorial powers, and without whose approval nothing whatever could be done. It was determined, however, to raise an army for the liberation of Peru; and although Lord Cochrane had vainly asked the year before for a small land force to capture Callao, an army was now raised without difficulty by the dictators, and General San Martin was placed in command. This man had rendered good service to Chili when, in conjunction with O'Higgins, he had led the movement of independence; but his success had turned his head. He was vain and arrogant, and at the same time dilatory and vacillating. He, like the dictators, was jealous of the success and popularity of Lord Cochrane, and was bent upon thwarting him to the utmost. His army, four thousand two hundred strong, was embarked at Valparaiso in the ships of the squadron. Lord Cochrane proposed to him to land at Chilka, the nearest point to Lima and Callao. San Martin, however, chose Pisca, and the troops were landed there on the 18th of September. For fifty days they remained there doing nothing, the fleet being compelled to remain inactive off the port.

On the 28th of October they were re-embarked. San Martin again refused to listen to Lord Cochrane's proposal for a vigorous attack upon Callao and Lima, and requested to be landed at Ancon, a port as unsuitable for the purpose as was Pisca. Lord Cochrane, however, determined that the fleet, furnished at such expense and effort by Chili, should not be wholly wasted, and when he sent his ships in to anchor off the port, he retained the *O'Higgins*, the *Independencia*, and the *Lautaro*, with the professed intention of blockading Callao at a distance. His real intention was, however, to cut out the *Esmeralda* from under the guns of the forts, and also to carry off another ship, on board which, as he had learned, a million dollars were embarked. The *Esmeralda* was a forty-four gun frigate, and was considered the finest Spanish war-ship in the Pacific. She lay under the protection of three hundred guns on shore, and a strong boom moored by chains at short intervals; while near her lay twenty-seven gun-boats and several vessels that had been armed for the defence of the port. Only two or three of his officers knew of his intentions until a few hours before his intended attack, when he issued a proclamation to the seamen and marines, telling them that they had now an opportunity for dealing the enemy a mortal blow, and repeating the triumph of Valdivia.

Volunteers were asked for, and the whole of the sailors and marines from the three ships offered to follow Lord Cochrane wherever he might lead them. This was a much larger force than he required, and one hundred and eighty sailors and eighty marines were chosen for the work. This force was gradually transferred to the flag-ship, and the other two vessels sailed out of the bay just before darkness came on, as if in chase of some ship they had sighted—a ruse well calculated to lull the Spaniards into security. The men intended for the service then took their places in fourteen boats that lay hidden behind the flag-ship. All were dressed in white, with a blue band on the left arm, in order that they might distinguish each other in the dark. At ten o'clock the boats pushed off in two directions, commanded respectively by Captain Crosby and Captain Guise, while the admiral led the way in his launch. It was just twelve o'clock when the boats arrived at a small opening in the boom. The oars had been muffled, and so perfectly had silence been observed, that the admiral's launch ran against a guard-boat lying at the entrance, without its approach having been observed by the Spaniards. There was a hasty challenge by the startled officer in command, to which the admiral himself replied by threatening the occupants of the boat with instant death if they gave the slightest alarm.

The threat, and the appearance of the boats dashing in through the opening, had its effect. No word was spoken by the Spaniards, and in a few minutes the flotilla of vessels rowed down in line upon the frigate, and boarded her at a dozen points simultaneously. The Chilians had been ordered not to use their pistols, but to rely wholly on their cutlasses. The sentries on the frigate shouted the alarm, and the Spaniards, snatching up their arms, rushed up from below. Many were cut down at once by the Chilians, the rest retreated to the forecastle and made a gallant stand, and it was not until the Chilians had made three charges upon them that they gave way, some leaping overboard, and others running below. The Spanish marines gathered on the quarter-deck, and they too fought with great bravery. Not one among them asked for quarter or sought safety in flight, but continued the struggle until the last man fell.

The admiral himself had been very unfortunate. He had swung himself up into the main-chains the moment his boat touched the frigate, and was about to leap upon the deck of the *Esmeralda* when he was struck on the head by a Spanish sentry with his clubbed musket and fell back into the boat. He fell upon one of the rowlocks, which entered his back near the spine, inflicting a very severe injury, from whose effects he suffered for several years after. In spite of the agony caused by the wound he again clambered up on to the deck, and was almost immediately shot through the thigh. He bound a handkerchief tightly round it, and managed to direct the operations until the capture was complete. The affair occupied but a quarter of an hour, the Chilian loss being eleven killed and thirty wounded, while a hundred and sixty of the Spaniards fell. While this was going on, the garrison of the forts, awakened by the uproar, ran to their guns and opened fire on the *Esmeralda*, several of the Spaniards, among them their captain, and two or three of the Chilians, being killed or wounded by their shot.

It happened that in the harbour at the time were two neutral frigates—one British, the other an American. It had been arranged between them and the Spanish authorities that in the event of a night attack they were to show lights in a particular position, so that they might not be fired upon. This they did, but by the admiral's orders similar lights were at once hoisted on board the *Esmeralda*, thus causing much confusion among the Spaniards. Both the neutral frigates were hit several times, while but few shots struck the *Esmeralda*. Lord Cochrane was now forced by his wounds to leave it to Captain Guise, the next senior officer, to carry out the orders that he had previously given, namely, that the brig with the bullion on board was first to be captured, then that every ship was to be attacked and cut adrift. The success of these operations was certain, as the Spaniards, directly they saw the *Esmeralda* captured, had taken to their boats and made for shore, and the whole of the Spanish vessels might have been either burnt or captured. Captain Guise had all along thwarted the admiral's plans to the utmost of his power, had fomented several mutinies, and should have been tried and shot long before. He now, instead of carrying out the orders, cut the *Esmeralda's* cables, hoisted her sails, and steered through the opening in the boom.

Although marred by the treachery, or at any rate gross misconduct of Cochrane's subordinates, the capture of the *Esmeralda* exercised almost as great an influence on the fortunes of the struggle as did that of Valdivia. It was a death-blow to the Spanish naval force in the Pacific; for although they had still two frigates and some smaller craft in those waters, they never afterwards ventured to put to sea, of which the Chilians now became absolute masters. The action, in fact, ensured the success of the Chilian effort to free Peru.

San Martin now requested Lord Cochrane to re-embark the army once more, and carry it to Huacha. This was done, and there San Martin remained without doing any more than he had done at the two other ports. After having landed him the fleet returned to Callao, where they used every effort to tempt the Spanish war-ships to venture out, but without success. The effect, however, of these operations showed itself in other ways. On the 3rd of December six hundred and fifty Peruvian soldiers deserted from the Spanish service, and two days later forty officers followed them, and from that time defections took place almost daily.

San Martin now made no secret of his intention to assume the dictatorship of Peru. He had for so many months kept his army inactive, in order that he might in time be able to enforce his authority. What he would not do, however, was accomplished by Lord Cochrane. Weary of the long delay he offered in the following March to capture Lima if two thousand soldiers were assigned to him. This offer was refused, but after some time he obtained a force of six hundred. With these he effected a landing at port after port along the coast, and so harassed the Spaniards that, on the 6th of July, Lima capitulated and Peru was free. San Martin at once proclaimed himself protector of Peru, and appointed two of his creatures as chief ministers. Lord Cochrane in vain attempted to obtain from him payment for the sailors of the fleet, who had been very many months without receiving a penny.

San Martin insolently replied that he would pay nothing

whatever to Chili, but that he would make Lord Cochrane a Peruvian admiral if he would leave the service of Chili for that of Peru. Lord Cochrane knew that Chili would decline to pay for work that had been done to make Peru, like itself, free and independent, since it was now as prostrate at the feet of San Martin as it had been at those of the Spaniards. The army it had raised had betrayed it and taken service under San Martin, as had the two mutinous scoundrels, Captains Guise and Spry. Lord Cochrane, therefore, determined to take by force the money due to the fleet. At Ancon there was a large amount of treasure seized from the Spaniards. It had been deposited by San Martin there, and in the middle of September the admiral landed, and took possession of it without opposition. Of the two hundred and eighty-five thousand dollars found there, he paid a year's arrears to every officer and man in the fleet, taking nothing, however, for himself, and reserving the small surplus for the pressing wants and equipments of the fleet.

In June, 1822, Lord Cochrane returned to Valparaiso, from which he had been absent twenty months. He was received with a popular ovation; but his enemies were still at work, and struck at him in the matter upon which he was most sensitive, by refusing any payment whatever to his officers and men, many of whom almost died of starvation.

In October a revolution broke out in Chili, and such indignities were heaped upon the admiral himself that upon the 12th of the month he formally resigned his commission, and in January, 1823, quitted Valparaiso in a vessel chartered by himself, taking with him several European officers and gentlemen, who, like himself, were tired of Chilian ingratitude, and were ready to follow him in whatever service he engaged.

Stephen had taken no part in the later operations of the fleet. After the capture of the *Esmeralda* he had been knocked down and very severely injured by a splinter, caused by a shot from the Spanish batteries passing through the bulwark close to where he was standing. Lord Cochrane had sent him, with other wounded, in one of the small war-ships down to Valparaiso, and there he was tenderly nursed by Lady Cochrane. It was three months before he fairly recovered his strength, and as soon as he was convalescent he took a berth in a craft that was sailing with stores and provisions for the fleet. They had been out four days when she was caught in a storm on-shore. In vain they tried to beat out; the vessel was a poor sailer, and drifted to leeward faster than she could work to windward.

"What sort of ground tackle have you?" Stephen asked the captain.

"I have two good anchors, señor lieutenant, but the cables are rather old."

"I should advise you to have them brought up on deck and overhauled, and if you find any specially bad places we can cut them out and splice the ends again."

The cables were brought up, but it needed a very short examination only to show Stephen that they were old and worn from end to end. "It will go hard with us if we have to rely upon these," he said. "They would not hold a bluff-bowed craft like this two minutes; the very first roller that struck her would snap them like pack-threads. The worst of it is, captain, that if we escape being drowned we have but the inside of a prison to look to, for we are off the Peruvian coast now, and any of us who get to shore will be seized at once."

"With such a sea as this, señor, there is little chance of any of us being saved if we once strike. We are now somewhere off the mouth of the San Carlos river. In calm weather there would be water enough on the bar for us to run in, but not now; we should strike and go to pieces to a certainty."

"Well, that would depend; we might bump over it. But even if we did break up on the bar, we should have a much better chance than we should if we went ashore anywhere else. Instead of being dashed on the beach by the waves, and then being swept out again, we should be likely to be carried on into the still water behind the bar, and so of making our way to shore. There are eight of the crew and ourselves. You had better get up ten small casks—those wine barrels would do very well—let the liquor run off, then bung them up again, and fasten life-lines round them; with their help we should have a fair chance."

"It is worth trying at any rate," the captain agreed. "The surf on the bar will be tremendous, but if we could stick to the casks we might get through it."

"Do you think that you are north or south of it now, captain?"

"North, perhaps two or three miles."

"Well, we will go on fighting as long as we can, captain; it is of no use throwing away a chance, and the wind may possibly drop or shift so as to enable us to make off shore; but if we do not see the land before three o'clock I would turn and run in towards it, and then when we get near enough to see objects plainer, head for the south until you see the entrance. When you do we will go straight for it. It is better at any rate to do it while there is daylight to help us."

The barrels were got up and prepared to serve as life-buoys. They had just finished when Stephen made his way a short distance up the rigging. "I can see the line of surf, captain; it is not more than three miles away. You had better take a look at it—you may be able to tell where we are. I think I can make out a place of some size a short distance along."

The captain joined him. "Just as I thought," he said; "that is San Carlos, and the mouth of the river is about a mile beyond it."

"Then you may as well bear away for it at once—the sooner we get it over the better."

"Make your casks fast to something, men," the captain ordered, as he stepped on deck. "The surf will get higher as we get inshore, and will, I have no doubt, sweep our decks. When the time comes let each man go to his barrel with his knife in his hand ready to cut the lashings just before we strike."

In half an hour the captain made out the entrance to the river and headed the ship for it.

"There is a heavy sea indeed on the bar," Stephen said as they neared the line of breakers. "You see, I have changed my togs since the gale began, for I saw that unless the wind changed we should find ourselves in difficulties. We have not much mercy to expect as Chilian sailors. I should have none if it were known that I am a naval officer. Will you tell the men that if we get ashore and I too am saved, they had best hold their tongue about my rank. In the first place it would do me harm, and in the next it would damage you all were it known you had one of Cochrane's officers on board, for it would show at once that you were on your way to our fleet; whereas if it is supposed that you are merely an ordinary coaster you may be let off unharmed."

"There is not much chance for us either way," the captain said. "If we fall into the hands of the Spaniards they will probably hang us at once, while the country people may cut our throats so as to save themselves the trouble of handing us over to the Spaniards. We are no more than a hundred miles from the frontier, and if we do get to shore our best chance will be to try and make our way down the coast, travelling at night and lying up in the daytime. But anyhow I will tell the men what you say."

"Get all the sail upon her you can, captain—the faster she is travelling the more chance she has of getting over the bar."

"I will shake out the mainsail," the captain said. "Then all hands had better gather aft—the masts are sure to fall over her bows as soon as she strikes."

In a few minutes the ship was nearing the breakers at a high rate of speed. The men were all gathered aft, each with his barrel. Stephen held his breath as they mounted the last great wave outside the surf. Borne along by the great wind and the impetus of the waves, the vessel plunged head-foremost into the surf, which poured in cataracts on to her deck. There was a slight shock, which caused the vessel to tremble, but she was swept along by the fury of the surf. Another wave lifted her high into the air, and as it passed from under her she struck again. This time the shock was tremendous. Every man was thrown off his feet, the masts went over with a crash, and most of the hands were swept overboard by the torrent that poured in over the stern. Stephen had grasped one of the back-stays, and though it seemed to him for a moment that his arms were being pulled from their sockets, he still maintained his grasp. Another and even greater sea than those that had preceded it thundered down upon them. There was a forward move and then another crash, and Stephen felt himself floating in the water, holding on to the keg. Glancing round he saw that the ship had gone altogether. She had broken up completely, and the sea was covered with floating timbers.

The danger from this was greater than from the waves, and he let go his hold of the barrel and dived, swimming under water at right angles to the run of the waves as long as he could hold his breath. When he came up he looked round. He was beyond the wreckage, and was also inside the line of surf. Had the wave carried the ship her own length farther she would have been out of danger. The river bank was but a couple of hundred yards away. The water was still rough, but it was a long heavy swell rather than a stormy sea, and Stephen, who had kicked off his shoes before the ship struck, at once swam for the shore, and was not long in reaching it. After resting for a minute or two he walked along the bank, and soon made out four barrels that had men still clinging to them. Gradually, too, these made their way ashore; the swimmers were all men who had been carried away by the first wave that had swept over the boat. Of the others he could see no signs. He thought he could make out two or three barrels in the middle of the wreckage, but of this he was not sure, and had little doubt that those who were with him at the time the ship went to pieces had all been killed by the floating timber.

"Now, men," he said, when the four survivors had joined him, "shall we keep together or try to make our way separately?"

The men consulted together, and then said that they thought they would have more chance of making their way south were they to separate. Stephen was glad of this decision, which he had no doubt was arrived at from the fear that if they were taken, and he was recognized to be an Englishman, it would make their treatment worse than it would otherwise be. He himself much preferred to go alone; he had no authority over these men, and five men together were more likely to attract attention than one alone. Looking across the river they saw a number of people on the opposite bank. They were evidently inhabitants of the town, who, having seen the ship running for shore, had come down to watch her fate, and to give any assistance in their power. Stephen saw that they were waving their hands for them to make up the bank, where there might be a ferry-boat to take them over. He pointed this out to the men, and said, "I am afraid we shall be pursued ere long. Of course, at present they take us for their own people; but when they see that we do not cross, they will suspect the truth, and will send over to see whether we have taken shelter in some village there may be on this side. When they hear that we have not done so, they will guess that we are Chilians, and there will be a hot pursuit for us. We will walk together for a little way along the bank as if going in the direction that they point to. They are not likely to stay long where they are; some will go back to the town now that there is nothing to see, others will no doubt remain on the bank to collect wreckage that may be washed ashore, a few may go on to the ferry and wait there for us. If there are any boats in the river you may be sure they will soon put out to collect floating casks and bales."

The little crowd was indeed just beginning to break up, and after going a short distance Stephen and his companions left the river and started south. After going two or three hundred yards they shook hands and separated, the sailors striking more inland, while Stephen took for the present a course that ran parallel with the sea-coast. It was already growing dark, and Stephen was worn out with the excitement of the day, so that after going on for an hour, he lay down in a clump of trees and went to sleep. It was broad daylight when he awoke, and on walking to the edge of the trees he saw a village a few hundred yards in front of him. He made a long detour to pass it, and was proceeding along a well-beaten path when he heard the sound of horses' hoofs behind, and looking round saw four Spanish troopers riding towards him. Escape was out of the question, and he walked quietly on in the faint hope that they might pass without stopping him. This, however, was improbable; his hair was matted with sea water, his clothes still wet—his whole appearance too evidently that of a shipwrecked man. They stopped when they reached him.

"You are one of the men who were cast ashore last night?" a sergeant said.

"I am," Stephen replied frankly.

"My orders are to take you back to San Carlos. Where are your companions?"

"I do not know," Stephen replied. "We separated at once; I went my way and they went theirs."

"You are a Chilian," the man said; "anyone can tell it by your speech."

Stephen by this time spoke the language so fluently indeed that he could have passed as a native. There was, however, sufficient difference between the dialects of Peru and Chili for it to be seen at once that he was not a Peruvian. He did not reply directly to the question.

"We were on a trader," he said. "The captain and four of the men were lost; five of us gained the shore. We were not on an armed ship, and cannot be considered enemies."

"The whole race of you are enemies," the sergeant said. "You are rebels and traitors every one of you. Gomez, do you and Martinez take this man back to San Carlos, and hand him over to the governor. I will ride on with Sancho and see if we can come up with the other fellows; as there are half a dozen parties out in search we are pretty sure to lay hands on them before nightfall."

On the way back Stephen, as he walked between the two horsemen, debated whether it would be better to allow them to remain under the impression that he was a Chilian, or declare himself an English officer. In the former case he would most likely be shot without ceremony, in the latter he might probably be sent up to Callao or Lima. It might make no difference in his fate, but at least might delay it; and if he could but manage to communicate his position to Lord Cochrane, the latter would certainly take instant steps to offer one or more of the many Spanish officers who were prisoners in his hands in exchange for him, or would threaten that if any harm came to him he would give no quarter to Spanish officers in future. At any rate the latter seemed to promise him the better chance, and accordingly when on his arrival at San Carlos he was taken before the governor, he replied boldly to the question, "Who are you?"

"I am Lieutenant Stephen Embleton, flag officer to Admiral Cochrane."

The words created a sensation among the officers standing behind the governor.

"You dare to say this!" the governor exclaimed furiously.

"I am giving a simple answer to your question, señor," Stephen said quietly. "When we ask the Spanish officers who fall into our hands what their names are, they reply as I have done, truthfully, and they are treated as I expect to be treated, honourably; especially as I have not been captured by you when in arms, but have simply had the misfortune to be shipwrecked on your coast."

The quiet tone of the reply had its effect. The officers spoke a few words together in a low tone, and the governor said more calmly than he had before spoken:

"How am I to know that this story is true?"

"I have no means of proving it now," Stephen replied; "but if I am taken to Callao, a message sent to Lord Cochrane under a flag of truce would speedily bring back a letter verifying my story."

"But how did you come to be on board that craft that was wrecked?"

"I was wounded, señor, at the action in the port of Callao. A splinter caused by a shot from one of your batteries struck me when on the deck of the *Esmeralda*. I was sent down to Valparaiso. Your surgeon can examine me and will find that the wound has but lately healed. Being anxious to rejoin my ship as soon as possible, I did not wait for a ship of war going up, but took passage in a Chilian trader."

"Doubtless conveying stores to the Chilian fleet," the governor remarked.

"She may have had stores of that kind on board," Stephen said, "but that was no affair of mine. I simply took a passage in her, and paid for it. The admiral is expecting me, and will, I am sure, be ready to exchange an officer of superior rank for me."

By the governor's orders Stephen was now taken into another room. In a quarter of an hour he was brought back again. The governor had left the room, but a Spanish colonel said to him:

"It has been decided to send you to Callao, where, no doubt, inquiries will be made into the truth of your story, and his excellency the Viceroy will himself decide upon your fate."

Stephen bowed.

"I can have no doubt, señor, that his excellency will treat me with the same courtesy with which some score of Spanish officers are at present treated by Lord Cochrane; especially as he will know that were I,—which I cannot for a moment believe, —badly treated, it is in the power of our admiral to carry out wholesale reprisals."

The colonel made no reply, but ordered the guards to remove the prisoner. An hour later a young Spanish officer entered.

"I have been ordered to accompany you to Callao," he said courteously. "I take four men with me, and I am told that I am to be responsible for your safety. It would be painful indeed for me to have to take any stringent measures to prevent you from escaping on the road, and if you will give me your parole not to attempt evasion it will be far more pleasant for us both."

"If you will give me a little time to think it over," Stephen replied, "I will give you an answer. It is too serious a matter for me to decide at once. However, whether I accept or refuse I thank you greatly for your courtesy in making me the offer."

"We shall start in an hour's time," the Spaniard said. "A meal, of which you are doubtless much in need, will be brought to you at once, and when you have concluded it I will return for your reply."

He then left the room, and in two or three minutes a soldier entered with a substantial meal. As he ate it Stephen thought the matter over. It did not seem to him that with four soldiers and an officer watching him he could have much chance of making his escape, and, even did he succeed in doing so, he would almost certainly be retaken, as he could have but a short start, and his dress and Chilian speech would attract instant attention. If overtaken he might be shot at once, and he therefore decided that his chances would be better as a prisoner at Callao than as a fugitive in a hostile country. Accordingly when the officer returned he at once gave him his parole not to attempt to escape upon the journey.

"I am very glad that you have so decided," the Spaniard said. "I will send you at once a suit of clothes to ride in. Your attire would at once attract attention and might lead to unpleasantness. We have a long journey before us, and may as well make it as agreeable as we can under the circumstances."

Stephen thanked him heartily for the offer, which he gladly accepted, for he felt ashamed of his appearance in his rough clothes, now shrunk and water-stained. The servant who brought the suit of clothes brought also a large basin of water, soap, and a towel, and Stephen was therefore able to make his toilet in comfort. The suit was an undress uniform—white breeches, jacket of the same material, with white braid, a pair of high riding-boots, and a broad-brimmed hat. As soon as he dressed himself, his guard conducted him downstairs. The officer and the four troopers were already mounted, and a horse stood ready for Stephen. Without a word he mounted, the officer took his place beside him, and the troopers falling in behind, he rode out through the gate.

"I thank you heartily for your thoughtfulness in providing me with the means of making myself respectable."

"You certainly look better," the young officer said. "Now permit me to introduce myself. My name is Filippo Conchas; my uncle is the governor here, and it is to that I owe the pleasure of this excursion with you."

"I should not have thought that a ride of five or six hundred miles was a pleasure, Don Filippo."

"Oh, yes, it is, when one can go one's own pace, and travel only in the morning and evening. Moreover, one gets terribly tired of a small provincial town, especially in times like these, when things are not going quite so pleasantly as one might wish, and one knows that half the inhabitants are bitterly hostile to one. Besides, señor, I have an attraction at Callao, and in fact am betrothed to a fair cousin, the daughter of another uncle who is the chief naval authority at the port. My uncle, that is the one here, is a strict disciplinarian, and as all leave is stopped owing to the doings of your admiral's ships, I am kept here; so, of course, directly I heard that you were to be sent to Callao I applied to him to appoint me to command the escort, and as I was the first applicant he had no excuse for refusing, although he was not in the most pleasant of humours. However, that I did not care about as long as I got my leave. He has gone down to the river with several of his officers to inspect the goods, of which a large quantity has been cast ashore. If he had been here I should not have ventured to effect this transformation in your appearance until to-morrow. Are you a good rider, señor?"

"No, indeed," Stephen replied, "I have had no opportunities for practice."

"It does not matter much," Don Filippo said; "I daresay you will be a good rider at the end of our journey, and your not being so at present will afford me an excuse for not making fatiguing journeys; so all is for the best, you see."

CHAPTER XV

FRIENDS IN NEED.

DON FILIPPO did all in his power to make the journey a pleasant one for Stephen. They travelled on an average about twenty-four miles a day, twelve in the morning soon after sunrise and as much in the cool of the evening. During the heat of the day they halted, sometimes in the shade of a grove, sometimes at the hacienda where they breakfasted. The young officer chatted freely to Stephen about himself and his life, and as they lay in the shade during the long hours of the heat, Stephen related his own adventures on his first cruise, and in reply to questions of the Spaniard, repeated to him what he had heard from his father of Cochrane's exploits. Don Filippo treated him in every way as a friend and an equal, and no one who saw them together would have dreamt that he was a prisoner. Even at night no guard was placed at the door of his chamber, the Spaniard having absolute faith in the honour of an English officer. The journey occupied nearly three weeks, by the end of which time Stephen was perfectly at home on horseback. As they approached Callao Don Filippo's gaiety deserted him.

"I do not conceal from you, Don Estevan, that I am anxious about you, very anxious. You can hardly understand the deep and bitter hostility that has been excited in the minds of my countrymen by the doings of your admiral. Our hold on Peru when you arrived here was absolute, and it was morally certain that, with the aid of the ships and men on their way out, we should have very soon recaptured Chili again. All that has changed. Our armies have been defeated, our ships captured by inferior forces, our prestige destroyed; we find ourselves insulted in our ports, our ships cut out from under our guns, the Peruvians ready at any moment to revolt, our flag almost swept from the Pacific, and with every prospect that the broad dominions won for Spain by Pizarro and Cortez will be wrested from us. You can hardly imagine the wrath and humiliation of every Spaniard at the misfortunes that have fallen upon us, the more so that these misfortunes have been inflicted by a naval force that we deemed absolutely contemptible.

"All this is due to Admiral Cochrane and his English officers. In the next place, in addition to the political hate there is the religious one. It is by heretics that we have been defeated, as we were defeated centuries ago by your people and the Dutch. You know how great is the power that the priests wield. We have still the Inquisition among us, and though its power in Spain is comparatively slight, the institution still flourishes on this side of the Atlantic. All this makes me anxious for you. No doubt your admiral would exchange some of his prisoners for you, or might, did he learn it, retaliate upon them for any ill-treatment dealt to you, but you see he may never get to know in time. He may hear that the ship in which you sailed was lost, but he may suppose that all hands were lost with it, for the four Chilian sailors were captured an hour or two after you were, and were at once shot. I am sorry now that I undertook this journey. We have been friends and comrades since we started, and I cannot bear the thought that any evil should befall you. You have an absolute right to good treatment, for your admiral has always treated his prisoners with the greatest kindness and consideration, but I regret to say that in the present state of the feelings of the Spaniards I am not certain that such treatment will be meted out to you."

"We must hope for the best, Don Filippo," Stephen replied. "I do not blind myself to the fact that my position is not free from danger, but I confide in the honour of your countrymen."

"Unhappily," the young officer said gloomily, "the ideas of honour on this side of the Atlantic differ materially from those in the old country. It has been so ever since we set foot in this country. Acts of treachery have been performed by men who at home would shrink from any deed that savoured of dishonour; and although even here one Spaniard would not transgress the code towards another, there are too many who feel no scruples whatever as to any course that they may pursue towards one of another race and another religion."

Stephen nodded.

"I understand that, Don Filippo, and I own that, while I have no great fear of ill-treatment on the part of the military and civil authorities, I feel that should I fall into the hands of the Inquisition my chance would be a slight one. From what I have heard I know that its power is so great that even the most powerful of the civil authorities have to give way to it. Of course, being a British subject, they have no shadow of right to meddle with me, and if they do so and it becomes known in England, it will be a very serious matter; but my fate might never be known, and even did it come to the admiral's ears that I had been brought a prisoner here, any application on his part might be met by a statement that I had been shot while attempting to escape, or that I died of fever in prison, and he would never be able to obtain any proof to the contrary."

"I am but too well aware of it," the young Spaniard replied. "Men are constantly missing—not military men, but merchants, land-owners, and others who have been known to entertain liberal opinions. No one knows what has become of them. No one dares to make inquiry. I tell you, señor, that I, a Spaniard, acknowledge that the state of affairs here is detestable, and I am not surprised at the efforts of the colonies to break away from us. Even in the middle ages in Spain priestly tyranny was never carried to a greater point than still prevails here. We have been here for centuries, and what have we done for the countries under our sway? So far from enriching, we have impoverished them. The great proportion of the population are little more than slaves, and we are hated as bitterly as Cortez was hated by the Mexicans when he overthrew the empire of Montezuma. It is three years since I came out here full of enthusiasm, and eager to bear a part in putting down the rebellion of Chili. Now I feel that Chili was more than justified, and that ere long we shall lose all the possessions that the swords of our ancestors won for us, and which were regarded with so much natural pride by Spaniards; and the worst of it is, that it is the outcome of our own work, our own oppression and misgovernment. Were I to speak like this in public, not even the influence of my two uncles could save me. I too should disappear and be heard of no more. I have been thinking," he went on after a few minutes' silence, "for the last two or three days whether it would not be better for me to give you back your parole and to suffer you to escape. Of course I should be blamed, but the offence would not be a tithe of the gravity of that of speaking as I have just spoken to you."

"I would not think of such a thing, Don Filippo," Stephen replied warmly. "I would not take my freedom at the cost of involving in my trouble one who has behaved so kindly to me. I have still a great hope that everything will turn out well, and that I shall be exchanged for some officer in the admiral's hands. He is sure to hear of my being at Callao, for his last letter said that many deserters were coming in, and from some of these he is likely to learn that I am a prisoner; and in that case he would not, I am sure, lose a day in sending in a flag of truce with a request for my exchange, and a notice that if this was refused he would quickly follow it by retributive measures if any harm befell me."

The Spaniard did not reply. He felt sure that every pains would be taken by the authorities to prevent the news of his companion's capture becoming public; and his uncle, on appointing him Stephen's escort, had laid strict injunctions on him to say nothing of the matter on his arrival at Callao until he had delivered his prisoner over to the authorities, and had received permission from them to speak of it. On the following day they entered the town. As they rode to the house of the military governor no one paid any heed to their passage; it was but two young officers returning perhaps from Lima or from some other station. On reaching the governor Filippo went up alone to make his report, leaving Stephen in charge of the soldiers. He was absent half an hour.

"I have said all I could for you," he said gloomily on his return. "The governor is one of the old type, obstinate, bigoted, and arrogant. I have not been all this time with him; in fact only a few minutes. He dismissed all I had to say with a wave of the hand:

"'You will take the prisoner, Lieutenant Conchas, to the military prison, and hand him over to the governor there. Until you hear further you will maintain an absolute silence as to his arrival here, and will simply state that you are here on a short leave.'

"I had nothing to do but to bow and retire, but if possible I will send a message to your admiral that you are here. At present, however, that is out of the question; for while I was waiting in the anteroom I learned that the blockading fleet has sailed away, and that there is no news whatever as to the direction which it has taken. It is very unfortunate, but you may be assured that, as soon as it returns, I will somehow or other communicate with the admiral."

Remounting they rode to the prison. They said good-bye to each other before they reached its door, for, as Filippo said, it would be better that he should part ceremoniously.

"We must not show any affection for each other," he said, "or, should the English admiral learn that you are here, or should you manage to make your escape, suspicion would at once light upon me. Believe me, Don Estevan, I shall do all in my power to aid you."

The parting inside was therefore brief. Don Filippo handed Stephen over to the chief official of the prison, saying that the orders of the governor were, that he was to be kept apart from all other prisoners and allowed no communication with anyone.

"Adieu, señor. I trust that you have had no cause to complain of your treatment during your journey hither."

"None whatever," Stephen said gravely. "You have treated me with the courtesy that an officer has a right to expect at the hands of his captors."

The young Spaniard bowed, saluted the prison officer, and left without another word. The governor struck a bell, and on an assistant entering he gave Stephen into his charge. "Place him in the end cell of the long corridor," he said. "If it is occupied at present, remove whoever is there to another cell. This prisoner is to hold no communication with others, and an extra strict watch must be kept on him. He is one of the heretic officers of the Chilian fleet, and will want looking after closely."

The cell happened to be untenanted, and Stephen was at once conducted there. It was apparently intended as a place of confinement for officers who had fallen into disgrace. It was some twelve feet square, and contained a table and a chair. From the window, which was very closely barred, a view of the bay could be obtained, and Stephen felt that his quarters were better than he had expected. As soon as he was alone he examined the apartment more closely. Looking down as well as he could between the bars he could see the top of a wall some twenty yards away, and decided that a courtyard surrounded the building, so that even could he find any means of descending from his window it would be necessary afterwards for him to climb this wall. At present, however, he had no idea of trying to escape. To do so would, were he caught, greatly prejudice his case, and might be used as an excuse for his instant execution. However, he concluded that if he could loosen the bars it would be as well to do so without loss of time, as it might be necessary to make the attempt at very short notice.

Upon examining the bars he found that they were so strongly built into the wall that it would be a task demanding a very long time to execute. Turning from this he examined the door. The framework was massive, and he had noticed as he had entered that it was fastened outside by two heavy iron bolts. "There is not much to be done that way," he said. "Now I must wait to see how my meals are brought in. The only possible way that I can think of is that of overpowering the warder and getting out in his clothes. I don't suppose that there is much order or discipline in a Spanish prison, and if I could once get down into the yard after dark, I might walk quietly out if there is a gate open, or climb that wall if there isn't."

That evening his supper was brought in by the warder into whose charge he had been given. He was accompanied by another armed with sword and musket.

"Two of them," Stephen said to himself, as, after retiring without having spoken a word, his guards closed and bolted the door behind them. "I think I could manage them at a pinch. It seems to me that an escape is possible, but the question is what should I do with myself when I got out. If the fleet had been still off the town I might have made along the shore, stolen a boat, and rowed out; but as it has gone there is nothing to be done that way. A journey on foot from here to the frontier and down through Chili would be a tremendous affair. I should be pursued, and as it would be guessed that I had gone that way, orders would be sent to every town and village to look after me, and a man in the dress of a Spanish officer on foot would be remarked by every soul I met."

Three days passed without incident, but at dinner-time on the fourth he thought that the warder, as he placed the hunch of bread on the table, gave him a significant glance. As soon as the door was closed he seized the bread and pulled it to pieces. Inside was a tiny pellet of paper. He opened and smoothed it out. In a female hand was written in tiny characters: "*The Inquisition has demanded you. You will be handed over to-morrow. If it be possible, make an escape to-night. If you can do so, turn to your right from the front of the prison, take the second street on the left, and knock three times on the fifth door on the right-hand side. A friend will be awaiting you. If you cannot escape, hope still. We will try other means. Destroy this when read.*"

Stephen read it through three or four times to be sure that

he had his instructions by heart, then he put the paper into his mouth, chewed it up and swallowed it.

"It must be done when they bring in my supper," he said to himself. "I know that I am the last to be served in this corridor, for I can hear them stop at the door next to me before they come here. That is an advantage, as they would go straight down the corridor on leaving me. The first thing is to tear up these two rugs into strips, and make ropes for binding them. Of course I shall have to tackle the soldier first. The warder has evidently been bribed and he will make no resistance. When I have once overpowered the soldier, I may get some hints from the other as to which is my best way of getting out of this. Of course this is Filippo's doing. What a good fellow he is to run such a risk! There is one thing, if I once get fairly out of the cell I will be killed rather than be taken and handed over to the Inquisition."

Although he had not once been visited between meals, he thought it prudent not to begin the work of making his rope until the sun was getting low. When it did so he tore up the blankets, twisted and knotted together the strips, and then sat down to await the coming of the jailers. He had already tried to wrench off one of the legs of the table, but it was too heavy and strongly made for him to succeed. He then thought of using the chair, but he could not feel certain of stunning the soldier with the first blow, and the latter might fire off his musket, or shout so loudly as to give the alarm; he therefore determined to trust to his hands alone. He knew that he was greatly superior in strength to any of the little Spanish soldiers, and that with the advantage of surprise he ought to be able to succeed without noise.

About an hour after it became dark he heard the footsteps come to the next cell, then he took his place close against the wall by the side of his door and waited.

As the bolts were drawn back he took a deep breath. The warder as usual came in first, followed closely by the armed guard. As the latter entered, Stephen sprang upon him, and his hands closed upon the man's throat with so fierce a grip that the musket fell instantly from the fellow's hands. Without losing his grasp in the slightest Stephen whirled him round and threw him against the warder, whom the shock brought to the ground, Stephen hurling the already almost insensible soldier upon him. Seizing the musket he brought the butt end down upon the soldier's head with a force amply sufficient to stun him; then he rolled him off the warder's body and helped the latter to his feet.

"I was obliged to be rough with you," he said, "in order that that fellow when he comes to his senses may confirm your story that you were at once knocked down. Of course I shall tie and gag you both."

"Yes, and before you go you had better give me a tap with that musket. You need not hit me quite so hard as you did him, but it must be hard enough to make a good bump. You needn't be afraid of hurting me. I am well paid for anything that may happen, though indeed I did not expect it to come like this."

"In the first place I am going to take your clothes," Stephen said. "You can say that you were insensible when I stripped you; but first I want you to tell me how I can get out."

"You won't have much difficulty about that," the man replied. "When we have taken round supper our work is done for the night, and half of us are free to go out and spend the evening. You turn down the first staircase you come to, follow it to the bottom, then take the corridor to the right and go on until you come to an open door. Two soldiers will be standing there on sentry, but they ask no questions of the warders. You had better wait when you get in sight of the door till you see that no one else is going out, or it might be noticed that you were a stranger and questions might be asked you. Now you had better lose no time, or the others may be out before you get there, and the door be shut."

As he spoke he was taking off his uniform, which consisted of a dark jacket, trousers, and cap, and a brown belt from which hung a sword. Stephen put them on, then tightly bound the insensible man, whose lungs were now playing, stuffed a portion of the rug into his mouth and fastened it there with a strip tied at the back of the head. Then he similarly bound and gagged the warder, and then gave him a heavy blow on the head, feeling that it was best for the man himself that it should be a severe one. Then he took the sentry's musket and hid it under the bed, so that, if by any chance he managed to free himself of his bonds, he could not fire it to give the alarm. Then putting the cap on his head Stephen went out, bolted the door, and proceeded down the corridor. Following the instructions that had been given him he made his way towards the door. Just as he neared it he saw a group of three or four warders going out together, and waiting for a moment till they had disappeared boldly followed them, and passed between the sentries into the open air. So rapidly and easily had the escape been managed that he could scarcely believe that he had escaped from the hands of the military authorities, still less from the fate that would have awaited him had he fallen into the hands of the Inquisition. Not knowing which was the front of the building, he followed the lane, upon which the side door opened, to its end, and then finding that he was now at the rear of the prison he returned; and gaining the street in which was the main entrance, followed out his instructions and tapped three times at the door of the house indicated. There was a little pause and then it was opened a short distance.

"Is it you, señor?" a female voice asked.

"It is the man whom you are, I believe, expecting, and who received your message."

With an exclamation of gladness the woman opened the door and, as he entered, closed it behind him.

"Follow me, señor," she said; "there is nothing in the passage to run against."

A few steps further Stephen heard a door open, a flood of light poured into the passage, and his guide said "Quick!" He entered and she closed the door behind him.

"Thanks to the saints that you have escaped, señor!" a voice said. "It seemed to us well-nigh impossible that you could do so; but, knowing how brave and enterprising you English are, Filippo said that he had great faith that you might manage it."

Stephen now saw that the speaker was a young and very pretty girl.

"I am speaking to the Señorita Inez Conchas," he said respectfully. "How can I thank you and Don Filippo sufficiently for your action in my behalf. You have saved my life, for assuredly had I not known that I should be handed over to the Inquisition no thought of making my escape to-night would have entered my mind."

"It is all Filippo's doing," she said. "He made me write the letter, and got me to come here because he could not come himself,—I and my old nurse with me. She is sitting in the front room on watch; it was she who opened the door to you. You see, we could not be sure whether the note would reach you; the man whom we bribed might have turned traitor and given it to the governor. My nurse arranged it; for it would never have done for Filippo to have appeared in the matter, and I am so well known in the place that it would have been very dangerous. However, we hoped that all would be well, for half the man's bribe was not to be paid to him until you were free. However, we placed her at the corner of the street this afternoon in order to watch if anyone came to this house or stopped to look at it earnestly. The people are away in the country, and my nurse, who knew the woman who is left in charge here, got her to lend her the key until to-morrow morning, on some excuse or other. Filippo brought me round just before dark; there is an entertainment to-night at the Viceroy's, and he had to be there. Indeed, it was the best place he could be, as no suspicion can now fall upon him of having aided in your escape. How did you manage it, señor?"

Stephen briefly related how it had been brought about.

"That was well done indeed!" the girl said, clapping her hands merrily. "I scarce thought that it could be your knock when you came, for we had agreed that if you did manage to make your escape it would not be until very late, and it seemed impossible that you could have got out so early. However, that is all the better, as you will now have a long start. Now, señor, the first thing for you to do will be to put on the disguise Filippo has prepared for you in that bag on the table. Here is a piece of burnt cork for darkening your eyebrows and eyelashes, and a false moustache that will quite change your appearance. I will go into the next room with nurse; when you are dressed you can call, and I will come back."

As soon as he was alone Stephen opened the bag and drew out an attire such as would be worn by a respectable Peruvian merchant. This he put on, darkened his eyebrows, and stuck on the moustache, and acknowledged when he viewed himself in a small mirror that he should not have known himself. On his opening the door the girl came in from the other room again.

"We have talked over, Filippo and I, the way you had best go, and we both agree that the journey south would be altogether too dangerous. It will naturally be supposed that you have gone that way, and the news will be sent down by horsemen, so that the troops and the authorities will be on the look-out for you everywhere. We both think that, although the journey is very long and toilsome, your best plan will be to ride straight inland, cross the Andes, and come down into Brazil. You are not likely to be questioned on that line, which no one would imagine that you would be likely to take. You may meet with adventures on the way, but you English people are fond of adventures. At any rate that plan will be safer for you, and indeed for us."

"Why for you, señorita?"

"If you were to be captured," she said, "you would be questioned as to who aided you, and there are means in these prisons by which they can wring the truth from the strongest and bravest. There are tortures, señor, that flesh and blood could not withstand."

"You are right, Donna Inez," Stephen said gravely. "For myself I should be ready to run the risk of getting through to the south, but what you have said decides me. I would die rather than say a word that could betray you and your cousin. But no one can say what one would do under fiendish tortures; therefore I at once accept your plan."

"That is right," the girl said. "Filippo said that he was sure that for our sake you would consent to it. Now for your instructions. Nurse will, in the first place, take me home; then she will return here; she will be back in half an hour. She will take away with her the things that you have worn, and will to-night cut them up and burn them, so that no trace may remain of your visit here. When she returns she will guide you through the town. At a cottage a quarter of a mile outside a muleteer with two animals is awaiting you; he does not know who you are, but believes you to be a Brazilian who has been on this side of the continent for some years, chiefly in Chili, and so speak that language, and now, being afraid to proceed by water, are about to return by the passes. How far you will be able to get him to accompany you I cannot say, but at present he has promised to take you over the Andes. The best course to take then you can talk over with the muleteer. You will find many details of the various routes in a letter Filippo has given him for you. And now adieu, señor. We shall think of you often, and I shall pray for your safe return to your friends. Possibly we may meet again some day, for Filippo has a powerful relation who, it is expected, may some day be the Spanish ambassador in London, and he says that he shall try and get him to take him on his staff."

"I should indeed be glad if it could be so, señorita. I shall to the end of my life entertain the liveliest feelings of gratitude to you and Don Filippo for your kindness. Have you a pencil and paper?"

The girl pointed to the table, on which stood writing materials. Stephen wrote his father's address upon it and handed it to her.

"That is my address in England," he said. "I pray you, when you return to Spain, to beg Don Filippo to write to me there, and I am sure to get it sooner or later. Directly I receive his letter I shall make a point of taking a passage for Spain in order to thank you more fully and heartily than I can now do. It would be dangerous were I to write to you here."

She nodded. "Adieu, señor."

"Adieu, señorita. May your life with Don Filippo be as happy as you both deserve!"

He put the hand she gave him to his lips. A minute later she and her nurse left the house, and Stephen remained wondering over the events that had happened.

"It is certainly the best plan," he said to himself. " I daresay there will be lots of hardships to go through, but it will be a glorious trip. Fancy going down the Amazon from almost its source to the sea! The señorita said nothing about money, but Filippo has shown himself so thoughtful in every other way that I have no doubt he has not forgotten that for such a journey some money at least will be required. Happily I am now in a position to pay anything he may advance me, so I need not scruple to take it. He told me that his father was very rich, but that money was very little good to him in Peru, and that he had a very handsome allowance, but no means whatever of spending it, especially in such a place as San Carlos. I will write him a line or two now, and will give it to the old woman after I have read his letter."

He sat down and wrote a note expressive of his warmest gratitude to Filippo, and concluded: "*In other matters too I am deeply your debtor, but this fortunately I can, as I told you, discharge far more easily than I can my debt of gratitude. As soon as I reach England I will pay in the amount to a house having connections in Spain, and order them to have it placed to your account with some good firm there, with instructions to write to you saying that they hold it payable to your order. My name will not be mentioned, so that in case of any accident the money will not be traceable to me. My other and greater debt must for ever remain unpaid, but to the end of my life I shall remain the debtor of you and Donna Inez. Wishing you both a long life and every happiness together, I remain always your grateful friend.*"

He folded the letter up and put it into his pocket, and then waited until he heard the three knocks on the door. Stephen blew out the candle, went along the passage to the front door, opened it, and went out. Without a word the old woman turned and walked along the street. He followed at a short distance, and was presently in a busy thoroughfare. Twenty minutes' walking took them beyond the town, and they presently stopped at a cottage where a candle was burning in the window.

"This is the house, señor," she said, speaking for the first time.

She went up to the door and tapped at it. It was opened by a man in the attire of a muleteer.

"This is the señor who will accompany you, Gomez," she said. "Now, señor, my work is done." And she turned to go.

"Wait a moment," he said. "Gomez has a letter for me, and I want to read it before I give you a note that I wish you to take back and to hand to Donna Inez."

"Here is the letter, señor," the muleteer said.

Stephen took it to the light and opened it. It was a long one, but he skipped the first part, which was full of directions and hints for the journey. Running his eye down it fell upon some figures, and he read: "*Gomez will hand you a bag containing eight hundred dollars. This, I have no doubt, will be sufficient for your journey down the Amazon and to pay your passage-money home. You are heartily welcome to it. Some day, if it please you, you can pay me back; but if aught befalls you on your way down do not let the thought of this paltry debt trouble you in any way. I know not whether this will ever reach your hands, but pray that it may do so, and that I may have the satisfaction of knowing that Inez and I have had some part in saving the life of a brave English gentleman.*" Then with a few more words of adieu the letter closed.

Stephen had already felt that there was some money in the pockets of his trousers, and he now handed his letter to the old woman and pulled out some gold.

"No," she said, drawing back; "I would die to please my young mistress, but not one penny would I touch from the hand of a foreign heretic."

A minute later and she was gone. The muleteer laughed at her outbreak. "Well, well," he said, "how people differ; now, for my part, when I receive payment for the work of my mules I care not in the least whether it comes from a heretic's pockets or those of a good Catholic. But I did not know that you Brazilians were heretics, señor."

"As a rule we are not," Stephen said, "but my case is an exception; I will tell you more about it on the journey. Callao is not the town where it is safe to be a heretic."

"No, indeed," the muleteer said with a laugh; "however, it is no business of mine, señor. A gentleman whose name I know not, but to whom I was recommended by a cousin of mine, who is a relation of the old woman who has just left us, made a bargain with me to take you to the Amazon or a river running into it. He agreed to give me my own terms. He paid me a third of the money in advance, and said that you would pay me the remainder at the end of the journey. He said that you were a Brazilian, and spoke Chilian better than our tongue; though, indeed, they are so much alike that one passes as well as the other, or did till this war began. That account of you may be true or it may not, it is no business whatever of mine. A man says to me, I want you to carry a bag of salt to such a place. I agree as to the terms, and it is no matter to me whether the sack contains salt or sand as long as the weight is the same. Your things all came up here to-day, señor—your wallet, and your sword, and a brace of pistols, a rifle and a bird gun. You will find everything right. I understood that it was your wish, for some reason which was again no business of mine, to start as soon as you arrived, and I have three mules standing saddled in the stable if you are ready to start."

"I should certainly be glad to do so, Gomez. I have, as you say, my reasons for wanting to be off as soon as possible."

Accordingly the three mules were at once brought round, the baggage divided between them, and five minutes later, after blowing out the candle and locking the door behind him, the muleteer mounted and rode off with Stephen.

CHAPTER XVI.

AN INDIAN GUIDE.

"OF course we must go through Lima," Stephen said as they started.

"Assuredly, señor, the roads over the passes all start from there, and it would take us a long circuit to avoid the town."

"Oh, there is no occasion to avoid it," Stephen said. "It is about five miles, is it not?"

"That is the distance; but, as the road ascends a good deal, we generally count it as six. It is a fine city Lima, and I hope that it will not be very long before we shall be able to enjoy it without the presence of the Spaniards; we think they cannot remain here much longer. If the Chilian army would but move from the sea-coast the whole country would be up in arms. We would rather have done without the Chilians if we could, for there has never been any great friendship between them and the Peruvians. I do not say between them and us, for I am almost as much Chilian as Peruvian, seeing that I was born within half a mile of the frontier and high up in the hills. But there is more money to be made here. In the first place, the Peruvians have more towns beyond the passes, and there is more traffic; and in the next place, in Chili most men are ready to work if there is money to be made, whereas most of the Peruvians are too lazy to pick up gold if it lay at their feet. Most men in our business come from the hills."

"And why don't the Peruvians and Chilians like each other?"

"Who can tell. The Chilians have a colder climate, and the people for the most part came from the north of Spain; they are hardier and more active; then, too, they are not so strict in church matters, and here they call them heretics, and a Peruvian hates a heretic a great deal worse than he does the father of all evil. We muleteers pray to the saints for protection on our journeys, and before we start on a long expedition burn a few candles at the shrine of our patron saint, and we never pass a shrine or a wayside cross without making a prayer; but we don't concern ourselves with other people's religion; that is their business, not ours. But that is not so with the Spaniards, and the Peruvians are just as bad. You may kill a man in a knife fight and no one cares much about it. But if you were to pass a village shrine without raising your sombrero they would be ready to tear you in pieces as a heretic."

"What is the country like when you once get over the mountains?"

"It is a tree country and generally flat. Here you see the hillsides are mostly bare; but on the other side of the ranges of mountains—for there are two chains—the forest grows almost to the top, and, as I have heard, they extend thousands of miles over the country beyond. In these great forests there are swamps and rivers, great rivers. Very few white men know where they rise or how they go, but they all run into the largest of them all, which, when it gets near the sea, is called the Amazon, but which has many names at different points of its course. They say that some of these rivers have many rapids and falls, and on almost all of them there are Indians who are more dangerous still; some of them they say eat men who fall into their hands.

"It is a terrible journey that you are undertaking, señor.

One thing is certain, you must take with you some man of courage and resolution, one who at least knows something of the country. No man knows much, but there are men, Indians, who make it their business either to trade or to guide traders. Of course they never go very far, but they have gone far enough to know much of the nature of the dangers and difficulties."

"Do you think that you would be able to find me such a man?"

"There are many," the muleteer said; "but it is not everyone that can be trusted. I know of one man who, if he happened to be at home and disengaged, would suit you well if he would undertake such a journey. He would go if anyone would, for no dangers terrify him, and he has made, before now, perilous expeditions with officers and others who have sought to discover the sources of the rivers. He lives in a village but a few miles from the summit of the pass, and if you have not as yet decided on your route, he will at any rate, if he cannot go himself, give you better advice than you can obtain from anyone else I know of."

They passed through the city of Lima unnoticed. There were still numbers of people in the streets, and the sound of musical instruments came from the open windows. Parties of ladies stood on the balconies and were enjoying the coolness of the night air, and it was evident that Lima had no thoughts of going to bed for a long time yet.

"You would hardly see a soul in the streets while the sun is high," the muleteer said upon Stephen remarking on the number of people still about. "The whole town goes to sleep from eleven to four or five, the shops are all closed, and save on a business of life or death no one would think of going out. About six the day really begins, and goes on until one in the morning; then people sleep till five or six, and for a time the streets are busy; the marketing is done then, the ladies all go to early mass, the troops do their exercises; by nine the streets begin to thin, and by ten they are deserted."

Stephen was much struck with the appearance of the town, which had been laid out with great care, the streets running at right angles to each other, and being all precisely the same width, dividing the town into regular blocks. It contained at that time some 70,000 inhabitants. He was surprised at the want of height in the houses, comparatively few of which had more than one story. On remarking on this to the muleteer, the latter said:

"It is because of the earthquakes; nowhere are there such bad earthquakes as here. If it were not for that Lima would be perfect. The country round is very fertile, there is an abundance of pure water, the climate is healthy, and it lies 600 feet above the sea. But the earthquakes are terrible, there has not been a bad one lately, but it might come at any time. Every twenty or thirty years there is a very bad one. The worst were those of 1687 and 1746; the first destroyed every house in Lima, and the second was almost as bad, but was much worse at Callao. There they not only had the earthquake but a tumult of waves such as never was before seen. The sea went right over the town, and almost every soul there, and at other towns along the coast, perished. There were twenty-three ships in the harbour at Callao, nineteen of these were sunk and the other four carried half a mile inland. Since then there has been nothing like that, but the Indians say that we may expect another before long. I don't know what they go by, but people say that they predicted the others long before they came. Have you ever felt an earthquake, señor?"

"No, there was a very slight shock when I was at Valparaiso, but it was not much more than the rumble a heavy wagon makes in the street, and did no damage whatever."

"I have never felt a great earthquake," the muleteer said, "but I have felt little ones. The animals always know when they are coming, and when I see the mules uneasy and apprehensive, I always choose some level spot where there is no fear of rocks coming rolling down on us, and halt there. The first shock may be so slight that one hardly feels it, but the mules know all about it. They straddle their legs and brace themselves up or else lie down on the ground. When I see them do that I know that the next shock is going to be a smart one, and I lie down too. It is nothing when you are out in the country, but in the towns it is terrible. People rush out into the streets screaming with fear. If they are near a church they make for that; if not, they kneel down in the streets, where they are pretty safe, the houses being so low and mostly thatched. I have never seen one severe enough to bring the houses down, but I have seen them crack, and parapets tumble down, and great pieces peel off the walls. What with the dust, and the screams of the women and children, and the ringing of all the church bells, it is enough to shake a man's courage I can tell you."

After proceeding some ten miles farther, by a road always ascending and often steep, a halt was made. The muleteer removed the valises and packs, gave a double handful of corn to each animal, and then, hobbling them, allowed them to wander about to pick up what they could. He and Stephen partook of some of the food they had brought with them, and then wrapping themselves in their cloaks lay down for a few hours' sleep. At daylight the journey was renewed. So they travelled on, halting for five or six hours in the heat of the day, and riding in the morning early, and late on into the evening. The climate, however, scarcely necessitated the mid-day halt, and at night they were glad to wrap themselves in a blanket in addition to the cloak. At last the summit of the pass was reached. In front of them rose another chain of mountains almost as lofty as that which they had climbed. Between those great ranges lay a plain varying in width. Several towns and small villages were visible.

"That is Jauja to the right," the muleteer said, "and that is Pasco to the left; they are both large towns. They do not look so very far apart from here. But the air of the mountains is so clear it is difficult to judge distances. You would not take them to be much more than twenty miles from us; they are nearly three times as far, and are fully eighty miles apart."

"Where does the guide of whom you spoke live?"

"It is some twenty miles down; it is where the roads from the two towns fall into this pass. It is convenient for him, because he is in the track of merchants going either north or south."

No stay was made on the top of the pass, for the wind was strong and piercing. There were snow-covered peaks on either hand, and so they hurried onwards, although they had already done a long morning's march. Five miles farther they halted in a wood, and although they had already made a descent of some thousand feet they were glad to light a fire. On the following day they halted early at a solitary hut standing at the junction of two roads.

"Bravo!" the muleteer said as the door opened and a man came out at the sound of the mules' feet, "here is Pita himself. I thought we should find him, for, since the war began, trade has gone off greatly, and he was likely to be out of employment. Well met, Pita; I was in hopes that I should find you here, for the señor has need of the services of a bold fellow like yourself."

"Enter, señor," the Indian said gravely, lifting his sombrero, for he was dressed in Peruvian fashion. "It is long since I have seen you, Gomez."

"Yes, a full year," the muleteer replied; "it was at Cuzco, and you were just starting with a party of traders."

The hut contained little furniture, but there was a pile of skins, the proceeds of the Indian's hunting since his return from his last expedition. He took off three or four of them, threw them on the ground, and motioned Stephen to take a seat while he busied himself in preparing a meal. Nothing was said of business until this was served. When it was finished the Indian rolled three cigars, and when these were lighted, and three cups of excellent coffee made, Pita said:

"Now, señor, in what way can I serve you?"

"I want to go down the Amazon to the coast."

"It is a long journey, long and difficult; I have never been so far. The farthest point that I have reached has been Barra, where the Madeira falls into the Solimoes."

"That is the Amazon," Gomez explained. "It is called the Marañon here in Peru, but from the frontier it is known as the Solimoes."

"As far as the frontier," Pita went on, "there are no great difficulties, and there are many towns on the banks; beyond that to Barra there are but one or two villages. The Mozon begins at Llata, some two hundred miles north of this. The road is a good one, for we pass through Pasco and Huanuco; there you can take boat, which will carry you as far as the frontier, and beyond that you will have to take another, for no Peruvians will venture so far from here."

"The señor wishes to escape towns," Gomez said. "He has no papers, and wishes to escape questioning. You know what Spanish authorities are, and how suspiciously they view the passage of a stranger. Could you not take him down the Madeira?"

"It is a terrible journey," the Indian said. "Very few white men have ever descended the river. There are bad falls and bad Indians. I myself have never gone down it more than a few hundred miles. It would need much courage, señor, and even then things might turn out badly. I would not undertake such a journey single-handed, though with a good comrade I might adventure it. You could not get a boat unless you bought one, and, as a rule, men travel on light rafts, as these are safer on the rapids than boats. That way has the advantage of being a good deal shorter than going round by the Marañon, but the difficulties and dangers are very much greater."

"Do you love the Spaniards?" Stephen asked.

The Indian's face darkened.

"They have been the destroyers of our race," he said; "the oppressors of our country. I hate them with all my heart."

"Then I may tell you at once," Stephen said, "that I am an Englishman. I am one of the officers of the English admiral who commands the fleet that has destroyed their war-ships and is blockading their towns. I was wrecked on the Peruvian coast and thrown into prison. They were about to hand me over to the Inquisition as a heretic when I escaped, so you can understand the danger that I should run in passing through any of their towns. I speak, as you hear, the Chilian dialect, therefore I would be detected as a stranger at once, and as I could give no satisfactory reply to questions, and have no papers, I should at once be seized and sent back again to Callao."

The Indian nodded gravely. He had heard of the misfortunes that had befallen the Spaniards, and knew that the fleet that had inflicted such damage upon them was commanded by an Englishman.

"The señor is provided with money," Gomez said. "I did not myself know that he was an Englishman, though I suspected from the manner in which I was hired that he had trouble with the Spaniards."

"I would have told you so, Gomez," Stephen said, "but I thought it better that you should not know, so that if I were seized by the Spaniards you could declare that you were wholly ignorant of my being an Englishman, and believed that I was only a trader travelling on business."

"They would not have believed me," Gomez laughed. "You had no goods with you, and your speech showed that you were not a Peruvian. I have often wondered on the way to what nation you belonged, and how it was that one so young could be ready to undertake so desperate an enterprise as you proposed; but now that I know you are an officer under the terrible English admiral I can well understand it."

"I would do much," Pita said, "for any enemy of the Spaniards; and more for this reason than for the sake of money. I am ready to undertake to do my best to take you in safety to Barra; beyond that I would not go. The river below that is, as I hear, quite open, and you could journey down without difficulty save such as you would meet with from the Portuguese authorities; but the distance would be too great for me to return. Even from Barra it would be a journey fully two thousand miles home again."

"What would be your terms for taking me to Barra?"

"I do not say that I would take you there, señor, I only say that I would try and do so. As I tell you, I have never journeyed far down the Madeira myself, and know not what the difficulties may be. For that reason I shall want half the money paid to me when we reach Cuzco, near which live my wife and family, and I must leave this with them in case I never return. I will think over what pay I shall require for myself and my comrade. It is not a matter upon which one can decide at a word."

"I can quite understand that, Pita. I must of course keep sufficient in hand to pay my expenses down to Para, where

I can doubtless obtain a passage by an English ship. But I am ready to pay any sum you may ask that is within my means. Now, Gomez, we had better go out and look to the mules, and leave Pita to himself to think the matter over."

"The Indian will not overcharge you," Gomez said when they were outside the hut; "the pay of these men is small. They value their lives lightly, and when, like Pita, they once take to the life of a guide, either to those who are searching for mines or to traders, they never settle down. They are proud of the confidence placed in them, and of their own skill as guides, and so long as they can earn enough to keep their families during their absence—and a very little suffices for that—they are contented."

"I suppose there are mines to be discovered yet, Gomez?"

"Assuredly there are," the muleteer said confidently. "The Spaniards have worked rich mines ever since they came here, but great as is the treasure that they have taken away, it is still insignificant compared with the store of gold among the Incas when they came here. Every Peruvian on this side of the Andes dreams of gold, and there are thousands of men who, as soon as they earn enough money to buy tools and provisions, set off to search for gold-mines or buried treasure. It is certain that the Incas buried a vast quantity of their treasure rather than see it fall into the hands of the Spaniards, and it has never been discovered. It is generally believed that the secret of the hiding-place is known to Indians, who have handed down the secret from father to son. This may be true or it may not. So many thousands of Indians have either been killed by the Spaniards or have died in their mines, that it may well be that all who knew the secret died centuries ago. But I do not say that it may not be known to some of them now; if so, it is more likely that these may be among the tribes beyond the boundaries of Peru. There are vast tracts there where neither Spaniards nor Portuguese have penetrated. The whole country is one great forest, or, in some places, one great desert.

"The Indians of Peru have become, for the most part, an idle, shiftless race. Centuries of slavery have broken their spirit altogether, and had the secret been known to many of them, it would have been wrung from them long since, especially as all are now Catholics and go to confession, and would never be able to keep such a secret from leaking out. It is true that there are little Indian villages among the mountains where the people are still almost independent, and here the secret may still be handed down; but I doubt if it will ever be known. Doubtless it is guarded by such terrible oaths that those who know it will never dare to reveal it. Pita has gone, in his time, with a score of expeditions in search of the treasure; most of these thought that they had obtained some clue to it, but nothing was ever discovered, and I doubt whether Pita himself was ever earnest in the search.

"In some respects he is like ourselves, in others he is still an Indian, and has a full share of Indian superstitions, so that his Christianity is no deeper than his skin. He would do his best to guide those who employed him to the neighbourhood where they thought that the treasure was hidden, but I doubt whether he would do anything to assist in their search, or would really try to gather from the Indians any clue as to its whereabouts."

"But, at any rate, the natives could not very well have carried away their gold-mines."

"Not carried them away, señor,—no; and that the Spaniards had such rich mines at first shows that they did learn from the natives—by torture, I daresay—where most of these were situated; but they got more silver than gold, and even now there is gold to be found in the sands of most of the rivers in

South America, so that I think it was from washings more than mines that the Spaniards got their gold. Still, we all think that there must have been rich gold-mines in the times before the Spaniards, and that when the natives saw how villainously their monarch and all his chief men were treated, and how the Spaniards thought of nothing but gold and silver, they may have blocked up the entrances to all their richest mines, and in a few years all signs of the sites would be covered by thick vegetation. You see, señor, these things are talked over whenever a few of us get together, and though there are not many other things that we do know, you will scarcely meet a Peruvian who could not talk with you for hours about the lost treasure and the lost gold-mines of the Incas.

"There are many places that I know of where the sand is rich enough to pay well for washing, but they are all far away from habitations. A man would have to carry his stores and provisions and tools with him; and then, it is hard work, and a Peruvian does not care for hard work. As to the natives, there would be no keeping them at it, they would desert and run away at once; for not only do they hate work, but, above all things, they hate to work for gold. They look upon gold as an accursed thing, which brought about the conquest of the country by the Spaniards, and the centuries of oppression that have befallen their race; and even should a native alight upon a rich spot he would go away and never say a word about it, fearing that if he did, all sorts of trouble would fall upon him."

"Pita is a fine-looking Indian, Gomez."

"Yes, señor; he is a mixture, that is, he is of pure Indian blood, but he belongs to two tribes. His father was a native of one of the villages highest up among the hills. He too was a hunter and guide. In one of his journeys down in the plain country he married the daughter of one of the chiefs of the wild Indians, and Pita was their son. I don't know which tribe it was that his mother belonged to, but I know that they lived in the forests on one of the greater rivers. Pita is not one who talks much of himself, or who talks much at all, but I know that he has the reputation of being one of the most daring hunters and guides in the country, and that he has gone through many adventures while travelling with traders. He has always been trustworthy and faithful to his employers. As he says, he cannot promise to take you safely down the Madeira, but if any man can do it, he will."

Half an hour later they returned to the hut, where the Indian was sitting in precisely the same attitude in which they had left him.

"Well, Pita, have you arrived at a conclusion?" Gomez asked.

"I have thought it over," he said, "and I calculate that it may be a year before I return, and the risk is great. Can the señor afford to pay three hundred and sixty-five dollars? That is for the services of myself and my comrade. He has no wife or family, and will therefore need less pay than I, who will have to leave money behind for mine. The señor will be at no other expense until he arrives at Barra, except for such things as tea and sugar, and any liquor he may wish to put on board at starting. If the señor cannot afford that, I will guide him down along by the foot of the mountains until we can cross over into Chili. It will be an arduous journey, but without perils, and we shall pass through few villages."

" How long will that take, Pita?"

" It would be a long journey, señor. As a bird flies it would be seven or eight hundred miles; but winding round the foot of the hills it would be two thousand."

"I would rather try the other, Pita," Stephen replied; for

the thought of the passage by water through unknown forests, and then down the Amazon, exercised a strong fascination over him, and the idea of a toilsome journey of two thousand miles was the reverse of attractive. The war was, he was sure, nearly over. He might arrive in Chili only to find that the admiral had gone away; and even when he reached the frontier he had another journey to make before he reached Valparaiso, whereas when he arrived at Para he could sail direct for England.

"I could afford to pay you the terms you ask," he went on, "and shall still have enough left to take me from Barra home."

"Then, so be it," the Indian said; "to-morrow we will start for Paucartambo, which lies but a few miles from the Mayutata. We shall pass through Cuzco on our way. You have arms, I see, señor?"

"Yes, and some ammunition, but I shall want a larger supply before we start."

At daybreak next morning they set out, the Indian walking ahead. Once or twice Stephen pushed his mule forward to endeavour to enter into conversation, but he could get but few words from him, and had to drop back to Gomez, who was willing enough to talk.

"It is no use trying to get anything out of Pita, señor. If you can get him in the mood by a camp fire, he may tell you some of his adventures; but the natives are not given to talking overmuch, and Pita, when he is once on his way as guide, will go on without saying a word for hours. I have made several journeys with him, and it is always the same. Of course there is nothing for him to look after here, but it is a sort of habit. I have no doubt that he could tell you how many birds have crossed the road to-day. He has noticed every lizard, could tell you where a mule belonging to the last party has made a false step, how many there were travelling together, and all about them. He takes it all in; and though here it might just as well be left alone, this watchfulness might save your life afterwards."

Day after day they journeyed on. Stephen did not enter Cuzco. As the capital of the Incas he felt an interest in it, but cared little for it as a great Spanish town whose glory had almost departed; and it was not worth running any risk when nothing was to be gained by visiting it. He therefore remained at Pita's Indian hut a few miles away, while Gomez went into the town with the guide to get the stores they required. Pita's comrade returned with them. Stephen was greatly surprised at the man's appearance. Pita himself was, for an Indian, tall; he was spare in frame, but very sinewy; his muscles stood up beneath the brown skin like cords. Hurka was so short that he was almost a dwarf, and, save for his face, he might have been taken for a boy of fourteen. He possessed none of Pita's gravity, but was soon laughing and chatting with the Indian's wife and children, and was evidently a special favourite with them. His face was bright and intelligent.

"You would not think, señor," Gomez said as, after telling him what they had purchased in the city, he stood watching Hurka, who was running backwards and forwards between the hut and the mules, carrying in packages, "that that little chap is one of the best guides on this side of the Andes. He and Pita are, I should say, the two best; and whenever they can, they work together. He is a wonderful shot—better than Pita. He can swim like a fish; and he does not seem to know what fatigue is. He and Pita are like brothers, although they are so different in their ways; and it is wonderful to see how they get on together. I would not mind where I went with them, for they can find their way through the thickest forest, and are up to every device that can be useful to travellers. I have never heard of their losing anyone under their charge, except, of course, from disease and heat, and perhaps a few shot by Indians. That is a thing that may always happen, there is no guarding against it—especially when you have got men with you who will go their own way, and make light of any idea of taking precautions. Sometimes they have had to fall back altogether when they have been with gold or treasure seekers, but never when they were with trading parties.

"In the forest country the natives are generally ready enough to trade, but there are parts where they never allow a white party to penetrate. Whether it is that there is really a treasure, or an extraordinary rich gold-mine, or whether it is only that in some sections the tribes are more hostile than in others, no one knows for certain, but there is no doubt that when any party approaches certain localities troubles begin directly. As they go through the forest, arrows come flying thick through the tangle of creepers, and poisoned darts from blow-pipes. The foes are invisible, but they make themselves felt, and it soon breaks down the courage of the bravest to be shot at when you never get a chance of shooting back in return. Both Pita and Hurka have been with parties that have been attacked and forced to fall back; but it has not been their fault, for they always warn those who employ them that the dangers are too great to be overcome. Still, men who think that they have got a clue to hidden wealth always seem to consider that their guides are interested in preventing their getting it, and will listen to no advice till they find out for themselves that the danger has not been exaggerated, and that it is certain death to push on further."

"I wonder that neither of them has been killed," Stephen said.

"It is a wonder, señor, and some have even declared that

they must be in league with the Indians; but it is due to their understanding the native way of fighting. While white men stand up and fire away into the bush, they quickly throw themselves down behind the trunk of a tree, and then crawl into the forest and fight in the same way as the Indians do; and they say that more than once those two alone have made the natives fall back, and so enabled the whites to retreat. You will see that they will both take bows and arrows with them; and though they would use their rifles if openly attacked, in these battles in the forests, or when hunting in dangerous neighbourhoods, they use their bows in preference to the rifles."

The next day the journey was continued, and in ten days they reached a stream which, as the Indians told Stephen, ran into the Beni, one of the principal feeders of the Madeira. Here was a village occupied wholly by Indians and half-castes. A large canoe was purchased, and the loads of the two mules stowed in it, a store of bread and fruit was obtained from the natives, together with ten skins sewn up as bags, and intended to be inflated and used for the construction of a raft. Two days were spent in making their preparations, and then Stephen took leave of Gomez, to whom he gave a handsome present, in addition to the sum that had been agreed upon. By this time Stephen had come to appreciate the good qualities of Hurka, whose unfailingly good temper and gaiety had lightened the journey, and whose humorous stories of his adventures, and of the obstinacy and folly of his employers, raised a smile even on the impassive face of Pita.

Stephen was delighted when the canoe pushed out into the stream, and they began their journey down the thousands of miles of river that had to be traversed before they reached the eastern sea-coast. Pita sat in the stern of the canoe, Hurka in the bow, while Stephen had a comfortable seat in the middle, separated from them by two piles of stores and provisions. Over him was a roof of green boughs, supported by four poles, connected by others, to which a thin curtain of cotton-stuff was attached. It was all made in one piece, and was rolled up in the daytime to allow the passage of air, but at night could be dropped all round so as to form a protection against insects and the vapours from the water. The tent was large enough for the three men to sleep in comfortably; and in the centre was a small stove, in which fire was kept burning for cooking purposes in the daytime, and to counteract the dampness of the air at night. As soon as it was dark, and the insects became troublesome, the Indians threw on the fire branches that they cut fresh every day from shrubs growing on the banks. This caused a pungent odour which effectually prevented insects from making their way in through the leafy roof.

During the daytime the canoe was generally kept close to one shore or the other, so as to be under the shade of the overhanging forest trees; at night they sometimes tied up to a tree, but more often one or other of the Indians sat in the stern of the boat giving an occasional stroke with his paddle to keep her drifting down in the centre of the current. While it was light they always had their guns close at hand, and sometimes brought down a bird from the trees overhead. Baited hooks on a long line were towed astern. They seldom caught anything during the day, but at night they frequently captured a few fish. This, however, was more often done by spearing them, the Indians having bought spears for the purpose at the village. On these occasions Stephen took his place in the bow with two lighted torches of resinous wood; the light attracted the fish, which were speared by the Indians, who seldom missed striking them, however far beneath the surface, though Stephen failed even to catch sight of them.

The fish formed the main staple of their food, helped out by the birds, which were, for the most part, of the pigeon tribe, though larger and differing much in plumage from the English species. They had brought from Cuzco a hundred pounds of flour, which was sewed up in two skins, so that in case of a misfortune to the canoe it would be uninjured by water. From this the Indians made flat cakes, which were an excellent substitute for bread.

For the first ten days Hurka while paddling generally sung Spanish songs that he had picked up, but gradually he ceased doing so, and became as taciturn as Pita himself.

"The Indians on this part of the river," he told Stephen, "are generally of a peaceful nature, and are quite willing to trade, but, as we have no merchandise, they would look upon us with some suspicion; and, moreover, the tribes are often at war with each other, and in that case it is always better that travellers should avoid them. Consequently it is better to travel silently."

For the same reason they generally timed themselves so as to pass the Indian villages at night, the fire on such occasions being kept very low, and ashes being drawn up over the embers so as to completely extinguish the light until the village was well behind them. Shooting was, for the time, entirely given up.

CHAPTER XVII.

DOWN THE RIVER.

THE time passed pleasantly to Stephen as he reclined on a heap of skins and blankets watching the forests that bordered the stream, or looking up through the overhanging canopy at the birds and monkeys, the latter of which afforded him great amusement by the way in which they chattered and gesticulated. The mothers with the little ones climbed to the top of the trees, while the males came boldly out on the lower branches to bid defiance to those in the boat. Often he slept, for the heat, and the almost noiseless fall of the paddles, and the tranquil easy motion of the canoe made him exceptionally drowsy. One day his eye fell upon something on a large branch of a tree that bent down to within twelve feet of the water. It was only some ten yards ahead when he noticed it. It was partly hidden by foliage, and for a moment it seemed to him to be a thickening of the branch. He would have passed it without a thought had it not been for a slight movement; then a glance showed him that it was an animal of some kind lying almost flattened upon the tree.

He caught up his rifle just as it rose to a crouching attitude, and was upon the point of springing upon Pita. The gun was loaded with shot only, but as he threw up the muzzle and fired almost instantly, the beast gave a terrible roar. Its spring was arrested, and it fell headlong into the water within a foot of the side of the boat. A tawny head, with two rows of big white teeth, arose from the water almost abreast of him, and a great paw was raised to strike at the boat, but Hurka's rifle cracked out, and the animal sank again below the water.

"You have saved my life, señor," Pita said gravely. "It was a jaguar, and had you not fired it would have struck me down and crushed in my skull with a blow of its paw. I wonder I did not see it, but I was thinking at the time that we had best tie up for an hour or two so as to pass the next village, which is a large one, after dark."

"It was almost hidden among those leaves," Stephen said, "and had it not moved I should not have noticed it."

"I think you blinded it, señor," Hurka said. "I saw it rise

to spring, and snatched at my rifle just as you fired. I think the charge struck it between the eyes, for I saw a sort of blur there just as it fell. I should have been too late; for though I might have hit it as it was in the air, it would assuredly have come down on Pita.

"It was not like you, Pita. This comes of thinking while you are paddling instead of keeping your eyes on everything."

"I was wrong," the Indian replied. "I should have known that an attack by a jaguar was always possible; but this is the first that we have seen since starting, and I had no thought of danger in my mind. I will be more careful in the future. It must have been well hidden, for you did not see it yourself, Hurka, until it moved for its spring."

"That is true," the little Indian replied. "The Englishman's eyes must be quick indeed, and his nerve steady. It was seeing him catch up his gun that first called my attention to it. You have laid us both under a great obligation, señor, for Pita is my best friend, and were aught to befall him I should feel that I had lost part of myself. Perhaps before the journey comes to an end we may be able to show you how grateful we are."

"It is nothing worth talking about," Stephen said. "In a journey like this, comrades may well save each other's lives more than once."

"That is true, señor; but it is our duty to save your life if need be, and it is turning the tables upon us for you to be the means of saving ours. However, you will not find us lacking when the time comes. Already we have agreed that this time of all others we must carry our business through successfully. You are not like these Spaniards. To them we are Indian dogs, mere dust under their feet, a people whose services they buy as they buy those of our mules; but you have treated us as if we had been comrades of the same colour as you yourself, have insisted upon our eating with you, and have talked with us as if we were friends together; and you will find that it is so if danger arises. We Indians are not accustomed to kindness or consideration from our Spanish masters. Could they do without us they would not suffer an Indian to exist in the land; but they need our labour, and so bear with us. But we, on our part, never forget that our ancestors were lords of this country, that they received these white strangers with kindness, and were repaid by the grossest treachery and ingratitude, and that, not contented with seizing our land and our possessions, they murdered all our princes and leaders, and reduced all whom they did not slay to slavery, keeping us only that we might work the mines and till the fields for them.

"Centuries have passed since then, but there has been no change; they are still our masters, we their beasts of burden. They may pay us for our services, but they have no thought or consideration for us. We may risk our lives for them, but they value ours no more than if we were dogs. Save among the muleteers, like Gomez, who long ago ceased to be Spaniards, and are now Peruvians, they look upon us as a conquered race, and as to friendship or a kindly thought for an Indian, they think more of their dogs than they do of us. Therefore, señor, you may guess that Pita and I do not feel towards you only as a master who pays us, but as one who has treated us as if we were the same colour as himself, and even the service you have rendered Pita binds us less to you than the kindness that you have shown us. If all Englishmen are like you it would be a blessing indeed to this country if, after your famous admiral had driven out the Spaniards, he would himself reign over the land and bring some of his people here to govern us.

"The white Peruvians are no better than the Spaniards. They are the same blood, and have the same ideas, and save that they are cowards, while the Spaniards, to do them justice, are often brave, there is little to choose between them. They are as proud of their white blood, and they despise us as heartily; they are as greedy of gold, but too indolent to work for it; and when the Spaniards have gone they will be despots as hard and as tyrannical as our present governors. We hope for the change, though we know well that it will do but little for us; while, if the people of your race came as masters of the land, we might have some share of freedom and happiness. Tales have reached even us that across the western ocean you rule over a people dark like ourselves, but infinitely more numerous than we were when the Spaniards first set foot here; and that your rule is a good and just one, and that the natives are happy and contented, and that there are the same laws for them as for us. Do you think, señor, that there is any chance of your admiral and your people coming here?"

"I am afraid not, Hurka. We English here are in the service of Chili. We are free ourselves, and our sympathies are with all men who are struggling to be free; but we have no idea of conquest here, and were Peru to offer to come under our rule we should not accept it. We have already wide possessions in North America and elsewhere, and need no further territories, especially in a climate that is unfitted for us. We might rule it as we do India, but the Peruvians would never be contented, and we should never attempt to keep them in subjection did they wish us gone. India, the country you speak of, is inhabited by many races and religions. Before we went, there were incessant wars, and were we to leave they would at once recommence. The people, then, feel that our rule is a real benefit, and that they are far happier under it than they were under their native rulers. When we went there we had no thought of conquering it; we only went there to trade. It was because we were attacked that we defended ourselves, and there are still portions of the country that are altogether independent, and so long as the native sovereigns leave us alone we are well contented that things should remain as they are. We do not enrich ourselves at the expense of the natives. They have to pay taxes to keep up the expenses of the army and administration there, but England draws no revenue from India. It does not, as Spain did, enrich itself with the plunder of the land; and it is free to people of all nations to trade there as we do ourselves. Individuals may gain wealth there by commerce, or by the growth of indigo and other things that we cannot raise at home, but as a nation we obtain no revenue whatever from India. The army there is for the most part raised from the people, who are free to enlist or not as they please, and who fight as faithfully for us as they would have done for their own rulers."

"Then what do you gain by being there?" Hurka asked.

"We gain in the trade that is carried on by our merchants selling English goods there, and buying Indian produce. The army and the civil government furnish employment to large numbers of Englishmen. These are the only material advantages that, so far as I know, we gain; although of course it is a matter of pride and satisfaction to Englishmen that they rule over so great a country, and that our presence there is of enormous advantage to the people."

"And are there no gold or silver mines there?" Pita asked.

"No; at any rate nothing that has been worked since we went there."

"Ah, if you would but come here," Hurka exclaimed, "what a blessing it would be to us! and I am sure that the Indians, when they knew that they would be fairly treated, would no longer preserve the secrets of the Incas, but would gladly open to you mines that have been hidden ever since the Spaniards came, and hand over vast treasures that have been left untouched all these years. They are useless to them, and are hidden only because they hate the Spaniards, and know that did they discover these mines they would compel the people to work at them as their fathers did; and ere long we should disappear altogether."

While they had been talking they had floated quietly down the stream, and Pita said that they were now but a few miles from the next village, and had better tie up until darkness came on.

"Have you any desire for gold, señor?" Hurka asked, after they had secured the canoe to an overhanging branch, and the two Indians had rolled and lighted their cigarettes.

"Not particularly, Hurka. I suppose everyone would like gold; but I have already enough to live upon, having been very fortunate in aiding to capture a vessel carrying a large sum for the payment of the Spanish troops. If I were to search for gold it would be rather for the sake of the adventure than for the treasure."

"You are the first white man I have ever met, señor, who would not undertake any risk in order to gain a fortune, and the richest are as ready to adventure their gold in any enterprise that promises even a chance of success, as the poorest are willing to risk their lives."

"The adventure itself would be very exciting," Stephen said, "and I do not say that I should not like to take part in one, just as I am glad to have the chance of such an adventure as going down the Amazon; but it would certainly be the excitement, and not the chance of making money, that would attract me. I don't say for a moment that I should refuse a share in the treasure, only that I would not run any great risks for the sake of the treasure alone. I suppose that every one could do with more than he has; for even if you have nothing to wish for, it would at least be a pleasure to give it away.

"I have been fortunate; although I am still very young,

I have been through a great many adventures, and if I were to settle quietly down at home now, I have more to look back upon than most men."

Day after day they floated down, sometimes on a broad tranquil sheet with a scarce perceptible current, and at others in a rapid headlong stream pent up between narrow banks. The volume of water had vastly increased since they started, owing to the number of streams that had flowed into the Beni, some of these being so large that they would be considered good-sized rivers in Europe. At last, a month after starting, Hurka said that next day they would reach the confluence of the Beni and the Madeira.

"There is a mission-station there, and if the señor likes to pause there for a day or two before descending the river he can do so."

"Not at all, Hurka. In the first place I shall be asked a great many questions which would be difficult to answer, and in the second, even two days in a mission-station would be frightfully dull."

"Very well, señor, then we will pass straight into the river and halt a few hours' journey further down."

"Why should we halt at all?"

"We shall want to construct a raft, señor. There are many dangerous rapids in the Madeira besides the falls, and the river is beginning to rise. You were noticing yesterday how thick the water had become, and some of the streams that run into it are laden with mud. That shows that the rain has begun on the western slopes. The Madeira is generally in flood two days before the Beni, and the water will be running down in a great stream; therefore it will be necessary to make our raft. We need not desert the canoe, but can let it float alongside of us, or we can haul it on to the raft; it will be convenient for sleeping in."

"We had better land at once and make our raft," Pita said, "before we reach the Madeira. I know of no high bank for a very long distance after we have entered the great river where we could manage it."

"Then by all means let us do so at once," Stephen said, "and perhaps we may get some sport."

Accordingly the boat was headed towards shore. When they reached the side they found that the Beni itself had risen, and the bank, usually seven or eight feet out of water, was now little more than a foot above its level.

"You may get some birds," Hurka said, "but nothing else. The instinct of the beasts tells them that the river is nearly full, and doubtless indeed the low-lying parts of the forest are already submerged. They will be off before this, and will travel on till they come to ground that is always above the floods. Some will, doubtless, be caught and perish. Such as climb will take to trees, but hunger will destroy them."

"How far do the floods extend?"

"In some places a hundred miles, and on the Amazon itself, as I have heard, a great deal further."

They paddled along close to the bank until they reached a spot where it was bordered by a vast number of reeds, many of them as thick as Stephen's arm.

"Now we are going to make our raft," Hurka said. "These reeds are far better than solid branches. They are very light, and we fasten them but loosely together, so that they can give to the water. When we have made it, we shall then want four young saplings. These we shall lash together firmly in a square, and under each corner we fasten the skins, and one also in the middle of each pole; you know we have brought eight with us. First we make the raft itself with the rushes. It is made about four feet larger each way than the frame with the skins. This frame is laid in the raft, and is fastened loosely to it. Thus you see the raft itself is complete without the poles and skins, which, so long as it holds together, simply rest on it, but if the raft gets broken up the skins will support the poles. We generally lash a few cross poles to the frame, and on these we sit, for the water splashes up between the reeds, making everything wet. As we are going to take our canoe with us, we shall not want the cross poles, but shall lay her on the reeds and get on board her. We shall pick out the largest reeds we can get to place under the spot where she will lie, and shall only get out of the boat when it is necessary to go to the front or sides of the raft to pole her off from any floating tree or other danger."

It took them two days to complete the raft, the second day's work being carried on afloat, for the stream rose very rapidly. The lashings of the reeds were of leather thongs, so tied that while they were held firmly in their places there was a great deal of play, an advantage that Stephen discovered as soon as they were afloat again on the stream. The rapidity with which the river was running raised it in a series of sharp waves, and a rigid raft would have had one end or the other constantly immersed. The raft, however, undulated with the water almost as a carpet of the same size would have done, the lashings of the buoyant reeds permitting each side to rise and fall, while the structure upon it lifted or fell with the motion. The canoe half floated and was half supported by the raft below it, and Stephen was surprised to find how slight the motion was even in the broken water. Presently the two Indians left the canoe, and seating themselves on the poles, paddled towards the shore to the left, and getting out of the current made their way along the edge of the forest.

"We are close now," Hurka said, "to the Madeira, and the struggle of the two swollen rivers will raise a turmoil so great that even this raft might break up in the waves."

This Stephen could well believe when the canoe reached the

angle where the rivers joined. The width was nearly two miles, and the scene presented the appearance of the sea in a violent gale, except that it was a chaos without order or regularity. The cross currents seemed to crash against each other, hurling the spray many yards in the air. Waves leapt up in conical form as if lifted bodily from below. The position of the centre of the stream changed continually as one current or the other gained the mastery. Here and there were whirlpools and eddies that would have engulfed an ordinary boat in a moment. The whole was white with foam.

"It is like a huge boiling pot," Stephen said as he watched it.

"No boat ever made could live in it," Hurka said. "I have seen boats on the great waves that break on the coast, but there was an order in the waves, and those skilled in the work could wait their opportunity and come in on the top of one of them. Here all is confusion, and a boat would be thrown into the air by one of those suddenly rising lumps of water, and if caught between two of the waves would be crushed like a shell. No one would think of descending the river when the Beni and the Madeira are in flood, except by doing as we are doing now, keeping in the dead-water, or, if in canoes, making their way through the submerged forests. But even this would be hazardous work, for the canoe might be torn by unseen boughs below the surface of the water. Therefore at times like these, most men wait until the floods have abated, unless they are in a great hurry, and this is seldom, for neither Indians nor Peruvians are ever in haste about anything.

"The greatest danger to inexperienced travellers is that of being lost in the forest. Many streams come in, and when the water is very high it is difficult to know whether one is crossing a tract denuded of wood or one of the many channels of the river; and once lost in the forest a traveller's fate is sealed, for the current there is insufficient to enable him to judge in which direction is the main river, for he may be in a back eddy or in the current from a cross channel. The trees are so interlaced with creepers that every foot of the way has to be cut, while among the foliage are snakes of all kinds, from the great boas to the little tree snakes, a bite from which causes death in a few minutes. There too are starving jaguars, leopards, and wild cats, who, once they get over the terror caused by the inundation, are all on the look-out for food. Amidst all these enemies the inexperienced traveller speedily loses his presence of mind and even his reason.

"Once when I was going down this very river we heard a noise of wild laughter, intermingled with strange piercing cries. We knew at once that it was a traveller lost in the forest. It took us two hours to cut our way to the spot where we heard the sounds. We guessed who were the sufferers. Two Spaniards had hired a large canoe, and had taken with them six village boatmen. They had refused my offer to go with four men of my tribe who were accustomed to the river and its dangers, as we demanded a much higher sum than the villagers were ready to go for, and we said when we saw them put off that they would never get down to the mission. When we reached the spot one man was lying dead at the bottom of the canoe. One of the Spaniards and one of the villagers were missing, having no doubt leapt overboard in their madness. The others were all raving madmen, some with scarce strength to raise themselves in the boat, others making the dreadful laughing and screaming that we had heard.

"When they saw us they took us, I believe, for devils, and it was not until we had lassoed the strongest that we were able to overpower them. We bound them and laid them at the bottom of our canoe and took them down to the mission, which was some fifty miles below us. I was told afterwards that only one of them ever recovered his senses; the others either died raving or were hopelessly mad. From the one who recovered it was learned that as soon as they came to the point where the stream became rapid they made for the edge of the forest. At night they tied up their canoe to a tree, but in the morning when they awoke they found that the line had become untied, and that they had drifted into the forest. There they had been three days when we found them. They had lost all idea of direction, and had we been a few hours later the last voice would have been silenced, and when the flood subsided the canoe and its occupants would have rotted away, and no one would ever have known the fate that had befallen them."

"How do you find your way through a flooded forest, Hurka?"

"It is born in us as it is born in birds to make their way back to their nests. It may be that a careful examination would show that the trunks on one side are more thickly covered with creepers than the other; but we do not need to take notice of such things, or if we notice them it is without knowing it, as we are sure of our direction. We have seen Spanish travellers who had the things with which they said they could direct their course at sea, with a card that goes round and round and always when it is steady points in one direction. This is no doubt very useful out on the plains or in a forest where there are no obstacles, but here where the woods are intercepted by numberless streams and with wide swamps, such a machine is useless to any one unless he is intimately acquainted with the country and the course of the streams. Even Indian dwellers on the shores of the river often, in the times of floods, get lost in the forest and lose their lives, so changed is the aspect of everything by the water."

"It must be terrible," Stephen said, as he glanced between the trunks of the trees at the still, dark water under the thick canopy. "Of course the sun must be a help."

"We do not often see the sun in times of flood, señor. Rain often falls very heavily, and even when it does not do so there is, you see, a mist in the air rising from this vast expanse of water. Besides, it is only when it is directly overhead that the sun's rays penetrate the foliage, and at that time it is too high for the shadows to afford much guidance. Among us, three shots of a gun at regular intervals is a call for aid, but in flood time it is a useless one, for the Indians, like the wild beasts, all leave, save when their huts are on eminences, and the chances of the shots being heard by human ears are small indeed. To one lost in the forest at other times it is all but certain death, but when the floods are out a man would do wisely to fire the first shot into his own head."

Day after day they travelled on, keeping just far enough out to get the benefit of the current without allowing themselves to be drawn towards the centre of the river. Even this at times was very difficult, especially when they were passing round curves, for much of the water, instead of following the channel, made its way through the forest to the next bend in the river, and they had the greatest difficulty in preventing themselves from being drawn in among the trees by the current. At such times they were forced to launch the canoe overboard, to roll up the bottom of the raft, and to lay the great bundle of rushes across the poles now supported by the inflated skins. Only then by vigorous paddling, in which Stephen bore his part, were they able to tow this behind them across the current until they reached a point where the force of the stream was confined to the regular channel. At one point, where the river was broader than usual and the current in consequence slower, they crossed to the other bank.

"We are getting near the rapids now," Hurka said, "and this bank is the least dangerous of the two. Hitherto we have had nothing but the force of the stream to contend with, but now we shall have rocks. It is for this that we constructed the raft. Up to now we should have done far better to have come down in the canoe alone, but, once among the rocks, a touch would break her up, while the raft can scrape against them without injury. You will see that the aspect of things will change altogether; the banks where the rapids are, are high and steep, and the inundations will cease for a time. Once beyond the falls we shall again be in a flat country, and the inundations will extend almost all the way down until we reach the Amazon."

"There is no way of avoiding the rapids, I suppose?" Stephen asked.

"None but by getting out and carrying everything round. At the falls this has to be done, there are no other means of passing them. In some respects it is safer to go down the rapids now than it is in the dry season, for the greater portion of the rocks are far below the surface, and we shall pass over small falls without even noticing them."

The days as a rule passed pleasantly enough, save where the voyagers had to work against cross currents, but at night, when they tied up to a tree, the noise was prodigious. The howling and roaring of wild beasts was incessant. Monkeys chattered in terror, and occasionally an almost human scream proclaimed that one of them had been seized by a snake, or some other enemy. The hissing of reptiles could at times be distinctly heard, and Stephen often thought that he could hear their movements in the boughs above him.

At length they approached the rapids, and the stream became still more impetuous. The Indians had cut long poles, and as they drifted down one stood at each corner of the raft, using their poles occasionally as paddles to keep it straight. Stephen remained in the canoe in the centre. He would gladly have shared in any work that was to be done, but here he felt that he could be of no use.

"To-morrow we shall be in the full force of the rapids, señor," Hurka said. "I should advise you to lay yourself down in the bottom of the canoe and to pass the day in sleep. It will be safer so should there be an accident, for, with your weight at the bottom, the canoe will be more likely to keep upright than it otherwise would. You cannot aid us, and the speed at which we shall do the next hundred miles will be great indeed. In eight hours we shall be at the foot of the rapids."

"I will sit down at the bottom of the canoe, but I must see what is going on. I am accustomed to the aspect of a sea in a violent gale, and this great body of water, however fast it rushes, will not be more trying to the nerves than such a scene as that. There is one thing that I should wish you to do. Let each tie a light rope round his waist and fasten the other end to the canoe, and then if the raft does go to pieces you will be able to get on board, and at any rate, if she upsets we shall be together."

"We will do it if you wish, señor, but there would be danger of our capsizing the canoe."

"Not so much danger as there would be of the canoe upsetting if I were alone in it, for I should be powerless even to keep her straight, and she would go broadside on to a rock and be dashed to pieces."

"The señor is right, Hurka," Pita said gravely; "we will do as he wishes. But the ropes must be long, so that if we are flung off the raft there will be no sudden pull on the canoe. Should there be such a misfortune I will shout to you, and we will then swim towards the boat, taking up the ropes as we go, but putting no strain upon them; when we reach the boat, one will aid the señor to steady it while the other climbs in; after that it will be easier to get the second on board."

"You still think that it is better to make a passage than to carry the whole kit and the canoe over?"

PITA TRIES STEPHEN'S PLAN

"It would take many weeks, señor. Besides, though I have never been here before, I have heard that the difficulties are so great that the river Indians never attempt to carry even a light canoe over. I am at your service, señor, and am willing to try if you give the order, but I have been told by Indians that when the river is, as now, in flood, the danger is by no means great. Of course, we shall keep out of the full strength of the current."

Accordingly they started the next morning, and an hour after setting out were in the sweep of the rapids. The passage was an intensely exciting one. The Indians stood, paddle in hand, one at each corner of the front of the raft; their poles lay ready to snatch up in case any rock was approached, but the paddles were needed to keep the raft from being dragged out into the full force of the current. Here the water rose in steep ridges, and had the raft got among these it would have been torn to pieces almost instantly. At the same time it was desirable not to go too near the shore, as the risk from submerged rocks would be greater there. But Stephen saw that unless rocks came absolutely above the surface they would be swept over them, as the raft drew but two or three inches of water. Except in the middle, the stream rushed along with a surface broken only by tiny eddies. It was only by seeing how they flew past the banks that any idea could be formed of the speed at which they were travelling.

In eight hours it was over. Several times the paddlers had to exert themselves to the utmost to avoid spots where great swells of water showed that there were rocks below the surface, but on no occasion did the Indians have to use their poles. The bed of the river widened sharply at the foot of the rapids, and just as Stephen congratulated himself that the passage had been safely made, he saw by an increase in the labour of the Indians that something was wrong. Standing up in the canoe he perceived that they had been shot out of the current into the back-water formed by the sudden widening of the stream, and that in this back-water was a very strong eddy sweeping round and round in a circle. This was about a hundred yards in diameter, with a depression in the centre, and round this the raft was carried at a rate that defied the efforts of the two paddlers to check.

At one moment they were within twenty yards of a flat forest-covered shore, and the next were near the edge of the torrent pouring down the rapids. In vain the paddlers tried to edge the raft out little by little from the whirlpool. Not only was the current too strong for them, but its surface was dotted with floating logs and branches of trees that, like themselves, coursed round and round. As long as all were travelling at the same rate and in the same direction the danger of a collision was comparatively slight, but more than once when the rowers succeeded in gaining a short distance towards the outside edge of the whirlpool, they were forced to desist suddenly and paddle straight with the current, to avoid a great log bearing down upon them.

Pita took a lariat from the canoe and prepared to throw it, so as to catch one of the branches when they neared the shore. He tried several times, but the distance was too great; and indeed it was necessary to catch the trees at some little distance before reaching the point opposite to them, in order to pull diagonally across the current, for a jerk when the canoe was at right angles would have torn the raft to pieces.

"Could we launch the canoe and paddle out of the whirlpool in that?" Stephen said.

"We might do that," Hurka replied, "but a touch from any of these logs would sink her in a moment; and besides, we should be sorry to lose the raft, for we have no skins to make floats, and the rushes of which we constructed it only grow in the quiet waters of the upper river. We might take to the canoe as a last resource, but we should be very loth to do it."

"How long would the lariats be, tied together, with that piece of thin rope you brought to check the raft in dangerous places?"

"The rope is a hundred and fifty yards long, señor, the lariats reach about thirty yards."

"That would be plenty," Stephen said. "My idea is that you might fasten the end of the rope to an arrow and shoot it among the trees. It might not catch the first time, but no doubt it would after a few trials. The rope will, of course, be coiled up so as to pay out easily, and we could pull it in or pay it out as we went round and round. Each time as we approach the shore we could pull on it a little and edge the raft a few feet out, slackening out again as we came to the nearest point to the trees. If there were any logs in our way of course we should not pull; thus, by choosing our opportunity, we might get her out little by little till we are outside the full force of the stream."

The Indians did not quite understand Stephen's plan, but at once agreed to try it. Pita chose his heaviest arrow and lashed the end of the rope firmly to it, close to the feathers. Stephen knotted the lariats to the rope, and coiled them up so that they would run out easily, and they then prepared for the first attempt.

CHAPTER XVIII

CAPTURED BY INDIANS.

DRAWING the bow till the point of the arrow almost touched the wood, Pita stood like a statue until the boat was opposite to the trees, then he loosed it, and it flew far into the foliage. The instant the boat reached the opposite side of the whirlpool Stephen and Hurka drew in the rope hand over hand.

"Leave go, Hurka," Stephen said as the rope tightened. "I will try as we pass whether it has caught in the trees."

As the canoe passed on he put a slight strain on the rope. It yielded for a moment, and then flew through his fingers rapidly.

"It has caught on something," he said. "Now, haul in rapidly this time, Hurka, as soon as we pass the opposite point, so as to get the strain on as quickly as we can. Pita, do you keep your eye on the logs, and shout if there is anything in the way."

As soon as they had passed the half-way point on their way back to the shore, Stephen and Hurka began to pull. They could get but little tension on the rope, for the boat was travelling almost as fast as they could pull it in. Still, once or twice they were able to put their strength on it for a moment, and the raft moved a foot or two through the water. Again and again this manœuvre was repeated, and little by little they gained ground, until at last they edged the raft so near to the edge of the current that the two Indians, seizing their paddles, were able to get her into the still water beyond. They rowed to the trees, and there tied up.

"That was a good plan, señor," Pita said. "I should never have thought of it. I did think of shooting an arrow across to the trees, but I saw that the jerk would be so great that it would tear the raft to pieces."

It was some time before Stephen was inclined to talk; for the exertion necessary to pull the rope in at a rate exceeding that at which the boat was travelling towards the trees, coming as it did after the excitement of the passage down the rapids, had completely exhausted him. He was drenched with perspiration, and was glad to lie still in the bottom of the canoe for a time.

"Well, what next, Pita?" he asked when his breath came quietly.

"We shall float down as before, señor. It is a flat country for the next fifty miles, and the great inundations will rob the river of its power. We shall have several more rapids to pass, but I do not think they will be worse than these. Then we shall get to the falls. There are several small ones, round which we shall have to carry our boats, and there is a great one where the whole river leaps down a hundred feet in a mass. On still nights you can hear it, I am told, nigh a hundred miles away. It is the greatest fall in South America, though a traveller I once met told me that in North America there was a fall that was higher, but that there was nothing like the same quantity poured over it as over this at floodtime. Once beyond that there remain no more falls or rapids, and a ship can sail up there from the Amazon. Good-sized craft do come up sometimes, for there is a mission-station there, and the fathers carry on a trade with the Indians, who come from the lower districts to purchase goods."

"I shall be very glad when the water gets clear enough for us to take to fishing again," Stephen said. "We have caught no fish of late, and have got but a few birds, and I am getting very tired of these cakes."

Another three weeks and Stephen stood at the foot of the fall of the river Madeira. The flood of water that poured down in one unbroken sheet was enormous. The noise was like that of continual thunder, and Stephen, as he stood watching the swollen waters at his feet and feeling the very ground shake beneath them, felt spell-bound at the grandeur of the scene. The mission-house was inhabited by only two or three old monks, and from them they learned that there had been a bad outbreak of fever there, several had died, and the rest were so weakened that it had been determined that the monks, with the exception of these men, who had passed through many fevers and were thoroughly acclimatized, should go down by boat to Barra, and remain there until the season of the floods terminated and the sun had dried the inundated country.

Stephen was glad of a rest, for since entering the rapids the work had been hard and continuous. The Indians would have undertaken all the portage round the various falls and bad rapids, but he insisted on doing his share of the work, and had day after day toiled with heavy weights over a rough country. It was all over now, and the prospect of a week spent at the mission before proceeding on their voyage was very pleasant.

"You must be careful," one of the monks said, "not to stray too far from the house. The natives of the neighbourhood have long since been Christianized, but we are visited by parties from long distances belonging to some of the other tribes who are still wholly wild and eat human flesh. Here they behave peaceably, because they credit us with supernatural powers, seeing the respect and devotion with which we are regarded by the natives here, of whom indeed we generally keep a strong body on guard during the time that the strangers most frequently visit us; that is to say, at the time that the floods are out. At that time most of the people who live near the river are forced to retire to a great distance from their homes, and being deprived of their usual pursuits, they take that opportunity of coming here to purchase the articles they require. I do not say that they would harm you, but assuredly they might do so, and it would therefore be best for you to keep near the mission-house. Here you are safe from any danger whatever, for even the wildest Indian would not venture to set foot inside these walls, fearing that if they did, some terrible calamity might befall them."

Stephen took the advice, for although he was not much affected by what the old man said, Pita and his companion both confirmed his words, and told him that many bad Indians, who would kill and eat any white man who entered their district, frequently visited these mission-houses.

"Always carry your gun with you, señor. They have not the same terror of firearms as their forefathers had, but they have heard enough to know that they are weapons of war, and much more formidable than their own bows and arrows, or the poisoned darts of their blow-pipes."

Stephen accordingly never went out, even to visit the falls, where he spent the greater portion of his time, without his rifle. Generally one or other of the Indians accompanied him, but seeing that no strangers visited the mission-house, they gradually abstained from doing so. Stephen preferred being alone—the tremendous roar of the water rendered conversation impossible—and he was quite content to lie and dreamily watch the flood pouring down unceasingly. On the evening before the day on which they were to start, the moon was shining brilliantly, and Stephen, taking his gun as usual, went out without mentioning his intention to his companions, and strolled down to take a last quiet look at the mighty fall, whose fascination grew upon him the oftener he looked at it and came to realize more and more its marvellous power and energy. He had been seated there for about an hour, when, without the slightest warning that anyone was near him, he received a sudden blow on the head that rolled him over unconscious. When he recovered his senses he found himself in the bottom of a small canoe paddled by three Indians.

Overhead he could see the branches of trees, and knew from this that they were following the bank of the river. Presently, to his surprise, they turned sharply off, and were at once in the gloom of the forest. They paddled for an hour, and then tied up the canoe to a tree. One of them lit a torch at the fire that smouldered on a flat stone, and the three gathered round it. Stephen could see that they were closely examining his rifle, pistols, watch, and money. Few remarks were made, but Stephen gathered from the tone that they were well satisfied with the capture.

"I have fallen into bad hands this time," he said to himself. "There is no doubt about their being stranger Indians. I can understand my arms being regarded by them as a most valuable capture, but why they did not finish me at once, instead of taking me away with them, is more than I can understand, unless it be that they are cannibals."

After examining his bonds and assuring themselves that they were tight, the Indians lay down to sleep, but in the morning continued their journey as soon as daylight broke. From the absence of undergrowth and of lianas stretching from tree to tree anywhere low down, Stephen came to the conclusion that they were following what was in the dry season a track through the forest. The Indians were quite young men, and laughed and talked without any of the gravity that distinguished the older men among the natives. For some hours they paddled on, then their progress was stopped by a deep tangle of creepers stretching from tree to tree across their way. There was an exclamation of surprise and, as Stephen thought, of apprehension; they began to talk rapidly and eagerly together, one pointing in one direction and another in quite an opposite one.

"They have lost the path," he said to himself, "perhaps they took the wrong turn at starting."

The argument between them was an animated one, until one pointed to a ray of sunlight that penetrated the foliage and fell on the trunk of a tree near the water's level. All looked surprised and even graver than before. The head of the canoe was turned, and they started in the direction from which they had come, by which Stephen concluded that they had unwittingly made half a circuit. They now paddled steadily and gravely, watching the darts of sunlight, and evidently steering by them. Before they had gone far the character of the forest changed, the trees grew somewhat further apart; but an undergrowth of smaller trees rendering it extremely difficult for them to force their canoe onward, their knives had frequently to be brought out to cut a way through the creepers. Angry words were frequently exchanged between them, each, it was evident to Stephen, accusing the others of being the cause of the disaster. The quarrel became more and more embittered, until at last two of them started up, and, drawing their knives, fell furiously upon one another. In the struggle they almost capsized the boat, and catching at each other to save themselves, both went overboard together.

The struggle was continued in the water, the men stabbing each other fiercely, while the Indian on board endeavoured in vain by his shouts to induce them to abandon the strife. Presently one of them, struck to the heart, threw up his arms and sank; the other turned to swim back to the boat, but after one or two feeble strokes he too sank lower and lower, and the water soon closed over his head. The remaining Indian stood for a time immovable, with terror and consternation in his face, and then he shook his fist threateningly at Stephen, whom he evidently regarded as being in some way the author of their misfortune, and then, taking up his paddle, proceeded to row. His manner, however, was indecisive. He had lost all confidence, and turned aside whenever the way was barred by creepers, instead of trying to cut through them. At times he ceased paddling altogether, and sat gazing restlessly around him, at other times he paddled with feverish energy. Some water had come in over the gunwale during the struggle between the Indians, and Stephen managed to turn round, face downwards, to take a hearty drink.

When evening came on, the Indian was paddling almost mechanically, when from a branch of a tree above something dropped down. For a moment Stephen could not discern its nature. There was a swift, rapid movement, a piercing cry from the Indian, followed by the sound of cracking bones, and then the man was lifted bodily out of the boat. Stephen could now see two great coils wrapped round his body, and the head of a gigantic python; then, overcome by the horror of the scene he became unconscious. When he recovered he found that the canoe had drifted away from the tree. He now set to work desperately to loose his bonds, and after great efforts and suffering severe pain, succeeded in getting one hand loose. After that the rest was easy, and in a few minutes he was free. Seizing the paddle he rowed away from the scene of the tragedy, and presently tied up to a young sapling, whose head was just above the water.

His next step was to examine the contents of the canoe. It contained, however, nothing but two or three fish dried in the sun, and some cakes, of whose composition he was ignorant, save that they were certainly not made of flour. Having satisfied his hunger and taken a long drink from the water alongside, he fired his rifle three times, but no answering sound came back. Knowing that he might only be paddling away from the river, he stretched himself in the bottom of the canoe, and resolutely postponing all thought of his position until daybreak, fell asleep. He awoke as soon as it was light again, loaded and fired his gun three times, and again listened for a response.

"It is of no use my waiting here," he said to himself, after some thought. "Pita has no shadow of a clue as to what has become of me, and as I may be thirty miles away from him it would take an army to find me. I had better try and push on until I got to dry land. I may then be able to work round the inundations until I reach the rocky ground and can make my way along it to the mission. As soon as the sun rose he was able to determine the points of the compass, and paddled steadily on, his eyes fixed upon the trees above him. Other snakes might be lurking or wild beasts taking refuge in the branches. That there were many of these indeed he was sure, by the number of uneasy howls that he had heard before the sun rose. Several times as he rowed he caught sight of leopards and jaguars in the trees; one of the latter, unobserved until he had passed beyond the branches, sprang down from above, narrowly missing the stern of the canoe, and starting in pursuit as soon as it came to the surface again. Stephen, however, was able to drive the boat through the water at a much higher rate than the beast could swim, and it was not long before he had left it far behind him.

He continued to paddle all day, but felt that his nerves were beginning to fail him, and it was only by a great effort that he was able to keep a fixed direction by the aid of the sun through the leaves. He tied up again at night, and paddled all the next day, finding to his gratification in the afternoon that the water now did not average more than four feet deep. By noon the next day he saw a break in the line of water, and a few minutes later stood on dry ground. He did not attempt to go further, but throwing himself down fell at once into a deep sleep. It was evening when he awoke; the fire still burned on the hearth in the canoe; he had been careful to keep it alight by breaking off pieces of dead wood from the trees. He now collected a large store, built up a pile a few feet beyond the water-level, and bringing some brands from the fire set it alight. His scanty stock of provisions was now nearly exhausted; he ate half of what remained, and then lay down before the fire with his pistols ready at hand in case any wild beasts should come near. The next morning he started in what he believed to be the right direction, keeping near the edge of the inundation. His memory of what happened afterwards was vague and indistinct. He remembered that for several days he kept on, sometimes plucking fruit as he went, and occasionally firing a gun three times. Rapidly his strength failed as he went on, he often stumbled and fell from exhaustion and hunger, and the power of thought altogether deserted him.

At times he fancied he saw men approaching, but only to find that his imagination had converted trees into moving objects. He had long since left the edge of the inundation. He was parched with thirst, his mind wandered, incoherent cries proceeded from his parched lips. At last he thought he saw a native village before him; as he drew towards it figures came out from the huts and gazed at him. A moment later he fell headlong to the ground, and lay there insensible.

When he came to himself he felt so weak that he could neither turn nor raise his head, but lay wondering vaguely where he was. As he looked upwards he thought he was still dreaming, for the well-known face of Pita was looking down upon him.

"Do you know me?" It was certainly Pita's voice, and being unable to move, Stephen closed his eyelids quickly in reply to the question.

"The saints be praised!" the Indian exclaimed, using the ejaculation common among the Peruvians. "He knows me, Hurka—he is sensible again, after all this time."

Hurka hurried up on the other side of Stephen. "It is true!" he exclaimed; "he knows me also."

The Indian brought a gourd, and poured some liquor into Stephen's mouth. "Do not talk," he said; "we shall have plenty of time for that later on."

Stephen closed his eyes obediently. Even now he was not certain but that he was still in a dream. So many times of late he had had a vague fancy that his Indian guides were still with him that he doubted the evidence both of eye and ear. However, he soon went off to sleep again. When he awoke, Hurka was at hand, and ready to pour some hot broth down his throat. It was long before he was strong enough to ask questions, and the Indian positively refused to talk. At last the time came when he was able to be propped up into a sitting position on his bed, which was composed of leaves covered with blankets.

"I am strong enough to hear about it now, Pita. Tell me where I am and how you come to be here."

"Hurka will tell," the Indian replied; "it is a long talk."

Stephen looked to Hurka, who at once began.

"When you did not return that evening, señor, Pita and I went out to search for you. We knew where you generally sat, but you were gone. We went to the mission, got some torches, and searching in the sand between the rocks we found traces of Indians' feet, and were able to follow them up to a point nearly a mile below the falls. There they ceased, and we were sure that you had been carried off in a canoe. As we found no sign whatever of blood or marks of a struggle we felt sure that you had not been wounded, but concluded that you had been suddenly seized, bound, and carried off. We roused some of the mission Indians, and I with three of them took to our canoe and paddled down the river for twelve hours. As we had no weight to carry and had four paddles, we felt sure that by that time we should have overtaken you had they held on down the river, for we concluded by the footmarks that there were but three of them, and they had your weight in the boat.

"They could hardly have counted on being pursued so

closely, and would not, therefore, have made any special effort. Then we turned and paddled back, keeping close to the trees in hopes of getting some sign of where the canoe had entered the forest. We found none, and as soon as we got to the mission, I set out to follow Pita, who had started inland. We thought it likely that the Indians had come across the inundations, and that he might obtain some news as to which tribe they belonged to. Of course he followed the high ground and passed through several Indian villages, but he was sure that they had not come from these, for in that case they would have gone on foot to the mission instead of taking the trouble to pass through the forest in a canoe. He walked sixty miles the next day and then reached the farthest edge of the inundation, and leaving the high ground followed it.

"He had taken with him a bag of flour from the mission, and kept on for a week; then he thought he must have gone beyond the spot where you had been landed. He had walked, he thought, fifty miles a day, and was more than three hundred from the high ground, and concluded that unless the canoe had come a long distance up the river they would never have made so long a passage through the forest. Then he went back again, keeping further away from the water. Four days later he came upon a group of Indian huts, and there heard that a strange white man had arrived at a village twenty miles distant, two days before. None knew from whence he came, for he had fallen down as soon as he arrived, and was lying ill. Pita could not understand how you could have arrived in such a state, unless indeed you had killed your captors after landing, and had then wandered in the forest until you chanced upon the village. He hastened there, greatly disturbed in his mind, in the first place, at the thought of your illness, and next because the tribe was a very savage one and ate human flesh.

"When he entered the village the natives crowded round him. He was an Indian like themselves, but his dress showed that he consorted with the hated white men. Pita, however, pushed them aside, and to their astonishment spoke to them in their own language. Pita's mother, indeed, had been one of that very tribe, and her father a great chief among them, so that when he told them who he was, he was heartily welcomed and treated with great respect. It was lucky for me that he arrived, for only the day before I too, when I gained news of your whereabouts, had reached the village, and upon entering had at once been made prisoner. I gathered from what I could understand of their language that I was to be eaten. I think that the manner in which you entered their village, and the mystery as to how you could have come there, saved your life. It seemed to them as something supernatural, and they were attending you carefully in order that if you recovered they might learn from you how you had come there, after which they would no doubt have killed you. Pita had some difficulty in obtaining my release, but upon his saying that, although belonging to another tribe, I was a great friend of his, they handed me over to him. Since then we have been as natives of the village. We have taken it by turn to nurse you, and by turns have hunted with the men."

"How long have I been here?"

"Nigh six months, señor."

"Six months!" Stephen repeated; "surely not, Hurka. I never could have been ill all that time; I must have died long ago."

"You were ill for six weeks, señor, with fever. When at last that passed away, your mind did not come back to you. Sometimes you raved about a great snake that was about to seize you; sometimes you thought that you were wandering in the forest; more often you lay quiet and without saying anything. We gave you plenty of food and you got stronger, but there was no change in your mind. A month before your mind came back the fever seized you again, and we had little hope that you would live; but we had got medicine from the mission, and just when it seemed to us that you were on the point of death, you fell into a deep sleep, and when, after lying for twenty hours so, you opened your eyes and knew Pita, we found that your mind had come back to you again. That is all."

"And you and Pita have remained here for six months nursing me!" Stephen said, holding out his hand to the Indian; "you are indeed good comrades and faithful friends, and I owe my life to you."

The exhaustion caused by listening to Hurka's story prevented Stephen from saying more, and in two minutes he dropped off to sleep. The next day he related to the two Indians the story of his passage through the forest.

"It was wonderful indeed that you should have alighted upon my mother's village," Pita said. "It was not to this that the three Indians belonged, but to another thirty miles away. Their disappearance has been the subject of much talk. It was at first thought that they had lost their way in the inundation and so perished, but when their canoe was discovered at the edge of the water-mark, long after the inundation had ceased, no one could account for it. The village was but three or four miles from the spot where the canoe was found, and there was no possibility of their missing their way. They could hardly have been all three devoured by wild beasts, unless, indeed, they had fallen in with a herd of peccaries; and this, it is now thought, must have been their fate. Fortunately, no one associated your coming with the discovery of the canoe."

Gradually Stephen regained strength, but it was some weeks before he was fit to travel again.

"I suppose," he said one day to Hurka, "that you will

follow the track straight through the forest to the mission, instead of going all the way round as you did."

"I don't know yet, señor. We shall have some difficulty in getting away. Our skill with the bow and gun have so impressed them that they want to make Pita their chief and keep him here, and they want to adopt me into the tribe for the same reason. Till you began to get stronger we could roam about as we liked alone, but of late we have noticed that we are always watched, and Pita has been told that unless he consents to remain, you and I will both be killed and eaten. Pita has put off giving them a decided answer, but he cannot do so much longer; and now that you are well enough to travel, we shall have to make off as soon as we can. He has been told that if he and I consent to remain with them, they will take you to a place among the hills, eight days away, where you can find much gold and return rich to your own country."

"It is very awkward, Hurka, but I should think that you and Pita can contrive some plan for getting off."

The little Indian nodded.

"We can manage that," he said. "We have only been waiting until we were sure that you were strong enough to travel. I know that even now you could not go far, but once in the forest, we shall be able to outwit them and to travel slowly. Pita and I have been hiding up a store of food for the journey, and if you are willing we will try to make our escape to-night. There have, for the last fortnight, been men posted round us as soon as it became dark, but we shall be able either to crawl through them or to dispose of any who may bar our way."

Pita presently returned from hunting. He carried a dozen large pigeons in his hand.

"We must go to-night," he said briefly. "I have been told that I must give an answer to-morrow."

"I have been telling the señor," Hurka said, "and he is ready to make the attempt at once; but I wish that they had given you a day or two longer, for there will be extra vigilance to-night."

Pita made a gesture of contempt.

"They will but throw away their lives," he said. "Let us go out."

As they walked along the village the women looked curiously at them, while men watched them closely with scowling looks.

"Do you see that large tree at the edge of the forest, señor?" Pita asked presently; "it has lost its bark, and the trunk is white."

"I see it, Pita."

"Well, señor, as soon as we start to-night do you make straight for that. We will join you there. Do not stop if there should be fighting, and have no fear for us. The great point is for you to get to the edge of the forest. You are not strong enough to run fast yet; but once in the forest we shall be all right. The night is dark, for the moon will not rise till some hours after sunset. Do you think that you will be able to find the tree?"

"I think so, Pita. I will fix its bearings in my mind, and notice the direction I have to take on leaving the hut. I wish I had my gun and pistols."

"You can have my gun when we are once in the forest, señor; but we must fight at first with our bows. There are a hundred and fifty men here, and as we wish above all things to hide the way we have gone, a gun must not be fired unless we are so surrounded that escape is impossible."

"How shall we leave the hut, Pita?"

"By the back. We will cut a hole through that mud wall as soon as it gets dark; but we must not leave until all save the watchers are asleep, or we should have them all down upon us instantly, on the alarm being raised. When we are through them, Hurka and I will run in another direction, and make a long round before we come back to the tree, so that they will not know in which direction to seek for us. They will be sure, indeed, that we shall take to the forest; but it would be useless for them to begin the search for us until the morning, and they will be in no great haste, for they will know that you are not strong enough to walk very far, and that when they once strike on our track they will have no difficulty in overtaking us."

"I feel strong enough to walk a good distance," Stephen said.

"You may feel so, señor; but you have not tried. For months your limbs have done no work, and they will soon feel it. Besides, even had you your full strength and vigour, the Indians could easily outwalk you, for they would run in four hours as much as you could do in eight. If we escape, it must be by craft, and not by speed."

"I am quite sure that you will do all that you can, Pita, but remember that it is my express wish that you should not throw away your lives in a vain attempt to save mine. I will do all that I can; but if they come close to us, and I can go no further, I charge you to leave me, and to make your way to the river. You have already done too much for me, by throwing away eight months of your lives in this wretched place. Few indeed would have done so much, and it is my most earnest wish that you should not sacrifice your lives for my sake in a hopeless struggle against overpowering odds."

Hurka laughed. "That is not our way, señor. We are comrades, and comrades stick to each other to the last. You are our employer, and we have undertaken to carry you through all dangers. You have been kind and good to us, and our lives are yours. We shall either all get together to the mission, or none of us will reach it. In all other matters we are ready to obey your orders, but our lives are our own to dispose of as we choose."

They had by this time re-entered their hut, and Pita at once began to examine the wall, and to decide where it had best be cut through. After some conversation with Hurka they determined to make the hole in the side wall, near the rear corner of the hut.

"They are more likely to be watching at the back," Hurka explained to Stephen, "as it is there they will consider it most likely we should make the attempt to escape. We can begin the hole as soon as night comes on, but we must not complete it until the village is quiet. The knives will make no noise in cutting through this soft stuff, and the moment the hole is large enough, and the part remaining is so thin that we can push it down, one of us will stand, bow in hand, ready to shoot any of the watchers who may stop before it. Once out, señor, do not make straight for the tree, or the men at the back of the house will attack you. Turn sharp off, and run along close to the backs of the next huts until you are fifty or sixty yards away, then strike out for the tree."

Accordingly, as soon as it was dark the two Indians began to cut through the wall. When they considered that they were nearly through, they thrust the blades of the knives in. As long as they found the wall still firm they continued to remove further portions of the earth, until, on pushing the knife through, they found that it moved freely, and knew that they were within half an inch or so of the outside; then they continued their work until the hole was large enough for them to be able to issue out one at a time as soon as the thin skin remaining was cut away. This, as they told Stephen, would be but the work of a moment, for, starting at the top together, they should run their knives round the edge of the hole down to the ground, and let the whole of the wall so separated fall inside together, when they could ease it down noiselessly to the ground. The sounds in the village diminished, but they could, by listening attentively, hear an occasional footstep outside.

"Will each of them watch at a given spot?" Stephen asked.

"No, there is no chance of that; the five or six men on guard will wander round and round as they please, sometimes separately and sometimes together—more often together, for they have never got over the mystery of your arrival, and have, as I have noticed several times when I have returned late, an objection to coming near the hut. I have often seen them cross the road to the other side when they came along, in order to keep as far away from the hut as possible. Of course, we have never given them any explanation of your coming here, but have said that your memory is weak, and that all we know is that you were with us at the mission, and that we found you here."

Presently Pita announced that the time had come. He handed his gun to Stephen, while Hurka swung his across his back. Each of them took up their bows, drew half a dozen arrows from the quivers, and held them in readiness for instant use. They then placed the bows against the wall, close to the hole, opened their long knives and thrust them through the thin wall together, then each swept his knife down until it reached the ground, and cut along it until the inclosed strip gave way and fell inwards. They caught it as it moved, lowered it gently down, and then Hurka crept through the hole into the open air.

CHAPTER XIX.

IN BRAZIL.

PITA followed him, while close on the latter's heels Stephen came out, and turning off at once behind the next hut, started at a run.

As he did so he caught the sound of the twang of a bow-string, followed by a stifled cry and a fall, then came a loud yell, checked almost before it was uttered. But the alarm had been given, and loud shouts rose from several throats. He ran, as directed, some fifty yards behind the huts, and then turned and struck off across the open towards the tree. No sooner had he done so than he felt the justice of what the Indian had said. His feet seemed heavy and his joints stiff, and it needed an effort to maintain the speed at which he started, until he stopped at the tree, panting and trembling from head to foot. He had been conscious while he ran of a great uproar in the village, but his whole mind was centred on his efforts, and it was not until he paused that he heard the full volume of the outcry. A hundred voices were shouting, dogs were barking, and the women's cries could be heard in the uproar. Far away to the left he heard occasional shouts, and it was in this direction that the men of the village were evidently running. The two Indians had no doubt led the chase in the opposite direction to that which he had taken. Stephen was wondering how far they would go before turning, when, almost noiselessly, the two men ran up to the tree.

"We have shaken them off," Hurka said; "there were but two who followed closely enough to keep us in sight, and our arrows soon stopped them. Now let us go."

Pita led the way, Hurka followed him, placing as he did so

one end of his bow in Stephen's hand, saying, "Our eyes are more accustomed to the dark than yours. Keep hold of the bow and follow me closely."

As soon as they were well in the forest the darkness was to Stephen absolute, and had it not been for the bow he could not have followed the little Indian, although treading almost on his heels. He appreciated more strongly than he had ever done before how much keener were the faculties of the Indians in some respects than his own, for they went along at a brisk rate, making their way through the trees with as little hesitation as if it had been broad daylight. Occasionally there was a pause for an instant as Pita slashed through a creeper barring his way.

"How can he see them?" Stephen asked.

"He does not see them, señor, he feels them. He holds his bow at arm's-length before him, and so touches even the smallest of the lianas; the large ones he can see plainly enough, and so could he the small ones were they level with the eye. It is those that are but a foot or two above the ground that are dangerous."

"It is marvellous to me how you can see anything, Hurka, for I cannot make out even the outline of your figure."

"We were born so, señor. Life in these forests accustoms the eyes to see in darkness. It is the same with the wild animals that run at night."

It was not long before Stephen's breath began to come in short gasps. The perspiration streamed from him, but he held on until Pita came to a halt.

"We will stop till you get your breath again, señor. There is no fear of them to-night, but we must hold on until morning, so as to get as long a start as possible before they can find our track and take up the pursuit. Until we have light we can do nothing to disguise our trail, but we will stop frequently, and go at a slower pace, so that you shall not become exhausted. It would never do to wear you out at the beginning of our journey."

All through the night the march was continued. They stopped at frequent intervals for a minute or two, and Stephen found himself able to keep up with them without any great difficulty, although long before morning broke he felt terribly exhausted. At last Pita said:

"In two hours it will be dawn. We will wait here, señor, and you can take a short sleep before we go on again."

Without a word Stephen dropped on to the ground, and almost instantaneously went off to sleep. When he awoke it was broad daylight. Hurka was beside him.

"We must be moving now, señor," he said. "Pita has been away for half an hour, and has just signalled to me to join him."

Stephen rose to his feet heavily. He felt stiff and sore all over, but the feeling wore off after he had walked a short distance. From time to time a cry like the note of a bird was heard, and towards this they directed their steps. They found Pita standing by the edge of a stream some fifteen yards wide, and without a word he entered the water as they came up and began to walk down it.

"I should have thought," Stephen said to Hurka, "that it would be safer to go the other way for a bit, because they would naturally suppose that we should come this way."

"That is just the reason why Pita is leading us down it," he said. "It is, of course, the way we should take to get down to the Madeira, and because it is so they will think that we would surely go the other in order to deceive them. No doubt some will go up and some will go down, but in that case we shall not have so many to fight."

A mile further another stream fell into that which they were following, and they turned up this and walked until they came to a bough some eight feet above the water. Pita sprung up and hauled himself on to it, then he leaned over and stretched his hands down to Stephen, and, with a strength the latter had hardly given him credit for, hauled him up beside him, and then similarly aided Hurka. They made their way along the bough to the main trunk, then followed another great bough on the other side, and dropped from its extremity nearly thirty yards away from the bed of the stream; then they struck off through the wood until they came upon another stream, and after following it for another half an hour left it by another tree as before.

"Now we can go on," Pita said, "it will take them hours to find our track."

They now continued their course steadily, Pita before they started taking off Stephen's boots and wrapping a broad band of soft leather he had brought with him round and round his feet.

"The heels of your boots make tracks an Indian might almost follow in the dark. You had better throw them into the next clump of bushes you come to; we can get another pair at the mission."

In the course of the day they crossed two other streams, and at each of them took measures as before to throw the Indians off their track. They kept on till nightfall, and then Stephen and Pita lay down, Hurka saying that he would watch until midnight.

"You don't think the Indians will follow at night?" Stephen asked.

"There is no fear of that, señor. They dread the wild beasts; there are so many in these forests, and they can scent a human being a long distance away. We have chosen this tree because, as you see, the lower branch is near the ground, and it will be easier to climb up into it if I give the alarm."

The next morning shortly after starting they came to a

bank of a stream larger than any of those they had passed on the previous day. Here they had a short consultation, and then Hurka and Pita set to work to cut down a large number of great rushes growing in the water, taking care to cut them some inches below its level. With the aid of some creepers a raft capable of sustaining them all was speedily made, and on this they took their places, and the Indians having cut two poles to steer by, they pushed off into the middle of the stream. The current was very sluggish, and they would have made but small way had not the two Indians poled vigorously. Stephen was thankful indeed for the change; upon the previous day he had only been enabled to keep up with the greatest difficulty, and had felt that another day's labour would bring him to a stand-still.

"They will walk quite as fast as we are going," he said presently.

"Yes, señor, faster; but they are probably still far behind us. They will, no doubt, find our trail at the points where we have left the streams, but, thanks to the pains we have taken to throw them off, will lose much time in having to search very carefully up and down every stream they come to. It will be the same if they trace us to the spot we started from on this raft; some must go up and some down, and both sides of the stream must be carefully searched. We are going nearly as fast as they will be able to do; besides, now we can travel at night. If they do not overtake us by evening, of which I think there is no chance, we shall be so far ahead by next morning that we shall be perfectly safe."

The Indians seemed tireless; all through the next night, whenever Stephen awoke he found them still at work. Soon after daybreak they stopped at a spot where there was another great bed of rushes, numbers of these they cut down, largely increasing the size of the raft, and adding to its stability. It was now some twelve feet long and eight wide, and composed of a great bed of rushes two feet deep, and which, with their weight upon it, floated more than a foot above the water. Four days later they emerged from the forest on to the Madeira. The stream by which they had come had received on its way so many accessions that it was now a river of some size. It took them four days of hard work to make their way up to the mission-station, although the distance was but fifty miles, and it was only by keeping close to the shore, and utilizing every eddy and back-water, that they succeeded in stemming the current.

The mission had now its full number of occupants, and they were received with the greatest kindness. Their effects had all been carefully stowed away in case they should ever return, although none thought that there was the least probability of their doing so, as nothing had been heard of them since six months before, when an Indian brought a message from Pita begging a supply of quinine for his white companion.

They waited some days at the mission. Stephen had regained much of his strength during his journey on the raft, and was willing to make a start at once; but the good fathers of the mission insisted upon his staying with them for a few days, and he felt that he benefited a great deal by the good food and wine they gave him. There was no longer any occasion for their original raft, and although it had done them good service they were all glad when they took their places in the canoe and started with a steady stroke down the river. It was no longer a rapid stream, and the falls, though still grand, were as nothing in comparison to the scene they presented when the river was in full flood. Still, there was enough stream to help them materially, and to allow the Indians to lay in their paddles at times and let the boat drift by itself.

At the mission-house they had taken in a supply of food

sufficient to last them to Barra, and as they were able to catch as many fish as they could eat, they fared well. The journey took them three weeks of somewhat monotonous travelling. There was no change in the scenery, a thick forest bordered the river on both sides; but as they got lower down there were clearings and small villages, and they met a few boats passing between these or going up to the mission. It was a glad day indeed to Stephen when the great river entered the still mightier Amazon, which was here several miles wide. Crossing it they made their way to Barra, a place of considerable size, with churches and many large buildings. His long companionship with the two Indians had, by this time, made Stephen as familiar with the Peruvian Spanish as with the Chilian, and enabled him to pass with great advantage among the Portuguese-speaking Brazilians as a native of Peru, since, had he been known to be a Chilian, they might have doubted whether he was a good Catholic, and he would, moreover, be viewed with disfavour by the Portuguese officers as one of a nation who had rebelled against Spain, his lawful master. He therefore, on landing, made his way to an hotel close by, representing himself as a traveller who had come down from Peru by the Madeira, and who wished to continue his journey down the Amazon to Para.

Stephen's next step was to purchase some clothes; those in which he left Peru, as well as the suit in the wallets, were unfit to wear. The first had remained at the mission during his long absence; he had indeed discarded it as worn out, but was glad to find it there on his return, for the other suit had been torn into absolute rags during his journey through the woods. He had no difficulty in obtaining country-cut garments, and his host, who had looked somewhat doubtfully upon him on his first arrival, was evidently relieved in his mind when he came down from his room in his new purchases.

"How are you thinking of travelling, señor? Do you desire to have a boat to yourself, or would you travel in a public boat? There are many such constantly going up and down the river. Some go through to Para, but the greater number stop far short of it, making voyages only two or three hundred miles up or down, and stopping at all the villages; these are cheaper than the long-distance boats, and you would have no difficulty in exchanging into another when it reaches its furthest point."

"I do not care which it is," Stephen replied, "and would as soon take a passage in a local craft as in another. Indeed, there is the advantage that if one does not find one's companions agreeable one can make a change and try one's luck in another boat."

"Then, if you are content with that, señor, you will not have long to wait. If not to-morrow, on the next day there is sure to be a boat going down the river."

"I also wish to take passages up the river for these Indians, who have served me most faithfully and well, and whom I regard as my friends."

"There will be no difficulty about that either, señor. Boats go occasionally from here up to the frontier, and sometimes beyond it."

Stephen talked the matter over with Pita and Hurka, and found that they would prefer to make a bargain for themselves with some native boat carrying merchandise.

"We shall be more at home so, señor; we shall go at a much lower price than it would cost by a boat carrying passengers; indeed, by offering to help at the oars when the current is strong we shall probably pay nothing whatever for our passage, as they are glad enough of help going up stream. All we shall have to do will be to buy our own provisions at the villages we stop at, just as the boatmen will do."

"You must give me an address where a letter will find you, Pita. Is there anyone at Lima to whose care I could send it?"

"Yes; Juan Fernandez, a merchant, in Santa Maria Street of Callao, number ten, knows me well, and has several times recommended me to traders and gold-seekers as a trustworthy guide, and if you address Pita, Indian guide, care of Señor Juan Fernandez, he will, I know, keep it for me until I call upon him."

"You will understand, Pita, that in paying you and Hurka only the balance of wages agreed on, I do so because I have no more money with me than is needed to carry me home; it in no way represents the deep obligation which I feel towards you both."

"Say no more of that, señor; we have done our duty, and should have done as much had you been one to whom we felt bound in no way beyond our agreement, but with you it has been altogether different. Had we been men of your own race you could not have treated us more kindly. We have been comrades and companions. If we saved your life, you must remember that you saved mine; say nothing, therefore, of an obligation. Hurka and I will always remember our journey with you as one of the most pleasant that we ever took. The toil has not been great, for we always went with the stream, while as to danger, we have both passed through many vastly greater perils. If you are satisfied with our services we are content, and more than content."

Two days later Stephen took his place in a large boat, with a long cabin on deck, carrying a mast and great sail. He parted with the Indians with deep regret, and watched them as, after looking after the boat until it had gone far down, they turned and went along the shore to a little craft on which they had arranged for a passage, and which was to start half an hour after he sailed. Then Stephen turned round to look at his fellow-passengers. One end of the deck was reserved for the whites. Here was a priest who had been up at Barra on a visit, two traders who had disposed of their merchandise and were returning to Para, an old Portuguese official, his wife, and two daughters, who had, he learnt, been staying for a month with a married daughter at Barra; besides these, there were three or four petty traders, who had come up from villages on the bank to replenish their stock of goods.

In the fore-part of the vessel were fully a score of natives, among whom were several women. An awning was extended over the after part of the upper deck, and it was not long before Stephen entered into conversation with his fellow-passengers. Hitherto he had thought of nothing but obtaining his passage, laying in a stock of provisions—for he was warned that each passenger catered for himself—and saying last words to his Indian companions; he had, therefore, had no time to obtain news of what was going on. After telling them that he had come down the Madeira, and had been laid up for more than eight months by illness, he said to the priest:

"I have now been some sixteen months away from all news, and feel like a man who has dropped from the moon."

"Then you are ignorant," the priest said in surprise, "that the southern portion of Brazil has declared Dom Pedro emperor."

"Dom Pedro!" Stephen repeated in surprise. "Is his father, King John, then dead?"

"No, he has returned to Portugal. You know that he was driven from that country by the French, and retired here and ruled over Brazil."

"That I know," Stephen said; "also that there were incessant plots and insurrections."

"That was so. Well, the war being over in Europe the

Portuguese wanted their king back among them again, and last year King John returned there, leaving Dom Pedro as his lieutenant and regent. The Portuguese having got back their king wanted to bring Brazil back to its former position as subject to Portugal. This provoked a great opposition in the southern provinces, and Dom Pedro was persuaded to throw off his allegiance to his father. In October the independence of the colony was publicly declared, and by this time Dom Pedro has probably assumed the title of Emperor of Brazil. How long he will maintain the title I am unable to say. Our northern provinces of Para, Bahia, and Maranham are still Portuguese, and are held by a large number of Portuguese troops. They have a strong navy, which keeps the sea and compels the few ships of Dom Pedro to remain in port under shelter of the guns of their batteries. There can be but one end to it. The insurrection will be crushed, Dom Pedro sent to Europe as a prisoner, and all who supported him executed, or, if their lives are spared, all their possessions will be confiscated.

"Truly it is a sad time for Brazil. Everywhere there are two parties, the one for independence, the other for the Portuguese; but such as hold to the former naturally keep silent. What may happen in the future no man knows; but at present none have any hope that the southern provinces can resist the great force the Portuguese can bring against them by sea and land. The mass of the people take no interest in the struggle. The natives, who are indeed the mass, care nothing whether they are governed from Lisbon or from Rio; they have to pay their taxes whoever is master. Of the whites, those families who have long been settled here are silent, that is to say, they are for independence; while those who have relations and connections in Portugal vehemently and loudly support its cause, and persecute all whom they suspect of entertaining opinions to the contrary. But all these things concern the population of the great towns; we in the interior take but little heed of them. Here we cultivate our fields, we say our masses, we carry on our trade, and politics interest us but little. If they do interest us, at least we do not speak of them. Silence is golden, my son, as you have doubtless learnt for yourself in Peru. How came so young a man as you to undertake so terrible a journey as you have made?" he asked, changing the conversation.

"It may be, father, that I did not sufficiently recognize that silence was golden. In any case my friends recommended me to take a long journey, because they thought it would be better and safer for me to travel to Brazil; and as there were reasons against my taking a passage by sea, there was nothing for me but to strike across the continent."

"You must possess courage and resolution to have ventured out on such a journey. Nevertheless, I can understand that your risk was greater had you remained. You have heard, I suppose, that Peru is now independent?"

"No, indeed," Stephen replied. "Was there a great battle?"

"There was no fighting at all. The Chilian fleet so hemmed in the Spaniards that neither supplies nor reinforcements could reach them, so they agreed to evacuate the country. San Martin was made dictator, or rather made himself so; but so great were the oppressions and tyrannies of himself and his officers that there was a revolution some months ago, and San Martin had to fly to Chili, where he has since remained, as far as I know."

"It served him right," Stephen said. "He was an ignorant, vain, and traitorous brute, and if the Peruvians had hung him he would only have got his deserts."

"I can understand, my son," the priest said with a smile, "that Peru was not a healthy place for you; and I should doubt whether, if you come to take an interest in politics here, Brazil will be a safer place of residence for you than Peru."

The voyage was pleasant but very slow. When the wind was favourable a great sail was hoisted; when it was not, the boat drifted down the river. The passengers passed the time away in eating many meals, consisting principally of the bread and fruit they purchased at the villages where the boat stopped, and in sipping coffee and smoking innumerable cigarettes. Of an evening the three ladies brought out guitars, and there was much singing by them and the male passengers, several of whom were able to take a turn at the musical instruments. Lines were put over, and occasionally fish caught. So week after week passed. The passengers changed frequently, but Stephen found all to be cheerful and sociable. Twice he had to change his craft for another of precisely the same size, rig, and slowness. The shores afforded but slight amusement, being low, and for the most part wooded, and indeed the river was for a time so wide that the land on either hand was invisible. Once or twice they met with strong winds, and the waves got up rapidly. The craft rolled heavily, and the passengers were for the most part prostrated by terror and sea-sickness.

At length after two months' passage they entered that branch of the great river upon which Para is situated, and a few days later moored alongside the quays of the town. Stephen at once went to an hotel, gave a Peruvian name, and then, having indulged in a bath and a very comfortable meal, sallied out into the town. In the streets were large numbers of Portuguese soldiers; while a short distance down the bay several fine ships of war lay at anchor. A good many merchant ships were moored alongside the quays, and Stephen determined on the following day to ascertain about them. On his return to the hotel he found a Spanish official talking to the landlord.

"This is the gentleman," the latter said, motioning to Stephen.

"I have to ask you for your papers?" he said politely.

"I have none, señor," Stephen replied. "I have just arrived from Peru, having come down by the river Madeira into the Amazon."

"But how did you pass the frontier without papers?" the official said in an altogether changed manner.

"Simply because there is no frontier line on the Madeira, and so far as I know no Portuguese official or soldier within at least fifteen hundred miles. At any rate, I have never been asked for papers until now."

"But how is it that you started without papers?" the official said sternly.

"It was a matter that I never even thought of, señor. I had been engaged in a quarrel, and the authorities wanted me to leave. My friends furnished me with money, and I left at an hour's notice. I have gone through several perils by the way, was captured by Indians, who took all that I possessed, and would certainly have taken the papers had I had them about me. I was nearly killed and eaten, and was only saved by the courage and fidelity of two native guides who accompanied me."

"Well, señor, this is not a time when strangers can travel about Brazil without papers. You may be an emissary of the usurper Dom Pedro."

"If I had been," Stephen said quietly, "I should have come up the coast, and should hardly have gone round by Peru and returned here after a journey that has occupied me some eighteen months. It was only after I arrived at Barra that I learned that King John had left the country, and that his son Dom Pedro had been appointed regent."

The officer looked doubtful. "Your story may be a true

one," he said. "I shall lay it before the authorities. Until you hear their decision you will remain here in the hotel."

"I am quite willing to do so," Stephen said. "In the meantime, señor, you will hear from the captain of the *Bahia*, now lying at the wharf, that I have at least come five hundred miles down the Amazon to this place, and there is one, Señor Vaquez, who is now in this hotel, or is at any rate putting up here, who came down with me all the way from Barra."

The official at once sent upstairs for the trader, who was fortunately in his room, and who at once confirmed Stephen's statement, that they had travelled together from Barra, and had left there some nine weeks before.

"This must be taken, señor," the officer said, "to relieve you from any suspicion of having come here from the insurgent provinces. At the same time there remains the fact that you have entered Brazil without passports or other necessary papers, a matter which will have to be considered by the authorities. At the same time, pending their decision there will be no occasion for you to confine yourself to the hotel, as the offence can hardly be considered a very serious one."

Two hours later Stephen was sent for to the governor's. Here a few more questions were put to him as to the absence of papers, and he was then asked what were his intentions as to the future.

"By your own confession", the officer who interrogated him said, "you are a fugitive from justice, and although we do not concern ourselves with crimes committed beyond our frontiers, we must concern ourselves with the movements of fugitives from justice who enter Portuguese territory without proper papers."

"I intend to take ship to Europe," Stephen replied. "My family have business connections there. I shall probably stay there until I hear that I can return home."

"Very well, señor. So long as you remain here you will be

under surveillance, but otherwise your movements will not be interfered with."

Stephen bowed and withdrew. At the hotel that evening he learned news that surprised him and altered his plans. Some officers who had dined there were talking together, and Stephen, who was sitting near them drinking his coffee and smoking his cigarette, heard to his surprise the name of Lord Cochrane.

"There can be no doubt as to the truth of the news," one said. "Not only has this English adventurer accepted the offer of Dom Pedro to take command of his fleet, but they say he is already on his way, and is expected to arrive at Rio in a few weeks. I am afraid that he will give us some trouble."

"Not he," another said scornfully. "One of our ships could dispose of the whole of the insurgent fleet. They are, as we know from our friends there, but armed merchantmen, the *Pedro Primeiro* being the only real war-ship among them. Moreover, their equipments are villainously bad, and their manning worse, the only real sailors they have being our countrymen, who will bring the ships over to us when the first gun is fired. Even the Englishman can do nothing with such ships as these against three well-appointed fleets like ours."

"He did wonders on the other side," one of the other officers said.

"I grant you he did, but the odds were nothing like so great. The Chilians are better sailors by far than the people here, and could at least be relied upon to be faithful. I should think it likely that he will throw up his command in disgust as soon as he sees what this so-called fleet is, and how hopeless it is to struggle against such tremendous odds."

"I hope that it may be so, major. I own the force of your arguments, and the apparent hopelessness of any attempt to meet us at sea; but after what he did on the other side I cannot but think that he will at least give us some trouble, and at any rate make our conquest of the insurgent provinces less easy than we have anticipated. The man's reputation alone will inspire even those who regard their position as most hopeless, with some sort of energy. Hitherto I have never thought that there would be any resistance whatever, but anticipated that they would surrender as soon as our fleet appeared off their shores and our troops landed; but I think now that this Englishman may infuse some of his own mad spirit into these indolent Brazilians, and that they will make at least a show of resistance."

"All the worse for them," the captain laughed. "There will only be so many more confiscations and so much more plunder for the troops. I hope myself that they will resist, for otherwise we shall gain but little prize-money or plunder."

"I think we shall get plenty of both in any case," the other said. "Two-thirds of the people down there are rebels, and whether there is resistance or not their possessions of all kinds will be justly forfeited."

"That is so; but it is the government who will forfeit them, and but a small proportion indeed will fall to the share of the army and navy."

The conversation then turning upon other subjects, Stephen rose and strolled out of the room, and going down to the wharf seated himself on a balk of timber to think the matter out. That Lord Cochrane should have been driven to resign his position in Chili he could well understand, for he had wondered many times that he put up with the treatment that he received and the utter ingratitude that had been the sole reward of his great services; but it was singular indeed that just as he himself arrived on the eastern coast of the continent he should receive the news that Cochrane would ere long appear on the coast to take command of the Brazilian fleet. Of course, now his plans would be changed, and instead of going to England he should endeavour to make his way down to Rio, and there join the admiral.

The question was how was it to be done? The journey by land would be out of the question; the distance was almost as vast as that he had already travelled, and he would be exposed to constant questioning. Upon the other hand, it was certain that no ships would be sailing from Para to Rio. He might get down to Bahia, but the same difficulty would present itself. It seemed to him that there was but one possible method of reaching Rio, namely to take passage by ship to the Cape de Verde Islands, and there to take another ship bound for Rio. The distance was great, but under favourable circumstances the journey might be made in a few weeks.

The next morning he was early down at the wharf. There were several ships lading for Europe, but one of them was English, and this he learned on going on board would, unless driven east by stress of weather, make for the Azores direct without touching at St. Vincent. There were, however, two Portuguese vessels that would touch at Cape de Verde, and would stay some days there. One of these would start the next day.

In this he secured a passage forward for a very small sum, on his saying that he knew something of the sea, and was willing to make himself useful. He had only now to purchase a few rough clothes suitable for the voyage, and he was ready for the start. The time the voyage would take did not much trouble him. It might be a month or six weeks yet before the admiral reached Brazil; and if what was said of the fleet were true, the work of getting it fit for sea would be a long one, as his experience in Chili had taught him. Even, then, if the voyage was much longer than he expected, he might still be in time to join the admiral before he sailed.

He went on board that night, and in the morning put on his rough clothes and assisted to make sail. In a short time the vessel dropped down the river, and in a few hours was fairly out at sea.

Stephen messed with the crew forward, and seeing his readiness to assist, and his handiness when aloft, he soon became popular with them, though they constantly expressed their surprise that a Peruvian should be so good a sailor. The wind was favourable and steady, and although the vessel was becalmed for three or four days, she dropped anchor in the port of Santiago three weeks after leaving Para. The mate of the vessel had been very friendly with Stephen during the voyage, and said to him the day before they arrived, that if he wished to go on to Europe he was sure that the captain would give him a free passage, as he was as good a hand as the best of the crew.

"To tell you the truth, señor," Stephen said, "I don't want to get to Europe, but to Rio. I have friends there who will give me employment, but the only way that I could see to manage it was to come here and take a passage in the first ship bound there."

"Very well. I will inquire directly we get in if there is a ship in harbour bound there, and if so you shall be rowed straight on board, which will save you the expense of living on shore, and perhaps a lot of bother with the authorities, who are always prying into people's business."

There were eight or ten vessels in harbour when they arrived; and the mate, after going ashore, brought back word that one was a British ship bound for Rio.

"She will probably sail in the morning," the mate said; "and as the port officials have already been on board and checked off the passengers, we can take you off after dark without risk of any bother."

Accordingly, as soon as it was dark two hands rowed Stephen across to the English barque.

"What do you want, my man?" the mate asked when he stepped on deck.

"I want a passage to Rio," Stephen replied in English. "I am a sailor and am ready to work my way if the money I have is not sufficient to pay for a passage. I do not look like it at present, but I am one of Lord Cochrane's officers, and as he is now either at Rio or within a short distance of it, I wish to join him there."

The mate went into the captain's cabin, and on coming out again asked Stephen to follow him. The captain looked at him attentively.

"This is rather a strange yarn of yours."

"It is a strange one, captain, but it is true."

"If you are one of Cochrane's officers what are you doing here? and why are you masquerading in that dress? Have you already served with him?"

"I was his flag-lieutenant on the Chilian coast."

The captain repeated incredulously: "Why, I should not guess you to be above twenty."

"That is about my age, sir; but what I say is nevertheless the fact. My story is too long to tell you now; but, briefly, I was wounded in the cutting out of the *Esmeralda*, and was sent back to be cured at Valparaiso. On my way up in a coasting craft to rejoin, I was wrecked on the Peruvian coast and made prisoner. I escaped by the aid of friends, and finding it impossible to make my way down to Chili, I crossed the Andes and came down by the great rivers to Para. There I heard that Lord Cochrane was about to assume the command of the Brazilian fleet. It was absolutely impossible to make my way there direct, either by land or sea, and I therefore took passage here in that Portuguese lying a hundred yards away, and now want to be taken on to Rio. The stock of money with which I started is reduced to twenty pounds. I must have something when I land, as the admiral may not have arrived; but I am ready to pay fifteen for my passage, and equally willing, if that is not sufficient, to work my way before the mast."

"Well, sir," the captain said, "if you are one of Cochrane's officers I shall be proud to carry you without any charge for the passage; but you can, if you like, pay five pounds for the cost of your food, which, as it belongs to the owner, I have no right to give away. Are the clothes you stand in all your kit?"

"No; I have a bundle on deck with another and somewhat more respectable suit. I bought it at Bahia, and although it is hardly the dress one would choose on board a ship, it is at least respectable, being that of a Brazilian merchant."

"I will lend you some togs for the voyage," the mate said. "We have no passengers on board, so that if they don't quite fit you it won't matter, although I think that we are pretty much of a size."

Stephen warmly thanked the captain and mate for their kindness, and then went to the gangway and told the men waiting in the boat to inform the mate that it was all right, and that he had arranged for a passage.

The voyage was a pleasant one. The mate's clothes fitted

Stephen very well, and he messed with the captain and officers, who were pleasant companions. They were five weeks on the voyage, and Stephen was delighted, on arriving at Rio, to hear that Lord Cochrane was still there, but that the fleet would put to sea in a few days. He resumed his Brazilian dress, and, after renewed thanks to the captain for his kindness, was rowed ashore as soon as the port officials had paid their visit.

CHAPTER XX.

FRESH TRIUMPHS.

NO sooner had Stephen reached the landing-place than he hired a native boat to take him off to the flag-ship, which, with several of her consorts, was lying some little distance off the shore and in front of the Naval establishment. Several others were close in by the wharfs.

"They look in a slovenly state indeed," he said to himself, "infinitely worse than the Chilian ships did when we first got out there. There are two or three by the flag-ship that look in a fair state of order, but the rest might be a fleet of big colliers, with their yards up and down anyhow, their rigging all slack, and everything dirty and untidy."

In ten minutes they were alongside of the flag-ship, whose appearance presented a strong contrast to that of the others.

Telling the boatman to bring up his bundle after him, Stephen ascended the ladder. A petty officer came up to him as he stepped on to the deck.

"What is your business?" he asked him in Portuguese, which Stephen now spoke fluently.

"I wish to speak to the admiral."

The sailor looked at him from head to foot. "Have you an appointment with him?"

"I have not, but he will see me, nevertheless, when he knows that I am here."

On looking round while the man hesitated, Stephen saw the admiral speaking to an officer in captain's uniform. The petty officer, after some hesitation, went up to the officer on watch, who at once came over to Stephen.

"You want to speak to the admiral?"

"I do, lieutenant. I see him yonder, and if you will be good enough to inform him that Lieutenant Embleton is here and ready to report himself for duty, you will find that he will not mind being disturbed."

The officer looked at him doubtfully. "You have neither the appearance of an Englishman nor of a lieutenant," he said.

"That may be, sir, but it does not alter the fact."

At this moment the captain left the admiral's side and walked forward.

"What is it, Lieutenant Romoro?" he asked as he passed them.

"This gentleman," and he hesitated over the word, "says that he is Lieutenant Embleton, and desires to speak to the admiral."

"Lieutenant Embleton!" the captain repeated in English; "not the admiral's flag-lieutenant in Chili, surely? If so, Lord Cochrane will be delighted to see you; he has spoken of you to me several times. He believed you to be dead, and but yesterday he was saying how he missed your services."

"I am the man, sir," Stephen replied. "I have been eighteen months in crossing the continent, and to get here from Para had to make the voyage to the Cape de Verde and back again."

"I congratulate you on your escape," the captain said, shaking his hand warmly. "My name is Crosbie, I am Lord Cochrane's flag-captain, I will take you to him at once."

The admiral had left the deck and retired to his cabin. Captain Crosbie took Stephen there, and at once knocked at the door and entered.

"Excuse my troubling you now, admiral," he said, "but my object will, I am sure, excuse my intrusion. I have a gentleman here that you will, I know, be glad to meet."

Lord Cochrane looked earnestly at Stephen; he had not seen him since he had sent him down to Valparaiso after the capture of the *Esmeralda*. The two years that had elapsed had greatly changed his appearance, and he had grown from a tall lad of eighteen into a powerful young man. A flash of recognition came into his face, he made a step forward and exclaimed: "Good heavens, can it be—"

"Stephen Embleton, sir. I have come on board to report for duty."

"My dear boy, my dear boy," Lord Cochrane said, holding out both hands and wringing those of Stephen, "I am glad to see you indeed. I thank God that I see you alive and well again, which I never dreamt that I should do, for I thought that you had died or had been tortured to death in the dungeons of that accursed Inquisition at Callao. But where have you sprung from, where have you been all this time, by what miracle are you here?"

"I escaped the night before I was to be handed over to the

Inquisition," Stephen replied, "then finding it impossible to make my way down to Chili I crossed the Andes and have come down the Amazon. I had an unfortunate adventure which detained me for eight months; at least, I thought it unfortunate at the time, but I cannot think it so now, as I have just arrived in time to join your lordship here."

"And now, admiral, if you will excuse me I will be off to my duties," Captain Crosbie put in. "I could not deny myself the pleasure of bringing in Mr. Embleton, but his story will assuredly be a long one, and, as you know, my hands are pretty full."

"Well now, lad," the admiral said when they were alone, "sit down and tell me all about it. Here I am with my old worry again, but worse. I thought the Chilians were as bad as could be in matters of business, but these fellows are infinitely worse. I have had no end of trouble with them, and have been obliged to threaten, three or four times already, to resign. As it is, I have only been able to get four ships out of a dozen ready, and even these, with the exception of this ship, are in a shameful state, and deficient in every necessary. What is worse, I cannot even rely upon the crews, which I always could do in the Chilian service. Well, before you begin your story I must tell you that I did not forget you, but tried every means in my power to effect your release. When I got a letter from my wife mentioning that you had sailed in that store-ship that had been so long missing, I set about making inquiries, and sent a boat ashore with a white flag to inquire if any such ship had been wrecked on the coast, for there had been a heavy gale at the time that she was making her passage. I was informed that she and all hands had been lost.

"From some deserters, however, I learned that this was a lie; a few sailors had got ashore and had been killed. I then sent a frigate down to the place where the wreck had been and sent a letter ashore to the governor. He replied that an English officer had been captured, and had been sent to Callao and handed over to the authorities there. When the frigate returned with the news I sent a furious letter ashore to the governor. He replied that he was not before aware that the officer in question had belonged to the ship that was wrecked, and that the person I spoke of had escaped from prison and had not been recaptured. A few days after this a fresh governor was appointed at Callao. I wrote to him, and he gave me substantially the same reply that the other had done. However, I opened negotiations with a merchant there and got him to make inquiries. He sent word that he had talked to some of the prison officials, and that they told the same story as the governor had done; they said that you had, in some extraordinary way, overpowered two prison officials and had made your escape. Of course I did not believe this, and supposed that instructions had been given to all the people connected with the prison to tell the same story. So I sent again to the merchant, and told him to use whatever means were necessary to get at the truth, as bribery will do anything on that coast. He found that the new governor on taking the command had found a book with a record as to the disposition of the prisoners on leaving. Some were marked merely discharged, others as returned to their regiments, many as having died in prison. There were also a large number of official documents relating to these matters, and among them the governor found an order for you to be handed over to the

Inquisition on the day following that on which you were said to have escaped. As soon as I heard this, it seemed to me that there was no doubt about your fate. You had been handed over, and this cock-and-bull story was only intended to throw dust in my eyes if I captured Callao. I therefore sent a demand to the Peruvian authorities for your release and surrender, saying what I had learned; and in reply they declared that I had been misinformed, for that you had escaped, and that the authorities of the Inquisition denied positively that you had ever been handed over to them.

"I wrote a strong letter in reply, saying that no one ever believed the word of an inquisitor, and that if it should ever be my good fortune to capture Callao I would burn their buildings to the ground, and hang every official, priest, and layman belonging to it. There the matter dropped. Of course I did not get the chance of carrying my threat into execution, but if I had done so I should have certainly carried it out; and even if I had found afterwards that I had been mistaken about you I should not have regretted it, for they have deserved the fate a hundred times over. Well, tell me about your escape; the story afterwards must keep. You know the state the Chilian navy was in when I took the command; well, this is much worse, and the factions here are even more bitter and unscrupulous than they were in Chili, impossible as that may seem to you."

"The affair was a very easy one, sir, for it was by bribery rather than force that I got away." And he then related the manner in which he had been befriended by Don Filippo Conchas and his cousin.

"A noble young fellow!" the admiral exclaimed when he

brought his story to a conclusion. "Of course there are fine fellows among the Spaniards as among other nations, but we have heard only of their worst side, that told by people who hated them bitterly. Well, I shall like them better in future, and I hope some day that I may run across that young fellow and his wife—no doubt she is his wife long ere this. Let us call Crosbie in. He is a fine fellow, and I am very certain he will be heartily glad to have you with him, for at present he has not a soul he can rely on."

On Captain Crosbie's arrival the admiral told him that Stephen was ready to set to work at once, in any capacity in which he could make himself useful.

"I shall be glad indeed of his aid," the captain said, "for there is not an officer or man who knows his work."

"Knows!" the admiral repeated; "there is not a man who has the faintest idea of it. I should have liked Stephen, above all things, for our first lieutenant, but our complement is complete."

"I think you might manage it," Captain Crosbie said after a few minutes' reflection. "No captain has yet been appointed to command the *Carolina*. You might appoint Morales to it. He belongs to a powerful family here, and they would be pleased at his promotion. So it might be a politic step, as well as serving our purpose by making a vacancy for Embleton."

"That would be just the thing," the admiral said.

"I am sure I should be delighted," Captain Crosbie went on, for Morales is of very little use; and with Mr. Embleton to aid me I should be able to get the crew into something like shape in half the time that it would take me to do it single-handed."

"Very well, then; the thing is done. I have full powers

to make any changes and appointments in the fleet, so I will write out the orders at once. If you will send Lieutenant Morales in here, Captain Crosbie, I will announce his promotion to him and tell him to take up his duties at once, and then Embleton can enter upon his as soon as he has provided himself with a uniform."

Stephen was about to leave the room with Captain Crosbie when the admiral stopped him.

"I have no doubt that you are short of cash, Stephen," he said, "and just at the present moment of course you cannot draw upon your bankers in England, for your father will naturally have long since believed you dead, and the account will be transferred to himself; so I must be your banker for the present. Here are two hundred and fifty dollars. Tell the fellows who make your uniform—Crosbie will tell you where to go to—that you will pay them something extra to get one suit finished by to-morrow. We shall sail in a couple of days."

After thanking the admiral, Stephen retired just as the lieutenant entered the cabin. On asking the captain as to the address of the best firm of tailors the latter said:

"I am just going ashore myself to see about some stores from the dockyard, and will go there with you. As I am known to them they will probably sharpen up more than if you, a stranger, went by yourself."

As they rowed ashore Stephen learned from Captain Crosbie that the fleet ready for sea consisted, in addition to the flagship, of one fine frigate, the *Piranza*, the *Maria da Gloria*, a converted merchantman mounting thirty-three small guns, and the *Liberal*, about the same size.

"We take with us two old vessels that will be used as fire-ships, and the *Carolina* and another ship that are not yet equipped will join us later on. We are first going to attack Bahia, where we shall have all our work cut out. The Portuguese have three line-of-battle ships, five frigates, five corvettes, a brig, and a schooner. The worst of the thing is that we cannot depend upon our crews. I think that our ship will be all right, but the others are all largely manned by Portuguese, who are as likely as not to mutiny directly we get near the enemy, and to take the ships over to them. Besides that, our equipments are simply miserable—the cartridges are all unfit for service, the fuses of the shells are absolutely untrustworthy, the powder is wretched, the marines know nothing either of working the big guns or of the use of the small ones, and are moreover an insolent, lazy set of rascals, and consider themselves as something infinitely superior to the sailors. Lord Cochrane will doubtless add to his own great reputation by the deeds he will perform here, but assuredly he will find that he will be harassed well-nigh to death by the different factions, and will have difficulties placed in his way at every turn, will be unable to obtain justice for his crews, and will ere long find his position altogether insufferable. The emperor is well-intentioned and honest, but is altogether devoid of any real power, and he is as completely in the hands of the clique of schemers round him, as was the President of Chili. There is not an English officer now in the service of Don Pedro who would not be delighted to leave it if they could obtain an appointment at one-fourth of the pay elsewhere."

On the 3rd of April the little squadron set sail. They arrived off Bahia on the 1st of May, and the Portuguese fleet at once sailed out of the harbour to meet them. The force was altogether too formidable to be engaged by four ill-manned and ill-equipped ships, but Lord Cochrane manœuvred so that he was able with his flag-ship to cut off the four rearmost ships of their fleet. He signalled at once to his consorts to join him in attacking these vessels, but to his astonishment and anger the signal was disregarded, and not one of them made the slightest movement to join him. Hoping that when they saw him actively engaged they would bear down and take part in the fight, he opened fire upon the Portuguese; but the guns and powder were alike so defective, and the crews so incapable of handling them, that he did but little damage to the enemy and was forced to draw off. He found that the Portuguese on his other three ships had absolutely refused to obey their captains' orders, and even on the flag-ship the Portuguese employed in sending up ammunition from below, had so wilfully delayed in their work that the guns were often idle for want of ammunition.

He wrote at once a very strong letter to the Brazilian authorities as to the manning and equipment of the ships, and declared that he could do nothing until these matters were remedied, for that it was necessary for one-half of the squadron to be incessantly watching the other. However, it was not in his nature to wait until his complaints were attended to, for his experience had already taught him that this would be to condemn himself to protracted inactivity. He consequently sailed to the nearest Brazilian port, and there transferred all the best men and the most serviceable fittings to his flag-ship and the *Maria da Gloria*. Leaving the other vessels to remain in port until properly refitted and until their captains could obtain disciplined and sufficient crews, he sailed with the *Maria da Gloria* for Bahia. As the commander of the smaller ship, Captain Beaurepaire, was an active and efficient officer, good results were soon obtained by the change. Several small captures were made of vessels coming in with supplies. The port was completely blockaded, and the Portuguese squadron, cowed by Cochrane's great reputation, dared not venture out to engage him.

After remaining there for three weeks the admiral returned to the port to see how the other ships were getting on, and in six days was back again. The Portuguese fleet had ventured out, but as soon as Lord Cochrane arrived they withdrew again. A week later information was obtained from a ship captured while attempting to leave the port, that the Portuguese were seriously thinking of evacuating the place altogether, before the fire-ships that were, they had learned, in course of preparation, should arrive. The admiral despatched the *Maria da Gloria* to the port to lay in water and victuals for three months. The other ships there were also to be victualled, and the *Piranza* was directed to join at once. In the meantime Lord Cochrane determined to increase, if possible, the alarm of the Portuguese, though he had now only the flag-ship off the port.

The enemies' fleet lay ten or twelve miles up the bay under shelter of the guns of the fort.

"As to attacking them by daylight," he said when talking over the matter with Captain Crosbie and Stephen, "it would be altogether too desperate. Were this ship manned with English sailors I would do it without hesitation, and even with Chilians a good deal might be effected; but although the crew have gained greatly in discipline since we got rid of the Portuguese, I could not count upon them. The Chilians had gradually gained experience and confidence in themselves, but our crew are altogether new to the work and could not be trusted to fight against such enormous odds. Still, by going up at night we might get in among their fleet unnoticed, and might even capture one or two vessels. At any rate, it would heighten their alarm even to know that we had got up through the channel into their midst."

As soon as it became dark on the evening of the 12th of June the *Pedro Primeiro* sailed up the river, sounding her way as she went. Absolute silence was observed on board the ship. Unfortunately just as they reached the outermost vessels the wind began to drop so light that the ship could hardly stem the tide that was running out; however, she made her way some little distance further. Even in the darkness so large a ship was noticed; the alarm was given and the drums beat to quarters on board the Portuguese ships of war. In answer to a hail as to who she was the answer was given, "An English ship". This satisfied the Portuguese; but as the wind had now altogether failed and the tide was growing in strength nothing more could be done. An anchor was dropped, but with enough chain to allow it to drag on the ground, and stern foremost she drifted out from the shipping and regained her old position at the mouth of the river. But although no material advantage had been gained the moral effect more than answered the admiral's hopes. When it became known that his ship had been in the midst of the Portuguese squadron, something like a panic took place on board, and this was increased by the news they received that the fitting out of the fire-ships had almost been completed.

Dependent, as the garrison and shipping were, almost entirely upon provisions brought by sea, they were already very seriously inconvenienced by the blockade. Accordingly, on the 2nd of July the whole squadron of war-ships, and seventy merchantmen and transports carrying the troops, evacuated Bahia. All on board the flag-ship were delighted when they saw the great fleet sail; for even Lord Cochrane had felt that even with the whole of his little squadron it would be a desperate undertaking to attempt to attack them when supported by the guns of their forts; now, however, that they were at sea he could at least harass them, for if the ships of war turned upon him he could bear away. Already an immense service had been performed, for the evacuation of Bahia practically handed over the whole of the province of that name to Brazil. The admiral had not been joined by the two ships left in port, but the *Maria da Gloria* had returned, and the *Carolina* and *Nitherohy*, which had been left at Rio to complete their outfit, came up three hours after the Portuguese sailed.

He directed these three ships to pick up any Portuguese vessels that lagged behind or made off to the right or left hand, while with the flag-ship he followed close on the rear of the main body. The Portuguese had intended to make for Maranham, where another squadron was lying, but Cochrane pressed them so closely that they were forced to abandon this plan and continued to sail south. The men-of-war did not attempt to turn on their pursuer, but kept steadily on, while the merchant ships and transports scattered right and left in order to escape from the reach of his guns. Those that did so were all picked up by the other Brazilian ships, while Lord Cochrane pursued the main body. Five days after they had sailed, he sent off the other vessels with their prizes to Pernambuco, the nearest port, with a despatch to the minister of marine, informing him that half the enemy's army, their colours, cannon, ammunition, stores, and baggage had already been taken. He stated that he should continue the pursuit, directing his attention at present to the transports, in order that he might if possible capture the whole of the troops and so lessen the risk of any future operations by the Portuguese against Brazil. After effecting this he should, he said, direct his operations against their war-ships.

For another week he followed the flying fleet. Each night he swept down among them, capturing many vessels and causing the utmost confusion and alarm among the rest. He chased them past the equator and more than half-way to Cape Verde, and then left them to make their way back to Portugal, and report that a single vessel had driven thirteen ships of war home, accompanied by only thirteen of the seventy vessels that had started under their protection. The pursuit would not have terminated even then, but would have been pressed until the rest of the convoy fell into his hands, but several of the transports had made their escape during the night attacks, and Lord Cochrane was anxious to prevent them from carrying their troops safely into Maranham. Upon abandoning the pursuit, therefore, he sailed for that port, and entered the river with Portuguese colours flying.

The authorities at once sent off an officer to congratulate their supposed friend on his safe arrival, and to express their satisfaction at this reinforcement to their strength. On arriving on board, the officer found that he had fallen into a trap. Lord Cochrane announced to him that the flag-ship would be followed by a numerous fleet with a military force, and that resistance would therefore bring about the destruction of the place and the capture of the fleet and garrison, and he then sent him on shore with letters to the governor to the same effect.

"You will already have learned," he said, "of the flight of the naval and military forces from Bahia. I have now to inform you of the capture of two-thirds of the transports and troops with all their stores and ammunition. I am anxious not to let loose the imperial troops upon Maranham, exasperated as they are at the injuries and cruelties exercised towards them and their countrymen, as well as by the plunder of the merchants and churches of Bahia."

The letter had a prompt effect, and on the following day a deputation came off and surrendered the city and forts. The Portuguese troops were at once embarked on their ships and allowed to sail to Europe, as, had they learned the truth, they might again have obtained possession of the forts and town, which the admiral had no means of preventing them from doing. The delight of the people at being free from the dominion of the Portuguese was unbounded, and they would have massacred the civilians remaining had not Lord Cochrane interfered and allowed all who were willing, to take the oath of allegiance to Brazil. Many of the leading Portuguese merchants and traders did so, but the admiral was obliged to remain two months in the port to protect them from the effect of the exasperation of the native population. But although compelled to remain inactive for a time, the admiral continued his work by sending off Captain Grenfell with a Portuguese brig, which he had seized in the river, to Para, the last stronghold remaining to the Portuguese, to follow there the example that he had set him, by reporting the capture of Bahia and Maranham, and announcing the coming of a great fleet and demanding immediate surrender.

The expedient was again completely successful. Astounded and cowed at the disasters that had befallen their countrymen, Para and the ships of war in the harbour at once surrendered, and the troops were embarked without delay for Portugal. Thus, in the course of six months, Lord Cochrane had with practically but one fighting ship put an end to the Portuguese domination in Brazil, had captured three strong fortresses, driven three large bodies of troops across the Atlantic, taken an immense number of prizes, a vast quantity of naval and military stores, and had annexed to Brazil a territory more than half as large as Europe, a record unapproached in the world's history. Upon his return to the capital Lord Cochrane was received with the greatest enthusiasm. The emperor came on board and personally tendered him his thanks. The title of Marquis of Maranham was bestowed upon him, and he was made a privy-councillor of Brazil.

These, however, were but empty honours. His sailors remained unpaid; by a system of wholesale fraud they received but an insignificant fraction of the prize-money due to them; for the Portuguese faction were still predominant in the Brazilian ministry, and Lord Cochrane was so openly insulted that he felt his position untenable. He remained, however, for a year longer in the service, in order to obtain for his sailors some portion of the arrears of pay and of the insignificant amount of prize-money that was admittedly their due. His resignation could not be much longer delayed, but finally it was brought about by accident. He was cruising in the

Piranza, to which he had shifted his flag, when he was carried far out to sea by strong easterly winds. These increased to a heavy gale, when it was discovered that many of the spars were so unserviceable that sail could not be set on them.

The rigging was absolutely rotten, as were the provisions on board. He could do nothing but run before the gale as long as it lasted, and by that time he had sailed far across the Atlantic. Return was impossible for him, seeing the condition of the ship, and the fact that there was not more than a week's supply of wholesome food remaining. He therefore decided that the only chance of safety was to continue his voyage to England. This he did, and reached Portsmouth in safety, and his first step was to advance £2000 to refit the ship. But his enemies in Brazil made out that his voyage to England was an absolute desertion, and sent instructions to the officers and crew no longer to obey his orders. He therefore sent off the letter of resignation he had so long intended. Thus, at the close of his two commands, in which he had brought about the expulsion of the Spaniards from the western coast of South America, and that of the Portuguese from the eastern, Lord Cochrane, so far from having reaped any personal benefit from his splendid services and daring exploits, was absolutely a poorer man by £20,000 than when he left the shores of England.

Stephen had, by Lord Cochrane's advice, resigned his commission as soon as the admiral saw that there was no hope of obtaining fair treatment from the Portuguese faction, who determined that the sailors should derive no benefit from the work they had done.

"Chili was bad," he said; "but in Chili there was some honest popular feeling, and this acted as a check and prevented the council carrying their rascally course too far. In Brazil there is practically no public opinion. The people are on a level with those in Peru, and naturally indolent; they have grown so accustomed to oppression that they dare not protest against any iniquity. I foresee that it will not be long before I, too shall resign; indeed, I would gladly do so now, were it not that I am forced to stay here to do what I can to obtain justice for the fleet. You are but one-and-twenty and your life is before you; you have had enough adventures to last an ordinary man for his lifetime, and you have acquired some six or seven thousand pounds by your rescue of that treasure, and your Chilian prize-money as lieutenant of the flag-ship. Here you ought to get more than that, but I can see already that the fleet will be cheated out of a great share of their prize-money. Still, however meagre the amount the scoundrels may consider themselves bound to dole out, you ought to get a thousand out of them as your share of the capture of a hundred ships, to say nothing of the men-of-war and the stores. With six or seven thousand pounds you can buy a ship, command her yourself and go in for trade; you can settle down on a little estate in the country, or buy yourself a share in some business. Were there any chance of further fighting here, I would keep you with me gladly, but as it is it would be a pure waste of time for you to remain."

Stephen took the advice, resigned, and went home. He had, of course, written to his father as soon as he arrived in Brazil, and when the vessel touched at Plymouth he posted a letter to prepare him for his arrival at home. He found him somewhat altered, but the lieutenant said: "I am in excellent health now, Stephen. Your disappearance, and Cochrane's letter telling me that he feared that he could give me no hope whatever, broke me down a good deal, and I felt myself that I was going downhill rapidly. However, I have been picking up fast ever since I got your letter giving me an account of your journey across South America. Now that I have you home again I shall soon be completely myself. I have invested all that money of yours in good securities, and as soon as I got your letter I sent the order, as you requested me, to Spain, for Don Filippo Conchas. I received a letter from him two months later acknowledging its receipt, and saying how pleased he and his wife were to hear of your safe arrival on the sea-coast, for they had long before given you up. Don Filippo said that he was a captain now, and that his regiment, the 15th Cavalry, was stationed at Seville, and that he hoped, when I had news again of you, I would write to him there."

"I shall go out myself, father, in the course of a month or two, to pay him a visit. He and his wife saved my life at the risk of disgrace and punishment to themselves, and I promised them that if I should get safely home I would go over to see them, and I will certainly do so."

"Quite right, Stephen. The sin of ingratitude is one of the meanest and basest that a man can commit, and I will spare you willingly on such an errand."

Captain Conchas and his wife were indeed delighted to see Stephen, and he spent a very pleasant fortnight with them. On the occasion of his first visit to London he made inquiries of Mr. Hewson, and found that Wilcox, the sailor who had been with him when they so nearly fell into the hands of the natives, was still in his service; and when, some time afterwards, the ship in which he was in returned to port, he had Wilcox down to Ramsgate, and installed him in the place of gardener and general factotum there. When Lord Cochrane returned to England Stephen went at once down to Portsmouth.

"I should have done better if I had come back with you, Embleton. I should have spared myself nearly two years of trial, humiliation, and disgust, and should have been a good many thousand pounds in pocket. What are you doing with yourself?"

"I am doing nothing at present, sir. These two long absences of mine, and the belief that I was dead, knocked my father down completely. He recovered a bit, but gradually went back again, and I fear that he has not long to live. However, my presence with him is a great satisfaction to him, and for the present I cannot think of leaving him."

"Quite right, lad. A man's first duty is to his father, especially when his father has been a kind one, and you are quite right in sticking to him until the end."

For this reason Lord Cochrane abstained from urging Stephen to accompany him, when, shortly afterwards, he was offered the command of the naval forces of Greece, which was at the time engaged in its struggle for independence. Stephen was the more pleased at his decision to stay at home with his father, that intrigues and want of means caused some eighteen months to pass before Lord Cochrane proceeded to take up his command. Even his experience of Chili, Peru, and Brazil had hardly prepared the admiral for the corruption, the incapacity, the faction, and the rascality of the Greeks. His efforts were always crippled; and although he accomplished all that a man could do in their service, and obtained many minor successes, he never had an opportunity of repeating the exploits that had made him famous in the service of his own country and in those of Chili and Brazil. When the battle of Navarino had practically put an end to the war he returned to England for a short time, heartily wearied of his struggle against men whom he pronounced arrogant, ignorant, despotic, and cruel, and "who were collectively the greatest cowards that I have ever met".

He returned after a short stay in England, but found that, now that his services were no longer indispensable, he was treated with such insolence that he resigned his commission and returned home, suffering from a sort of mental fever, the result of the trials, troubles, and disappointments that he had met with during his four years in the service of Greece. In 1831 he succeeded, on the death of his father, to the earldom of Dundonald, and applied himself to the work of obtaining restitution of the ranks and honours of which he had been so unjustly deprived. After the Reform Bill had passed in 1832, and the clique that had persecuted him so long had lost office, a free pardon was granted him. he was restored to his position in the royal navy, and gazetted rear-admiral. But naturally the Earl of Dundonald was still dissatisfied. The term "free pardon" for an offence that he had never committed galled him, and while he now devoted himself to various inventions connected with steam-engines and war-ships, he never ceased to strive for a full recognition of the injustice to which he had been subjected. His father had been devoted to scientific inventions, and as the earl inherited that talent many of his inventions were of the highest scientific value.

In 1848 Lord Dundonald was appointed admiral of the North American and West Indian fleet. Later still in life other recognitions of his character and services were bestowed upon him. He had been restored to his honours as Knight of the Bath by the Queen in 1854. He was appointed Rear-admiral of the Fleet, and a month later was named by Prince Albert as honorary Brother of the Trinity House. He died on the 31st of October, 1860, at the age of eighty-five.

Stephen Embleton went no more to sea. Contrary to his fears, his father lived for many years, but was a confirmed invalid, and suffered so severely from his old wound that he never went beyond the limit of his garden. Four years after his return from Brazil Stephen married, and before his father's death the cottage had to be enlarged to make room for the increasing number of its occupants; and Stephen Embleton continued to reside there until, a few years ago, he died at a great age.

www.ingramcontent.com/pod-product-compliance
Lightning Source LLC
Chambersburg PA
CBHW032016220426
43664CB00006B/268